Educating Teachers for Diversity

MEETING THE CHALLENGE

OECD

ORGANISATION FOR ECONOMIC CO-OPERATION AND DEVELOPMENT

The OECD is a unique forum where the governments of 30 democracies work together to address the economic, social and environmental challenges of globalisation. The OECD is also at the forefront of efforts to understand and to help governments respond to new developments and concerns, such as corporate governance, the information economy and the challenges of an ageing population. The Organisation provides a setting where governments can compare policy experiences, seek answers to common problems, identify good practice and work to co-ordinate domestic and international policies.

The OECD member countries are: Australia, Austria, Belgium, Canada, the Czech Republic, Denmark, Finland, France, Germany, Greece, Hungary, Iceland, Ireland, Italy, Japan, Korea, Luxembourg, Mexico, the Netherlands, New Zealand, Norway, Poland, Portugal, the Slovak Republic, Spain, Sweden, Switzerland, Turkey, the United Kingdom and the United States. The Commission of the European Communities takes part in the work of the OECD.

OECD Publishing disseminates widely the results of the Organisation's statistics gathering and research on economic, social and environmental issues, as well as the conventions, guidelines and standards agreed by its members.

This work is published on the responsibility of the Secretary-General of the OECD. The opinions expressed and arguments employed herein do not necessarily reflect the official views of the Organisation or of the governments of its member countries.

ISBN 978-92-64-07972-4 (print)
ISBN 978-92-64-07973-1 (PDF)
DOI 10.1787/20769679

Series: Educational Research and Innovation
ISSN 2076-9660 (print)
ISSN 2076-9679 (online)

Photo credits: Cover illustration © Dominique VERNIER/Fotolia.com.

Corrigenda to OECD publications may be found on line at: *www.oecd.org/publishing/corrigenda.*

Foreword

Increasingly multinational – and hence multicultural – societies have an impact on education and student achievement. Data from PISA 2003 and 2006 indicate that the educational challenges posed by family background, socio-economic context, and migration status are not only strongly linked to student outcomes, they are the main determinants of student performance over and above the influence of the school.* School education must therefore seek to overcome socio-economic inequalities and, at the same time, utilise the benefits that diversity brings to schools and classrooms. A key recommendation from the PISA studies was that schools should do better in building on the emotive capital of immigrant students as a driving source for enhancing their learning. One way in which they can do this is to use the strength and flexibility of their teachers – but of course for this to be effective teachers must receive appropriate support and training.

The foundations for this work were laid when migration was identified as a special theme by the Secretary-General and social inclusion issues were identified as key medium term themes for the Directorate for Education. This volume emerges from the CERI project Teacher Education for Diversity (TED), the analytical phase of which ran between December 2007 and September 2009. This activity examined how teachers are prepared for the increasing diversity of their classrooms and aimed to:

- Identify the common challenges and benefits which countries are currently experiencing in their teacher education as a response to increasing cultural diversity and the effectiveness of the solutions that have been proposed.

- Share experiences and examples of good teacher education and classroom practice and develop an analytic framework to further explore these issues.

---

* OECD Programme for International Student Assessment (PISA) 2003 and 2006: *www.oecd.org/edu/pisa.*

In recognition of the priority given to the themes of diversity, migration, and teaching, the TED project ran in parallel with the Directorate for Education's Review of Migrant Education and the CERI project Globalisation and Linguistic Competencies, and overlapped with the end of the first round of the Teaching and Learning International Survey (TALIS).

Educating Teachers for Diversity: Meeting the Challenge brings together key research findings and emerging themes that can be used to help strengthen initial and continuing teacher education to give teachers the tools required to effectively respond to their diverse students. It also explores moving into practice and approaches and principles used by school leaders and classrooms in their particular contexts.

Within the CERI Secretariat this report was edited by Tracey Burns and Vanessa Shadoian-Gersing, with the assistance of James Bouch, Therese Walsh and Cassandra Davis.

Acknowledgements

The analytical phase of this project, spanning from December 2007 to September 2009, would not have been possible without the support of the hosts of the expert meetings in Brussels, Belgium (Ministry of Education, Flemish Community) and Genoa, Italy (Regione Liguria, Centro Studi MEDI). We wish to acknowledge the contribution of the following individuals in organising the meetings from the host side: Gaby Hostens (Belgium), Luiza Ribolzi, Massimiliano Costa, Maurizio Ambrosini, Andrea Torre and Andrea Ravecca (Italy).

In addition we would like to thank the participants from all OECD countries who took part in the meetings to make them such a success, particularly the following: Victoria Chou, Marilyn Cochran-Smith, Maddalena Colombo, Gaby Hostens, Reva Joshee, Kristján Ketill Stefánsson, Winfried Kronig, Pat Mahony, Mirja-Tytti Talib, Dirk Van Damme, and Hiwon Yoon. We especially thank the contributing authors to this publication: Russell Bishop, Miquel Essomba, Bruce Garnett, Geneva Gay, Ben Jensen, Mikael Luciak, Claire McGlynn, Marieke Meeuwisse, H. Richard Milner IV, Milena Santerini, Sylvia Schmelkes, Sabine Severeins, Anne Sliwka, F. Blake Tenore, and Rick Wolff.

We would also like to acknowledge the assistance from our colleagues within the OECD Secretariat. First, an enormous thank you to Francisco Benavides, an original team member of the Teacher Education for Diversity project whose help in developing the concept and design was instrumental to the project's success. We also express our gratitude to team members (past and present) Ben Jensen, Henno Theisens and Tania Ullah for their very useful comments and input to the project and to this volume. In addition, we thank our colleagues Katarina Ananiadou, Michael Davidson, Nadia Hilliard, Francesc Pedro, Paulo Santiago and Dirk Van Damme for comments on previous versions of the Secretariat analysis.

And lastly, our thanks to the 3 196 student teachers, teachers, and teacher educators who responded to our online consultation of November-December 2008, and whose useful insights have served to remind us of the importance of connecting research, policy, and practice to continue to improve teacher education for diversity.

Table of Contents

Figures

Tables

Boxes

Executive summary

Increasingly multicultural societies have an impact on education and student achievement. Educational challenges posed by family background, socio-economic context and migration status are not only strongly linked to student performance, they determine student performance over and above the school's influence.[*] Schools and education systems must therefore seek to overcome such inequalities and at the same time harness the benefits that students and teachers from diverse backgrounds bring to classrooms. A successful school system treats diversity as a source of potential growth rather than an inherent hindrance to student performance. It uses the strength and flexibility of its teachers to draw out this potential, and provides them with the appropriate support and guidance to accomplish this task.

Educating Teachers for Diversity: Meeting the Challenge explores the concepts underlying diversity in various contexts and the challenges involved in creating an evidence base that could guide policy makers on this topic. It looks at the need to better articulate the links between initial and in-service teacher education and the necessity of addressing current gaps in our knowledge. Such gaps include how to attract and retain more diverse student teachers and how best to educate the teacher educators themselves. It also examines classroom practices and principles in a number of country contexts. Throughout the volume, issues raised by student teachers, teachers and teacher educators who participated in an online consultation are used to highlight emerging themes and key challenges in the field.

An important theme underlies all the contributions to this publication: that diversity is an asset for educators and societies in general and that efforts should be made to make the most of this rich resource. This approach contrasts with the view that diversity is a problem that needs to be avoided, or, if this is not possible, "solved".

---

[*]OECD Programme for International Student Assessment (PISA) 2003 and 2006: *www.oecd.org/edu/pisa.*

*The increasing complexity of the
globalised classroom – but how do
we measure successful teaching
for diversity?*

The issue of educating teachers for diverse classrooms needs to be addressed urgently. **Part One** presents an analysis of contexts, concepts, and research that have had an impact on how OECD countries prepare teachers for diversity in the classroom. In the Introduction, the OECD Secretariat sets the stage with key factors, including:

- an increasing proportion of migrants and immigrants in OECD countries;

- continuing disparities in scholastic achievement between first and second generation immigrant students and their native peers;

- lower scholastic achievement and graduation rates for indigenous populations in countries with a long history of migration;

- changing roles of teachers and continuing difficulty in attracting and retaining new recruits to the teaching force;

- a lack of empirical research on effective strategies for teacher education for diversity.

Also in Part One, international researchers examine the concepts and traditions underlying research on teacher education for diversity. Examples of using large scale data analysis to guide suggestions for policy and practice are provided. In Chapter 3, Ben Jensen provides analysis of the OECD's Teaching and Learning International Survey (TALIS) in regard to teachers' responses for teaching in a multicultural setting. The importance of disaggregating data when using large-scale data sets is underlined in Bruce Garnett's work in Chapter 4. Underlying the contributions to Part One are two questions: How can we measure the success of a particular initiative or policy? And what are the political and educational costs of the absence of strong and relevant research on this key topic?

*Preparing teachers: linking initial
teacher education to in-service
training and identifying knowledge
gaps*

Many practitioners who responded to the online consultation rated sensitivity to diversity issues as considerably important for becoming an effective teacher; far fewer reported feeling well prepared to handle diversity issues in the classroom. **Part Two** looks at teacher education itself and the different strategies used to prepare practitioners to respond to diversity in the classroom. In Chapter 5 Russell Bishop explores the distinction between diversity and disparity, in which *diversity* itself is a neutral concept (*i.e.* one can be short, tall, urban, rural, etc.) that is distinct from *disparity*, in which diverse situations are associated with different outcomes or differential treatment. This chapter looks in particular at a concrete example from a professional development programme aimed at improving educational outcomes for indigenous Maori populations in the New Zealand context.

This is followed by a special focus on two themes that are often overlooked in current research and policy making: *(a)* recruiting and retaining diverse teachers and student teachers; and *(b)* educating the teacher educators themselves. Chapter 6 highlights research from the Netherlands looking at three case studies of initial teacher education programmes and explores the experiences of the student teachers as they pursue their chosen studies and seek to find appropriate placements and practicum. In Chapter 7 Richard Milner discusses the preparation of teacher educators and offers planning principles and questions to help guide teacher educators in the crucial area of curriculum planning for increasingly diverse student classrooms. Part Two ends with a look at a teacher education programme in Italy, a country which is still developing its approach to diversity in the school and in society more generally.

Moving into practice: the importance of context, flexibility, and critical reflection

In the online consultation, teachers and teacher educators reported "creating an interactive environment to promote and support diversity" as their most favoured strategy to respond to diversity in the classroom. But how might one do this? **Part Three** focuses moving into practice and the realities that confront schools, principals, and teachers in the classroom in countries with uniquely different traditions and experiences of diversity. As these contributions make clear, context matters.

In Chapter 9, Anne Sliwka explores the process of change with an analysis of the steps taken to transition from a relatively homogenous society (Germany of the 1960s) to one more prepared to embrace its increasing diversity. Chapter 10 looks at Spain, a country that has experienced dramatically increased levels of migrants in a rapid period of time. By tracing the legal instruments used to effectuate change in teacher education and analysing how well these changes are reflected in current teacher education programmes, Miguel Essomba explores the process of moving from theory to practice.

Chapter 11 focuses on a country in transition: Northern Ireland. Claire McGlynn explores the different kinds of approaches that school principals have used in addressing diversity in such a context, including the important role of leaders in championing the explicit acknowledgement of diversity issues.

Lastly, this section ends with a look at the highly diverse American context, and explores how teachers can be best supported to choose the classroom practices with the most potential in light of their particular classroom context. In Chapter 12 Geneva Gay provides guiding principles and illustrative examples of how these principles can be translated into practice through the use of specific pedagogic tools.

The pending agenda – assessing the status quo*, highlighting gaps, and moving forward*

Part Four concludes the volume by identifying areas where further attention and action is needed in governance, research, and teaching. A number of gaps and areas for improvement that emerge from the publication are identified and described, followed by orientations for the pending agenda. It looks at common obstacles and resistance to change in teacher education for diversity and offers suggestions of discussion topics for policy makers and practitioners.

Educating Teachers for Diversity: Meeting the Challenge explores the evidence base that can be used to allow initial and in-service teacher education to prepare teachers for their changing classrooms. It provides concrete examples of challenges facing teachers in OECD countries and presents a range of policies, experiences and practices that are used in various contexts, from countries with long histories of diversity to those with more recent experiences. This publication also asks how these insights can inspire continuing educational reform and change in a globalised world.

Part I

Context, concepts and research

Chapter 1

The importance of effective teacher education for diversity

Tracey Burns and Vanessa Shadoian-Gersing
Centre for Educational Research and Innovation, OECD
Paris, France

Increasingly multicultural societies have an impact on education and student achievement. One way to harness the benefits that diversity brings to schools and classrooms is to use the strength and flexibility of teachers – but for this to be effective teachers require appropriate support and training. This chapter presents the main rationale for effective teacher education for diversity. It outlines common challenges and benefits countries are experiencing in their education and training of teachers. It also summarises specific issues faced by teachers in the classroom. In addition to calling for more empirical research on the topic, this chapter seeks to highlight major gaps in our knowledge base. These include the importance of attracting and retaining diverse student teachers (and teachers), better articulating the links between initial and on-going teacher education, supporting lasting change in teacher beliefs and practices, and researching the preparation and practices of teacher educators themselves.

Introduction

Increasingly multicultural societies have an impact on education and student achievement. Data from PISA 2003 and 2006 indicate that the educational challenges posed by family background, socio-economic context, and migration status are not only strongly linked to student performance, they are the main determinants of student performance over and above the influence of the school. School education must therefore seek to overcome socio-economic inequalities throughout societies while at the same time utilise the benefits that diversity brings to schools and classrooms. A successful programme treats diversity as a source of potential growth rather than an inherent hindrance to student performance. One way to do this is to use teachers' strength and flexibility. Of course, for this to be effective, teachers need to be given appropriate support and training.

This volume stems from the OECD Centre for Educational Research and Innovation (CERI)[1] project, Teacher Education for Diversity (TED).[2] This activity focused on how teachers were prepared for the increasing diversity in their classrooms, and aimed to identify the common challenges and benefits which countries are currently experiencing in their teacher education in response to increasing cultural diversity. The analysis focuses on:

- pre-service teacher education

- in-service teacher education

- training for teacher educators

This focus is deliberately broad as no matter how confident teachers feel about their pre-service education, it cannot prepare them for the evolving challenges they will face throughout their careers. Teacher education should thus be a continuum of development that includes pre and in-service training. System change and development involves the support of and dialogue with a wide variety of actors, including the teacher educators. Crucially, effective professional development is on-going and includes training, practice, feedback, and follow-up support.

This introductory chapter sets the stage for this volume by focusing on the concepts, themes, and definitions central to the discussion of teacher education for diversity. It discusses different approaches to diversity in the various OECD country contexts, explores reasons underlying these interpretations, and offers an analysis of how contextual factors have shaped country responses to increasing diversity in their classrooms and society. It looks at key challenges facing OECD teachers and classrooms with respect to diversity and the evidence base available to guide policy approaches to this issue. It also introduces an online consultation with practitioners that was conducted by the CERI TED team in order to better understand the challenges and strategies of those in the field. It concludes with an overview of the publication.

Underlying the analysis of and contributions to this chapter and the volume more generally is an important transversal theme: the conception of diversity as complex but potential positive, both for educators and societies in general. This contrasts with an approach that views diversity as a problem that needs to be "solved".

Defining diversity

It is important to state at the outset that "diversity" is a multi-faceted concept that can contain as many elements and levels of distinction as required. Work on the topic includes but is not limited to: age, ethnicity, class, gender, physical abilities/qualities, race, sexual orientation, religious status, educational background, geographical location, income, marital status, parental status and work experiences. In order to constrain the discussion and work of this volume to manageable levels and to recognise the specific focus on education, the definition of "diversity" for this work has been framed as: *characteristics that can affect the specific ways in which developmental potential and learning are realised, including cultural, linguistic, ethnic, religious and socio-economic differences.*

Implicit in this definition is a distinction between diversity and disparity, wherein "diversity" *per se* is a neutral concept that is an inevitable reflection of the richness of human experience (*i.e.* one can be short, tall, left-handed, right-handed, etc.). This it is thus distinct from "disparity", in which diverse characteristics are associated with different outcomes or differential treatment. All OECD school systems inherently contain diversity of socio-economic status, parental educational attainment and student abilities; what differs among them is how these differences are related to cultural, linguistic, ethnic and religious diversity, and the disparity associated with the various factors in particular societal and historical contexts.

Diversity and the importance of context

Although the challenges of increased diversity are shared by almost all OECD countries, the contexts in which they are addressed are quite different. In OECD countries with long histories of immigration as well as indigenous populations (*e.g.* Australia, Canada, New Zealand and the United States), classroom diversity reflects the long-standing diversity of the population as well as new arrivals to the country. Practically speaking, for these countries this means that diversity is reflected in cultural and historical terms but not necessarily in linguistic terms. As countries with long histories of immigration have traditionally perceived themselves to be built on the strength of their diverse immigrants, diversity and multiculturalism are often deliberately and formally celebrated in the classroom, in the present day at least.

The approach taken has varied among countries and over time, including the assimilationist vision of forging a unique American identity from a melting pot of diverse settlers, the quintessential approach of *e pluribus unum* ("out of many, one"). This is in contrast to the official Canadian policy of multi-culturalism, where ethnic groups are encouraged to retain their individual identities in order to achieve a cultural mosaic. These national core values are expressed in approaches to education and to teacher education programmes in particular, and include long-standing programmes to provide tools and strategies to help prepare teachers for diverse classrooms.

In other OECD countries, classroom diversity is more strongly linked to more recent international migration. In European countries with post-war labour recruitment (*e.g.* Germany, Sweden, Switzerland) and European countries with colonial histories (*e.g.* France, The Netherlands, the United Kingdom), immigrants have been settling (either through active recruitment for temporary workers or as long-term immigrants) since the 1960s and 1970s. In these countries (with the exception of the United Kingdom, which has taken a more multicultural approach in line with the description of the paragraph above), perceptions and discussions of national identity have remained, until rather recently, virtually unchanged from the image held prior to the arrival of the international migrants. In some of these countries it was assumed that the immigrants in the country would be there only temporarily (*e.g.* the "guest workers" of Germany and the Netherlands), while in others immigrants were welcomed rather freely with the assumption that they or their descendents would eventually become just like their peers in the host country, *e.g.* France, and thus no long-term targeted approach to integration was necessary. The French approach to teaching and the classroom reflected this virtually unchanged notion of a homogenous national identity, effectively excluding the experiences and contributions of these immigrants. Recent social upheavals such as the riots in the suburbs of Paris, as well as the poor scholastic performance of first and second-generation students from migrant backgrounds in many of these countries, have recently called this approach into question and refuelled debates on the nature of national identity and the long-term plan for immigration and immigrants.

Still other countries (*e.g.* Ireland, Italy, Portugal, Spain), have recently been transforming from immigrant-sending nations to immigrant-receiving nations, and as a result classroom diversity is a relatively new phenomenon. In these countries the impact of recent and proportionally large-scale immigration, especially in their inner cities, has been very keenly felt by those on the front lines of the classroom: the teachers. Having virtually no history of immigration (and certainly nothing on the present scale), most teachers in these countries had not been educated to address cultural or linguistic diversity in the classroom, and there were few tools available to help them. Although this is now evolving as these nations race to catch up with the rapid changes in classroom composition, the discussion of what these developments mean to national identity and how the core values of the nation are to be expressed in the classroom is very much under way.

Regardless of country history however, international mobility is likely to continue to increase. For countries where such mobility and immigration (and emigration) are new, the rapid pace of change poses an additional challenge for school systems and teachers, who may have had very little training in strategies to address the challenges of diversity. Countries that hitherto perceived diversity issues as low on the agenda (*e.g.* Korea, many Central and Eastern European countries) are now also facing debates on whether national core values should be changed to reflect these increasing demographic shifts. How this is expressed in education for all countries will continue to emerge as part of the tradition and history of a country and its experience of diversity through immigration or different native populations (including, for example, the Roma).

National responses to diversity and the priority given to diversity issues in teacher education programmes thus depend to a large extent on history and tradition. However they are also determined by the scale of the challenge and the perceived relevance of the topic at any given time. The scale of the challenge has a direct impact on the capacity and thresholds to adequately address diversity issues within systems. The scale can be determined nationally or system-wide, but often plays out locally, at the level of the classroom or school. For example, the presence of one student in the class who is not fluent in the language of instruction is a very different issue for a teacher than five or ten students who not only do not speak the language of instruction but also may or may not share the same first language as each other. Similarly, difficulties with retention or low graduation rates of particular populations (*e.g.* the Maori of New Zealand) manifest themselves very differently in classrooms with small numbers of these students *versus* classrooms (or schools) with a majority Maori student body. Yet strategies and policy responses to deal with these issues are generally decided at the national or regional levels and are usually not solely the realm of educational authorities. In discussions about migrant students in European countries, for example, the "concentration" of immigrants in schools and communities and the resulting impact on student achievement is a central theme of discussion. Yet the proportion of students in particular schools is strongly influenced by patterns of residential segregation, and this is in turn affected by housing and employment policy, discrimination and immigrant settlement practice (OECD, 2010).

Given the great sensitivity of these topics and debates, it is crucial to base analyses of the issue on a strong evidence base. The following section outlines challenges for the classroom being faced by a variety of OECD countries.

Challenges for the classroom

Immigrant students

Migration to OECD countries has been increasing in recent decades. Between 1990 and 2000, the number of people living outside of their birth countries increased by a half to approximately 175 million (OECD, 2006b). The effect of the retiring baby-boomer generation as well as the decline of native birth rates will only increase these numbers (OECD, 2008a). The appearance of resulting labour shortages, especially in areas unappealing to the domestic work force, has stimulated international migration movements and will continue to do so. Although temporary labour migrants currently outnumber permanent ones by a factor of three, temporary labour migration increased by 15% from 2003 to 2006, while permanent-type labour migration in the same period rose by over 50%. Migrants who enter into the resident populations with long-term permits also encourage migration of family members. In fact, family-related entries constitute approximately 44% of migrants to OECD countries (OECD, 2008a).

These statistics demonstrate that migrant families and communities are growing at a rapid pace and many are intending to stay for the long term. In terms of school performance, first-generation students often have difficulty because of the obvious challenges of immigration – learning a new language, adjusting to the culture and social structure of the host country, and adjusting to an unfamiliar school system (OECD, 2006a). One could argue that second-generation[3] students should fare better than the first generation because they were born in the host country and grew up speaking the native language. However data from PISA 2003 and 2006 indicate that, on average across all participating countries, native students perform better than both first and second-generation immigrants in mathematics. This overall pattern is particularly troubling as it appears that in a number of countries second-generation students do not perform as well as their "native" peers even though these students were also born and raised in the country. It is also remarkable because, while this is the average across all participating countries, in a number of countries immigrant students perform as well as their native born peers (*e.g.* Australia, Canada and New Zealand).

The performance of immigrant students in these countries suggests that it is not inevitable that first and second-generation students perform less well than their peers. These PISA data were key elements driving the argument that improving learning outcomes of migrant students is one of the most important reasons why educational systems have to become more effective and more equitable. It is thus crucial to isolate possible driving factors behind these performance scales and to think more broadly about key policy levers that might be used to address these inequalities. Given the diversity of the population of "immigrant students" in any one country context, there is also a need to disaggregate the data such that different patterns and performance of subgroups within the broader population can be perceived and appropriately targeted by policy and educational interventions.

One key factor underlying performance is the interest, enjoyment and motivation that students bring with them to the task of learning. Well-functioning school systems not only provide students with essential literacy skills, but also with the interest, motivation and confidence required to continue learning throughout life. PISA 2003 and 2006 show that first and second-generation students report a high level of enjoyment and satisfaction with the topic areas under study (*i.e.* science and mathematics). They also report comparable or higher future expectations for a career in that subject matter: first and second-generation students are more likely than native students to report that they expected to continue on to higher education although, in fact, children of immigrants are less likely to move on to higher education.

Why is there such a large gap between immigrant students' motivations and their scholastic performance? This question has no easy answers. The PISA data suggest that the effect of interest, motivation and a positive self-concept in one's studies can be overshadowed by the negative effects of other, more challenging characteristics of the learning environment. Several key elements come immediately to mind such as, for example, proficiency in the language of instruction. PISA data demonstrate that there is an effect of speaking a language other than that of instruction at home on students' mathematics and science performance, and that this is independent of immigration status (*i.e.* whether students are first or second-generation immigrants). As might be expected, these differences were more pronounced for the results on reading tests than science or mathematics. One obvious instrument would thus be better language support for second language learners, as well as methods of teaching to students of multilingual backgrounds (OECD, 2006a).

In addition to the language spoken at home, the educational background of parents, the socio-economic status of the family and parental occupation all have a bearing on the academic success of students in PISA and in other measures of performance. OECD-wide, a student with low socio-economic status is twice as likely to be among the low achievers (*i.e.* at the bottom quartile of the PISA reading literacy score) compared with the total student population (OECD, 2001). School systems can and do attempt to address these issues, and there has been a great deal of work done on how best to ensure equitable and efficient schooling (OECD, 2007b). A key challenge for OECD countries is to ensure access to fair and inclusive education for migrants and minorities, not only to help ensure successful academic performance of these students but also to enhance social cohesion and trust, essential elements of integration. From both a social and an economic standpoint, the long-term costs of educational failure are high, as those without the skills to participate socially and economically generate higher costs for health, income support, child welfare and security.

Of course, educational reform can be a long and slow process, and even in those countries or educational systems where strong migrant education policy has been formulated, implementation is often blocked or may progress slowly for a number of different reasons. The reality is that adjusting education systems to improve the achievement of immigrants may be given a lower priority than other pressing issues and lose out in the competition for time and resources (OECD, 2010). Practical constraints also include a lack of capacity, in terms of both time and money, to provide the necessary training and materials. A well-known impediment to change in education is the weak links between research, policy and practice, and the low level of assessment and evaluation of education policies (Burns and Schuller, 2007; OECD, 2009a).

Indigenous students

Australia, Canada, New Zealand and the United States have indigenous populations that pre-date the arrival of European settlers. Classroom diversity in these countries thus reflects the long-standing diversity of the population as well as new arrivals to the country. Despite the very different histories of colonisation and approaches to schooling these populations among the different countries, and despite strong performance of immigrant students on PISA in Australia, Canada, and New Zealand, there is a clear need to improve the learning outcomes of the indigenous people of these countries. The Aboriginals of Australia,[4] the First Nations of Canada,[5] the Māori of New Zealand[6] and Native Americans of the United States[7] have all been identified as populations that could be better served by their respective education systems.

Challenges identified across all countries include:

- difficulty in accessing and receiving the level of early childhood education and care recommended;

- lower levels of literacy and scholastic achievement;

- lower rates of graduation;

- proportionally higher representation in vocational education and training streams than their non-indigenous peers; and

- lower rates of participation in tertiary education in many of these countries.

These trends are of concern for equity imperatives as well as for economic reasons. Education plays significant role in improving many aspects of the quality of life, impacts on employment and earning potential, and is linked to improvements in health and well-being. It has been argued, for example, that education can help people to lead healthy lives by making healthier lifestyle choices, can help to mitigate ill-health by enabling people to better manage their illnesses, and prevent further ill health (OECD 2007d). Although they have had very different traditions of immigration, the educational situation of the indigenous populations of Chile and Mexico also share many of the same characteristics and have similarly been targeted as in need of improvement by policy makers, community members and practitioners alike.

Suggested improvements include investing in early learning programmes, improving higher education engagement by creating institutions designed for this population, and supporting the preservation of indigenous languages. These strategies emerge not only out of standard policy options for improving educational attainment and participation but also out of a recognition that, for indigenous communities and traditions, it is essential to recognise the importance of schools and communities working together. This includes involving indigenous people in the education system as providers, not just as users, as well as cultivating the leadership capacity for indigenous school leaders and teachers.

It is clear that in the effort to accommodate and reap the benefits of increasing diversity in today's classrooms, teachers will be on the front lines. Schools and communities depend on educators to help integrate students of different languages and backgrounds, to be sensitive to cultural, linguistic and gender-related issues, to encourage tolerance and cohesion, and to respond effectively to the needs of all students. Teachers are also expected to prepare students for the high-tech world – to help them learn how to use new technologies and to keep up with new and rapidly developing fields of knowledge. They are counted on to encourage students to be self-directed learners, and they play an active role in constructing their own learning environments and being open to the community. These shifts in the roles and duties of teachers come at the same time that attracting and retaining effective teachers is a challenge currently faced by many OECD countries (OECD, 2005).

A challenge for the system: educating and retaining effective teachers for diverse classrooms

Increasing diversity in the classroom is taking place against the background of a changing role for teachers. *Teachers Matter* (OECD, 2005) breaks this down to different levels and provides insight into how teacher roles that have been changing over time, on the:

- **Individual student level**: respond to individual learning needs, identify strengths and weaknesses of their students, and adapt their curricula and teaching in response to the increasing use and reliance on standardised tests.

- **Classroom level**: deal with multicultural learning environments and apply cultural knowledge of different groups of students.

- **School level**: develop and exercise management and leadership skills, become more interactive and collaborate with other teachers in order to plan and monitor school-level progress.

- **More broadly**: taking the initiative to engage parents and the rest of the community in their practices and classrooms.

Although most teachers perform some of the roles outlined above, there is a growing expectation that more and more of their classroom time will focus on practices and exercises consistent with these new roles. Viewing students as active participants in the learning process and personalising teaching and assessment to better suit individual (and multicultural) student needs require time and space to engage in these practices, as well as the support and training to learn them. Yet teachers seem to view these changes positively, reporting that they prefer a "constructivist" view of teaching (in which students are active participants in the process of acquiring knowledge) to a "direct transmission" view of student learning (which implies that a teachers' role is to communicate knowledge in a clear and structured way, to give students clear and resolvable problems, and to ensure calm and concentration in the classroom) (OECD, 2009b). This suggests that teachers are, at least in theory, prepared and able to offer the kinds of personalised instructional capacities that active learners require. However, reporting on a teaching *belief* is not the same thing as reporting on a teaching *practice*. Indeed, when teachers report on their teaching practices, *i.e.* what they actually do in the classroom, they report using practices that are more consistent with a direct transmission approach (*e.g.* explicitly stating learning goals, summarising earlier lessons and reviewing homework) than practices that would be more consistent with a constructivist view of teaching (working in small groups, encouraging student self-evaluation and student participation in classroom planning, making a product or debating arguments) (OECD, 2009b).

There is thus a disconnect between teachers' preferred beliefs and their expressed practices. Although the data from the OECD Teaching and Learning International Survey (TALIS) do not allow us to explore this link further, it is likely that one of the contributing factors is the time and focused attention required to engage in constructivist activities. There is also another, more subtle force likely to be at work however: the difficulty of changing behaviour once one has been trained or exposed to one type of model. Most teachers and teacher educators have had a lifetime of exposure to structured practices in teaching, as students, student teachers and teachers. In making teaching with constructivist patterns a part of the everyday routine, there is thus a need to break with previous learning, modelling and behaviour.

Breaking patterns and changing behaviour requires ongoing training and preparation on the teachers' part as well as support and capacity building from school authorities. How well are teacher's development needs being met in this domain? TALIS reveals that approximately 55% of teachers feel that they need more professional development than they have received in the previous 18 months (OECD, 2009b). When asked why they did not take part in development activities, the most commonly cited reasons were "conflict with work schedule" (47%) and "no suitable professional development" (42%). There is thus much room for improvement both in terms of better targeting types of professional development that reflect teachers' needs, and in terms of seeking ways to provide more flexible timing and delivery of training opportunities.

In order to address these issues, a key element is strengthening the evaluation, feedback and appraisal in the system to better identify strengths and weaknesses in teaching practice. Given that over 75% of teachers participating in TALIS reported that their appraisal and feedback was helpful in developing their work as teachers and that 63% also agreed that the appraisal and feedback they receive was a fair and just assessment of their work, there is room to use this process to effectively address training and development needs. Overall, there is a need for more research in this area. Despite work on teacher perception and the demographic shifts affecting classroom composition, we do not yet have clear answers to essential questions such as: what are the best ways to prepare teachers to deal with highly diverse classrooms while at the same time improving students' learning achievements? And, what education and training programmes for teachers have been demonstrated to be most effective?

Teacher education for diversity: key themes

Educating teachers for the challenges of diversity is a complex and multi-faceted endeavour. As already discussed, there is a serious challenge involved in changing practices and behaviour since, despite best intentions, the most common form of practice is that which has been observed and experienced personally. There is ample evidence that one-off modules on a topic – any topic – do not suffice to make lasting behavioural change. Rather, there is a need for ongoing and continuous support for planning, development and practice in order to break old habits and create new ones. Although most initial teacher education programmes include some form of diversity training, it is often in the form of a single module or elective, which is unlikely to have a major, lasting impact throughout teachers' careers. There is a need to holistically integrate the coverage of diversity throughout the programme. The question thus becomes: what is the best way to design a systematic approach to elements that should be covered in initial and in-service teacher education, and how should they be linked in order to create a true continuum between these two stages that, currently, are quite discrete?

In contexts where linguistic and cultural diversity in the classroom is a relatively new phenomenon, the scope and types of changes required can and do translate into resistance to change. This can lead to or stem from the temptation to think of diversity as a problem to be solved rather than a potential strength for both learning and teaching. Addressing this resistance is a long process wherein negative stereotypes, assumptions and values can be challenged – but changing such beliefs does not happen overnight. Part of the challenge inherent in this kind of change is preparing the majority as well as teaching to the minorities – that is, whole scale attitudinal change. Given the sensitive nature of this issue and the relationship to national identity and core values, it is crucial that policy approaches and levers be based on sound evidence regarding what works, and what does not.

The evidence base

Given the sensitive nature of the topic and the potential for political interpretation of what should be a scientific debate, an attempt was made to identify rigorous international research through a systematic review of the literature. Given the current high profile of the impact of migration on OECD countries and on education, in particular, a rational first step was to focus on migration issues as a relevant base upon which to build the analysis,[8] with teacher education as a subset of the review. The choice of a systematic review was a deliberate attempt to seek out the strongest possible evidence on the effectiveness of particular policies and programmes.

As such, the review question was: *what policies and practices have been demonstrated to support educational achievement and social integration of first and second-generation migrants?* The aim of the review was to systematically and transparently gather, analyse and synthesise research devoted to evaluating best practices and policies in 36 countries. A variety of academic databases, websites and key research journals were searched, using common keywords in English, French, Spanish and German (see OECD, 2008b for the full methodology, including keywords, journals and databases searched).

The result was disappointing as very few articles on teacher education met the relevance and quality assessment criteria for inclusion in the review. As was remarked in the review:

> *It should be noted that diversity training for teachers is well-investigated. However the empirical evaluations of programs and courses developed to assist teachers in addressing the challenges of diverse classrooms are scant. In a similar project Parker et al. (2004) conducted a systematic review of strategies for training pre-service teachers how to teach and increase achievement levels of children from diverse backgrounds. They too found minimal results. Their review of empirical and discursive literature located 5 studies out of their initial capture of 1 795 potentially relevant citations. Much of the research includes post hoc interviews and self-evaluations of what the teachers felt they learned during training and whether it will influence their practice. To a large extent the literature reveals positive responses from teachers, many of whom articulate a desire to become more critical and adaptive in their practice when addressing the needs of students from diverse backgrounds.[10, 11] (OECD, 2008b)*

One of the difficulties in reviewing the literature is that there are different ideas regarding what counts as "diversity training" and what the intended outcomes should be. Courses or workshops focusing on language appear to characterise diversity in terms of communication, noting that in order for one to integrate, one needs to speak, read and write the host language. This approach presupposes that diversity is primarily due to the linguistic complexity resulting from migration and immigration. Facility in the language of instruction is, of course, crucial, in the sense that literacy is a prerequisite for learning, and low levels of basic literacy have been linked to sustained underperformance. However, it is also somewhat misleading. In this case, "diversity" has been reduced to linguistic difference, and other elements of diversity and diversity training have been sidelined. A number of programmes have addressed this limited conception by attempting to provide a more holistic approach to diversity and diversity training, but again, very few contain an evaluation of the effectiveness of the initiatives or a comparative analysis with the effects of programmes that did not include such an approach.

Overall, while there is an abundance of theoretical research clearly pointing to the need for greater concentration on anti-discrimination programmes and policy development, and a number of individual programmes offered to combat this discrimination, this systematic review found very little that was empirically robust enough to allow decision-makers to feel confident about the effectiveness of programmes and policies prior to their implementation. This was also the case of the previous systemic review cited in the text (Parker *et al.*, 2004) and in a best evidence synthesis of Māori-medium studies and their review of international literature on improved outcomes for indigenous peoples (Timperley, Wilson, Barrar and Fung, 2007). The lack of evaluation of such programmes is unfortunate as it would both improve the accountability of policy implementation and provide useful and constructive feedback for the development of future policies and practices.

The lack of empirical research on this topic does not mean that other methods and other literature cannot and should not shed light on the current themes and issues that are important in this field. However, it is disappointing that there is not more research available that would give policy makers answers to questions on what works and what does not in this domain. Major gaps in our knowledge include:

- *How to better articulate the links between initial and in-service teacher education to provide a holistic approach to career development.* This would include paying close attention to elements of programme planning and design, as well as the development of initial and in-service policy and funding.

- *How to best utilise the induction period.* The transition between initial teacher education and the beginning of teaching is key to retaining new teachers in the profession. Gaps in our knowledge include the kinds of guidance that would be most successful, as well as the timing and delivery of this support.

- *How to recruit and retain diverse teachers*, important for harnessing their unique experiences and perspectives and for their role as mentors or role models. This would also include the types of selection criteria used to recruit and select student teacher applicants.

- *How to plan and implement the placement and deployment of new teachers such that the best teachers go to the schools that need them most.* This would include aiming to send the best and brightest teachers with the most preparation for diversity to highly diverse schools. It would also include planning and incentives to retain those teachers who are most effective in these environments.

- *How best to train the teacher educators.* Though teacher educators are responsible for preparing student teachers and teachers, very little is known about their own education and preparation, especially with respect to diversity. Professors in tertiary institutes, even those in the field of education, are expected to publish or perish, and extra attention paid to teaching development or innovation is not necessarily rewarded.

- *How to support lasting change in teaching beliefs and practices.* This includes providing ongoing support in areas of identified need and a better mapping of the options and timing of development opportunities.

- *How to mobilise knowledge effectively within the system.* There is a tendency to assume that higher education institutions are generators of knowledge while practitioners are merely consumers, such that any transfer of knowledge is unidirectional. Yet the knowledge emerging from the classroom about what works and what doesn't – and the resulting needs for guidance and development – can and should be an important tool to guide practice and policy.

- *How to evaluate the success of pedagogical tools.* What counts as success, and how would one measure it? Successful teaching includes improving student achievement, but that is not the only goal. Motivation, participation, self-esteem and satisfaction are all also important elements to consider.

Linking research to practice: an online consultation

In the absence of a large body of rigorous empirical research on teacher education for diversity, the CERI Secretariat engaged in an online consultation with practitioners in order to gather information on their preparation for and experiences with diversity in their classrooms. This exploratory exercise was aimed at inviting teachers, student teachers, and teacher educators to highlight key concerns that could be important for further research.

The responses to the online consultation reveal a number of intriguing results that suggest a need for more comprehensive data collection in the future (for a fuller discussion of methods, responses and key results, please see Annex A). Box 1.1 presents the key results.

Although not a representative sample, the teachers who responded reported the same demographic profile as the TALIS teachers in terms of gender composition, age range, the length of time employed as a teacher, and the percentage working in public schools. It should be noted however that, in this consultation (which was open to all teachers), a large number of respondents reported teaching in primary and upper secondary schools whereas TALIS only surveyed teachers in ISCED 2[11] level schools.

Box 1.1. **Key messages from the online consultation***

- 96% of student teachers and teacher educators and 70% of teachers who responded to the survey thought that sensitivity to diversity issues was important for effective teaching.

- 93% of the student teachers, 94% of teacher educators and 65% of teachers responding reported that diversity issues were covered in initial teacher education programmes in some form.

Yet...

- 47% of student teachers, 51% of teacher educators and 66% of teachers who responded judged that current teacher education is preparing teachers to be not at all or only somewhat well-prepared to effectively handle diversity issues.

- 78% of teachers and 69% of teacher educators reported no formal evaluation of the strategies they used to address diversity in the classroom.

* N = 3 196 respondents, non-representative sample.

One of the striking findings was the perceived lack of preparation to effectively handle diversity issues in the classroom. For student teachers and teacher educators, this is not simply a result of an absence of training. The vast majority of the student teachers and teacher educators that responded reported that diversity issues (*e.g.* working with different languages, cultures, religions) were covered in their teacher education programmes in some form. This suggests that there is a need to improve the design and development of the current training on diversity issues such that it better fits with the reported need. This is consistent with the findings from TALIS, which reveal that almost half of all teachers who reported a need for greater professional development did not engage in it due to an absence of suitable professional development.

In addition, the reported lack of systematic formal evaluations of teaching strategies fits with the already well-established observation that there are generally weak links between appraisal and feedback and evaluation systems in schools (OECD, 2009b). TALIS demonstrates that this weak link extends also to opportunities for professional development. For example, just under one-quarter of teachers reported that appraisal and feedback led to a moderate or a large change in their opportunities for professional development, which means that over three-quarters of teachers reported little or no change in their professional development opportunities as a result of school appraisal and feedback systems.

The key messages from this exercise provide food for thought and will hopefully inspire future analysis or versions of the TALIS survey. Throughout this volume, findings from this online consultation are used to highlight or counterpoint the contributions of the researchers authoring each chapter.

Overview of this volume

This volume could not and does not attempt to address all of the interconnected issues raised above. Instead, it focuses on key themes, including the increasingly diverse nature of our societies (and hence our classrooms) and the changing role and expectations for teachers. The challenges of addressing these themes in initial and in-service teacher education are discussed and examples of particular classroom practices are presented. In addition to calling for more empirical research on the topic in general, this publication also seeks to highlight areas where little research exists, notably on the importance of attracting and retaining diverse student teachers (and teachers) and the necessity of focusing on teacher educators and the preparation they receive, in addition to students and teachers.

The publication is divided into four main parts, and each chapter is introduced with a key theme or comment from the online consultation with practitioners. The intention is to harness the inspiration of practice to the results of research and shed further light on issues of emerging or continuing concern.

Part One looks at the increasing complexity of our societies and the concepts and challenges underlying teacher education for diversity. In Chapter 2, Mikael Luciak explores the broader concepts underlying diversity and the implications for schooling and teaching across OECD countries. In Chapter 3, Ben Jensen analyses the OECD's Teaching and Learning International Survey (TALIS) with regard to teachers' responses for teaching in a multicultural setting. The importance of disaggregating data when using large-scale data sets to explore issues of diversity is underlined in Bruce Garnett's work in Chapter 4. Underlying the contributions to Part One are two questions: how can we measure the success of a particular initiative or policy? And, what are the political and educational costs due to the lack of strong and relevant research on this key topic?

As outlined above, the vast majority of the practitioners who responded to the online consultation rated sensitivity to diversity issues as important for becoming an effective teacher; far fewer reported feeling well-prepared to handle diversity issues in the classroom. **Part Two** looks at teacher education itself and the different strategies used to prepare teachers to respond to diversity in the classroom. In Chapter 5, Russell Bishop explores the distinction between diversity and disparity and how this is reflected in current teacher and educational practice. He looks, in particular, at a concrete example from a professional development programme aimed at improving educational outcomes for indigenous populations in New Zealand. This is followed by a special focus on two themes that are often overlooked in current research and policy making: *(a)* recruiting and retaining diverse teachers and student teachers; and *(b)* educating the teacher educators. Chapter 6 highlights research from the Netherlands looking at three case studies of initial teacher education programmes and explores the experiences of the student teachers as they pursue their chosen studies and seek to find appropriate placements and practicum. In Chapter 7, Rich Milner discusses the preparation of teacher educators in the United States and offers principles and questions to help guide teacher educators in the crucial area of curriculum planning for increasingly diverse student classrooms. Part Two ends with a look at a teacher education programme in Italy, a country which is still developing its approach to diversity in the school and in society more generally.

Teachers and teacher educators in the online consultation reported "creating an interactive environment to promote and support diversity" as their most favoured strategy to respond to diversity in the classroom. But how might one do this? **Part Three** focuses on the realities that confront schools, principals and teachers in countries with uniquely different traditions and experiences of diversity. As these contributions make clear, context matters.

In Chapter 9, Anne Sliwka explores the process of change with an analysis of the steps taken to transition from a relatively homogenous society (Germany of the 1960s) to one more prepared to embrace its increasing diversity. Chapter 10 looks at Spain, a country that has experienced dramatically increased levels of migrants in a rapid period of time. By tracing the legal instruments used to effectuate change in teacher education and analysing how well these changes are reflected in current teacher education programmes, Miguel Essomba explores the process of moving from theory to practice.

Chapter 11 focuses on Northern Ireland, a country in transition. Claire McGlynn explores the different kinds of approaches that school principals have used in addressing diversity in such a context, including the important role of leaders in championing the explicit acknowledgement of diversity issues. Lastly, this section ends with a look at the highly diverse American context, and explores how teachers can be best supported to choose the classroom practices with the most potential in light of their particular classroom context. In Chapter 12, Geneva Gay provides guiding principles and illustrative examples of how these principles can be translated into practice through the use of specific pedagogic tools.

Part Four concludes the volume by identifying areas where further action is needed. This includes discussion of the research agenda and future plan of action as well as recommendations to encourage countries and research communities to consolidate their efforts and resources in order to provide sound evidence for further decision making for policy makers and educators alike. It looks at common obstacles and resistance to change, and also offers suggestions of elements of teaching practice that could be usefully used to help practitioners address challenges in their classrooms.

Throughout the volume, an attempt has been made to bring the views expressed by practitioners in the online consultation together with the analysis of researchers in the field. A number of key gaps in our knowledge and areas for improvement are identified and are presented with suggestions for policy, research and practice. These suggestions are necessarily general in nature since devising a "one size fits all" response to an inherently multifaceted issue such as preparing teachers for diversity is neither possible nor desirable. The end goal is that these suggestions could be used as a starting point for a series of further focused discussions and analyses within a specific context.

Underlying the four parts of this publication is the crucial transversal theme that sees diversity as complex but potentially positive for educators and societies as opposed to an approach that views diversity as a problem that should be "solved". Increasing diversity in our society and classrooms poses difficult questions about the nature of our national identity and how core values are expressed in education, questions we can no longer afford to ignore. It is thus imperative to insist on and support the development of a rich evidence base that can help policy makers answer questions about what works in teacher education for diversity and why.

Notes

1. *www.oecd.org/ceri.*

2. *www.oecd.org/edu/ted.*

3. "Second generation" refers here to native-born students, both of whose parents are foreign-born.

4. *www.abs.gov.au/Ausstats/abs@.nsf/39433889d406eeb9ca2570610019e9a5/649A 8316859C2BD7CA2574390014A031?opendocument.*

5. *www.ccl-cca.ca/solr.*

6. *www.socialreport.msd.govt.nz/knowledge-skills/educational-attainment-adult-population.html.*

7.   *http://nces.ed.gov/pubs2008/nativetrends/highlights.asp.*

8.   This exercise was part of a broader OECD transversal initiative on migration.

9.   See Vavrus, 2003.

10.   See Sobel, 2005.

11.   ISCED 2 is the equivalent of lower secondary education.

References

Australian Bureau of Statistics (2008), *The Health and Welfare of Australia's Aboriginal and Torres Strait Islander Peoples 2008. http://www.abs.gov. au/Ausstats/abs@.nsf/39433889d406eeb9ca2570610019e9a5/649A8316859 C2BD7CA2574390014A031?opendocument* accessed 14/10/09.

Burns T. and T. Schuller (2007), "The Evidence Agenda," in *Evidence in Education: Linking Research and Policy*, OECD Publishing, Paris, pp. 15-32.

Canada Council on Learning (2007), *The State of Learning in Canada: No time for complacency, http://www.ccl-cca.ca/NR/rdonlyres/5ACD85E3-4D4F-410D-B017-F5270CD3060D/0/SOLR_SummaryBrochure_Online_ EN.pdf*, accessed 19/10/09.

New Zealand Ministry of Social Development (2008), *The Social Report: Knowledge and Skills, http://www.socialreport.msd.govt.nz/documents/ sr08-knowledge-skills.pdf* accessed 14/10/09.

NCES (2008), *Status and Trends in the Education of American Indians and Alaska Natives: 2008, http://nces.ed.gov/pubs2008/nativetrends/high-lights.asp* accessed 14/10/09.

OECD (2001), *Knowledge and Skills for Life – First Results from PISA*, OECD, Paris.

OECD (2004), *Learning for Tomorrow's World: First results from PISA 2003*, OECD, Paris.

OECD (2005), *Teachers Matter: Attracting, Developing and Retaining Effective Teachers*, OECD, Paris.

OECD (2006a), *Where Immigrant Students Succeed: A Comparative Review of Performance and Engagement in PISA 2003*, OECD, Paris.

OECD (2006b), *International Migration Outlook*, OECD, Paris.

OECD (2007a), *PISA 2006: Science Competencies for Tomorrow's World*, Volume 1: Analysis, OECD Publishing, Paris.

OECD (2007b), *No More Failures: Ten Steps to Equity in Education*, OECD Publishing, Paris.

OECD (2007c), *OECD Seminar on Indigenous Education, Effective Practice, Mutual Learning*, *www.oecd.org/dataoecd/33/11/40626776.pdf*; accessed 15/10/2009.

OECD (2007d), *Understanding the Social Outcomes of Learning*, OECD Publishing, Paris.

OECD (2008a), *International Migration Outlook: Annual Report 2008*, OECD Publishing, Paris.

OECD (2008b), *Policies and Practices Supporting the Educational Achievement and Social Integration of First and Second Generation Migrants: A Systemic Review.* Commissioned to the Canadian Council on Learning [EDU/CERI/CD(2008)1].

OECD (2009a), *Working Out Change: Systemic Innovation in Vocational Education and Training.* OECD Publishing, Paris.

OECD (2009b), *Creating Effective Teaching and Learning Environments: First Results from TALIS*, OECD Publishing, Paris.

OECD (2010), *Closing the Gap for Immigrant Students: Policies, Practice and Performance,* OECD Publishing, Paris.

Parker-Jenkins, M., D. Hewitt, S. Brownhill and T. Saunders (2004), "What Strategies can be Used by Initial Teacher Training Providers, Trainees and Newly Qualified Teachers to Raise the Attainment of Pupils from Culturally Diverse Backgrounds?", in *Research Evidence in Education Library.* London, EPPI-Centre, Social Science Research Unit, Institute of Education.

Sobel, D.M. and S. V. Taylor (2005), "Diversity Preparedness in Teacher Education", *Kappa Delta Pi Record,* Vol. 41, No. 2, pp. 83-86.

Timperley, H., A. Wilson, H. Barrar and I. Fung (2007), *Teacher Professional Learning and Development: Best Evidence Synthesis Iteration.* Willington, New Zealand: Ministry of Education, *http://educationcounts. edcentre.govt.nz/goto/BES*.

Vavrus, M. (2003), "Incorporating a Transformative Multicultural Perspective into a State's Policy for Teacher Candidate Pedagogy Performance", paper presented at the annual meeting of the American Educational Research of Association, Washington, D.C.

Chapter 2

On diversity in educational contexts

Mikael Luciak
University of Vienna, Austria

This paper explores divergent meanings of diversity and the interrelations between history, tradition and perception. It discusses how long-standing cultural diversity in OECD member countries was handled in the past and highlights new challenges for educational systems stemming from increasing diversity due to migration. Different responses to diversity in the form of multicultural and intercultural education and implications for educational policy and practice are explored. The paper concludes with the role and responsibility of educators and policy makers to address these challenges – guaranteeing the educational achievement of all while strengthening intercultural understanding and social justice.

From the OECD online consultation: diversity as an asset

Practitioners place considerable importance on sensitivity to diversity issues. But there are different traditions and approaches to diversity which affect how it can be viewed – as a challenge, but also as an asset.

Introduction

In recent decades, pluralist and democratic societies worldwide have become increasingly diverse due to migration, globalisation and transnational mobility. These societal changes have had considerable impact on the educational landscape. According to the United Nations' International Migration Report 2006, almost 191 million people live in a country other than their country of birth. Since the 1970s, the number of international migrants has more than doubled, and developed countries have absorbed most of them. Among OECD member countries with at least 20 million inhabitants, countries where international migrants comprise over 10% of their population include Australia (20%), Canada (19%), France (11 %), Germany (12%), Spain (11%), and the United States (13%) (United Nations, 2009).

In the mid-1980s the anthropologist Clifford Geertz noted that social and cultural boundaries no longer arise mainly between societies but rather within them (Geertz, 1985). While the more recent migratory movements have made diversity a central topic of public and academic discourse and moved it toward the top of the policy making agenda, societal diversity is not a new phenomenon. Many countries have been inhabited by various ethnic, racial, linguistic and religious groups due to long histories of immigration and/or colonisation, and some were heterogeneous from the very outset of state formation. In addition, all societies are characterised by socio-economic and regional differences that account for socio-cultural and linguistic variations in the population. Jagdish Gundara, UNESCO Chair for Intercultural Education, suggests that in order to understand why issues concerning diversity are so closely related to recent migration in public discourse, we must account for "how many nation states obfuscate the underlying historical features of social diversity or (the) multicultural nature of their societies" (Gundara, 2008).

While it is true that the current rhetoric about challenges due to increased migration frequently tends to overlook long-standing social and cultural diversity, it must be emphasised that developed countries are indeed facing new challenges. This is due not only to new dimensions of increasing cultural diversity but also because enduring socio-economic differences between majority and immigrant populations risk creating a stratified society along ethnic lines characterised by inequality and inequity.

Discourses on the promotion or protection of cultural diversity vary in different fields and contexts. Robert Albro (2005), referring to the 2005 UNESCO Convention on Cultural Diversity, states "there is little consensus among cultural policy makers about what kind of diversity we currently live with, let alone should seek to promote". Nevertheless, in OECD member countries, there seems to be agreement that despite having unique histories, societal and political contexts, and relative representations of various migrant and minority groups, educational institutions must find adequate ways to respond to increasing diversity in schools and classrooms. To that end, this contribution addresses the following three questions: *what is meant by diversity and cultural difference? How is diversity promoted in educational contexts? What challenges come with increasing diversity in classrooms?*

Divergent meanings of culture and diversity

In 1952, United States anthropologists Alfred L. Kroeber and Clyde Kluckhohn described 164 distinct meanings of the term culture. As pointed out by Altman and Chemers (1984), "The concept of culture reflects a multifaceted set of things, from abstract principles about how to view the world to more concrete actions, such as ways of behaving and relating to the environment and ways of raising children." (p. 4) From a phenomenological standpoint, culture can be seen as a system of specific symbols such as patterns of interpretation, expression and orientation. The members of a culture internalise these orientations, interpretations and activity patterns.

The borders between cultures are not equivalent to language boundaries, to borders between nations or to borders between people or ethnic groups. A complex society exists of partial cultures, which can also be understood as *Lebenswelten* (*i.e.* "life worlds" [*e.g.* Schütz 1959]). Such "life worlds" contain a pool of interpretation patterns, which make up the common everyday knowledge. Persons living in it use this pool in order to orient themselves in the world, structure their perception and reflect on and initiate their activities. While culture can be regarded as a system of specific symbols and meanings, it is also argued that culture is not an object that can be definitely interpreted. "Culture is contested, temporal, and emergent" (Clifford, 1986, p. 19).

Culture is thus not naturally given or static but dynamic and altered by human beings. Ethnic, migrant or national groups might share similar cultural ways of being, but their cultures change over time and influence each other. Ethnicity, race and nationality are relational concepts that depend on self-identification and social ascription. While group affiliations and collective identities influence group members' perspectives and actions, individual group members can and do take a critical stance towards their own cultural background and do not necessarily abide by their group's cultural way of life. Also, others might see individuals as belonging to a particular cultural group while they themselves do not or no longer identify with that group's culture. Identities are multilayered and complex, and cultural identity is always hybrid (Hall, 1996).

Similarly, divergent meanings of diversity appear over time and in different contexts and fields. In general, the concepts of diversity are multifaceted, multilayered and, given their ambiguity, can be contested as well. Diversity can refer to long-standing intra-state cultural differences in societies with differing ethnic, racial, linguistic and religious groups or to new forms of cultural diversity brought about by demographic changes and migratory movements. In understanding diversity, it is important to recognise how cultural diversity interrelates with other diversity dimensions such as social and family background, gender, age, physical and mental abilities, or sexual orientation. Which dimensions of diversity receive attention in the public discourse at a given time and space, and the degree of importance placed on them, is a matter of choice and part of a political decision-making process.

Long-standing diversity in nation-states

Historically, the development of nation-states has promoted the homogenising tendencies of societies, frequently leading to mindsets along the lines of "one people, one culture, one nation, one history" (Bennett, 2001, p. 27). Depending on the country context, we speak of the existence of indigenous, aboriginal or autochthonous minorities as well as of national, linguistic and religious minority groups. Some groups were subordinated, colonised or even brought involuntarily into countries. In the process of state formation, members of these divergent groups were eventually expected to assimilate into the national majority culture or otherwise be excluded. The claims of these minority groups to cultural, linguistic or religious difference and to specific group rights were generally accompanied by struggle. Over the course of history, today's OECD member countries have responded differently to these claims. Some European states now recognise territorially-based ethnic and linguistic minorities and, for example, have signed the Council of Europe's Framework Convention for the Protection of National Minorities. Still, in several countries, struggles for the recognition of minority rights and autonomy have led to territorial conflicts or nationalist and separatist movements (for example, Francophones in Canada; Corsicans or Bretons on French territory; Scots in the U.K.; Basques or Catalans in Spain; Kurds in Turkey; or the Flemish in Belgium).

In contrast, claims to the recognition of cultural diversity in the context of migration focus on the paradigms of integration and interculturalism, dialogue, valuing cultural differences and mutual respect. These conceptions are more strongly orientated to liberal notions of individual rights and freedoms rather than to communitarian ideals about specific group rights. One definition of *cultural diversity* is that it "presupposes respect of fundamental freedoms, namely freedom of thought, conscience and religion, freedom of opinion and expression, and freedom to participate in the cultural life of one's choice" (UNESCO, 2009).

How long-standing diversity is managed in the school system differs across systems and traditions. Several countries grant *in situ* minorities the right to minority education, bilingual schooling and religious schools or have decentralised school systems that take into account the cultural and linguistic variations of the population in different (autonomous) regions of the country. These responses to diversity between majority populations and minority groups that have lived in nation-states for long periods of time can be distinguished from those efforts that are made to help schools adjust to diversity caused by ongoing migratory movements. The former responses often are geared to affording special group rights, maintenance of cultural identity, and the "preservation" of culture and language. Minority schools and school systems that serve populations in culturally and linguistically distinct regions are not aligned with the idea of a common national school system for all children, but they do not necessarily contradict notions of multiculturalism as long as the latter is conceptualised along the lines of a mosaic model of national community (*e.g.* Canada).

Given this variety of expression, it is not surprising that different understandings about the aims and processes in regard to the schooling of diverse student populations persist in schools and among teachers. The various perspectives include: assimilating all students into existing forms of schooling with a strong focus on learning the country's majority language and culture; or, alternatively, providing native language instruction and acknowledging cultural differences with the objective of promoting integration. They also extend to restructuring school organisation, curricular provision and teaching methodologies in order to reach out to all pupils and to develop inclusive settings.

Diversity and international migration

Considering contemporary trends of immigration, a variety of factors must be accounted for in order to better understand the implications of increasing diversity in OECD member countries. Depending on the country in question, migration takes many forms: immigrants from neighbouring countries or even from different continents, migrants who freely move within an economic and political union (*e.g.* European Union) and so-called "third country nationals" who need special visas and permits, refugees and asylum-seekers, and documented and undocumented migrants as well as repatriated migrants. Migration patterns change over time as outlined by reports on international migration such as the *International Migration Outlook* (OECD, 2009), the *International Migration Report* (United Nations, 2006) or the *World Migration Report* (International Organization for Migration, 2005).

Some migrants are highly skilled and educated professionals while others are low-skilled labourers with little formal education. Some come from countries with a long historical relationship with or even an established ethnic community in the reception country. Migrants come to work, study, seek asylum or move as part of family reunification. It should be noted here that while most OECD member countries experience immigration, some countries (*e.g.* Turkey, Mexico) also show strong internal migration, which includes minority groups and leads particularly to increasing diversity in urban areas.

The characteristics and size of individual migrant groups, the heterogeneity and size of the entire immigrant population, the reasons for entering and intentions for staying in a country, and the relationship between a country's majority population and the immigrant communities are only some of the relevant factors that must be taken into account in addition to cultural, social, linguistic or religious differences that are usually acknowledged as parameters of diversity. How nation-states responded to diversity in the past influences their current perspectives on immigration, *i.e.* whether they regard themselves as countries of immigration and positively value the multicultural nature of their societies, or whether they cling to views of homogenous nations and view immigrants over generations as foreigners.

School systems have responded to immigration in various ways, for example, by establishing special programmes for native and second language learning, by enriching the curriculum with multicultural content, by offering new courses for religious instruction, or by making teaching more culturally responsive and suited to the needs of immigrant communities. Today, in many ways, OECD member countries encounter new forms of diversity. Variations with regard to the size and types of immigrant groups or the time of their entry into the country must be taken into consideration in the development of school policies and programmes for these diverse student populations.

The multiplicity of diversity dimensions

As stated, policies regarding diverse populations that are distinguished by differing ethnicity, race, language, citizenship or nationality generally focus on the cultural, linguistic and religious diversity of these groups. However, policies and initiatives for mainstreaming, inclusion, anti-discrimination or diversity management also address other dimensions of diversity and markers of identity such as social and family background, gender, physical and mental abilities or sexual orientation.

Although measures specifically targeting gender equality, anti-homo-phobia, the inclusion of students from disadvantaged social backgrounds or those with disabilities have different aims than the types of diversity policies described above, these diversity dimensions must also be considered in the schooling of migrants. For example, gender roles in migrant communities might affect students' academic attainment while social background may play an important role in minority students' educational achievements as has indeed been shown by various comparative studies, including the OECD's Programme for International Student Assessment (PISA). The frequent over-representation of ethnic minority and migrant students among students with special educational needs is another example illustrating the importance of the interrelations of various diversity dimensions.

Research has shown how different dimensions of diversity are intertwined and that the experience of exclusion and subordination is based on multiple factors that can be additive or transversal, i.e. pervade and transform each other (Knudsen, 2006). Therefore, diversity policies targeting under-achievement and inequality of ethnic minority and migrant groups must also address the intersection of individual, cultural, and social factors. As a concrete example, a female migrant student might have a similar socio-economic background as a male student belonging to the majority, but she still might experience unequal treatment if faced with low teacher expectations due to her minority background or less support by parents if there are different gender role expectations in her ethnic community.

Cultural diversity, cultural differences and the role of schools

The number of different cultural groups cannot simply be added up to determine the extent of cultural diversity in a society. Rather, the character, complexity and relevance of cultural differences must be taken into account as well (Peters, 1997). There are diverse regional or local cultures, cultural differences between socio-economic classes and status groups, but also groups with different life-styles and cultural milieus, sub-cultures and professional cultures as well as groups that differ from the mainstream in regard to modes of communication and social interaction (*i.e.* Deaf culture) or sexuality and gender identity (LGBT culture). As pointed out by Bennett (2001, p. 27), these forms of internal diversity are usually not seen to contradict notions of unified national cultures:

> *Nationalist mappings of the relations between peoples, cultures, time and territory often depict the national culture as a rich mix of diverse regional or local cultures. But these are differences of a particular kind, ones which can be accommodated within nationalist projects to the degree that their qualities can be portrayed as harmoniously blending with one another in the context of an encompassing and unifying national narrative.*

How we conceptualise the cultural distinctiveness of minority and migrant groups and its relevancy depends on our definition and understanding of culture and collective identity. If we look at cultural differences in the context of education and schooling, we can pose various interrelated questions: what kind of cultural differences exists between groups? How do they arise? What is their significance? Who defines cultural differences and their implications? Depending on the social and cultural environment encountered during their upbringing, students in diverse classrooms differ in culturally-specific knowledge, competencies, skills, language use, communication patterns and discursive practices, in ways of behaving and relating to others, or in their value systems. These kinds of differences exist within and between societies. Cultural differences arise because societies live apart from each other in different natural and social environments, but differences also arise within one and the same society and are coined by the interrelations between various social and ethnic groups.

The process of overcoming cultural and language differences in the context of schooling might be easier for some groups than for others. Depending on their relationship to the dominant group and to schools, ethnic minority and migrant students may adopt a strategy of "accommodation without assimilation" (Gibson, 1988), which does not threaten their cultural identity. Alternatively, they may develop an "oppositional cultural frame of reference" (Ogbu, 1991) and resist overcoming these differences. For example, in countries that are traditional immigrant-receiving societies (*e.g.* Australia, Canada, New Zealand and the United States), newly arrived immigrant groups might have a different but not necessarily oppositional cultural frame of reference to the host society. Upon arrival, they differ from the host society in many respects, but their members strive to learn and get acquainted with the receiving countries' culture and language. These migrant students may face difficulties in schooling but over time they acculturate by learning the language of instruction and mastering their new cultural environment. However, they likely still maintain aspects of their original cultural ways and some even develop a bilingual and bicultural identity.

This process should be distinguished from that used by other groups, for example, members of historically subordinated ethnic minorities (*e.g.* African Americans, Native Americans or aboriginal groups in Australia). For these groups whose culture was, in the past, threatened and weakened by the imposition of forced assimilation (including school programmes and policies that devalued their culture), there may be more difficulty in overcoming cultural and language barriers. They might fear a loss of their minority cultural identity if they accommodate further to the majority norms. In explaining the differential academic performance between these lower achieving "involuntary" or "caste-like" minorities and higher achieving immigrant groups in the United States, Ogbu (1992, p. 7) argues that "the meaning and value that students associate with school learning and achievement play a very significant role in determining their efforts toward learning and performance". This immigrant-involuntary minority typology might be less helpful when attempting to explain the educational situation of migrant and minority groups in European nations which traditionally were not countries of immigration. It is more ambiguous whether migrants from former colonies can be considered to be immigrants or involuntary minorities (Gibson, 1997), and it is more difficult to assess the situation of indigenous (*e.g.* Sami in Scandinavia) or autochthonous national minorities (*e.g.* Roma in Central and Eastern Europe) in that respect (Luciak, 2004). Furthermore, for a long time in European nations, societal and educational integration of labour migrants and refugees was impeded by the fact that, in general, their long-term residence in the receiving countries was not assumed. Many European countries continue to struggle with the fact that they "unintentionally" have become countries of immigration.

As stated above, the process of overcoming cultural and language differences in schools is influenced by historical and current relationships between the majority and minority communities. In addition, the cultural frame of reference of a group affects individual group members' perceptions of schooling. However, teachers must be aware that in highlighting cultural differences and in ascribing specific behaviour patterns to individuals who, from their perspective, belong to a distinct cultural or ethnic group, they not only run the risk of essentialising inter-group differences (Dietz, 2007) but also – given that wider societal and structural factors are often ignored – they risk placing the "burden of success only in the hands of students and their families" (Nieto, 1995, p. 202). School and teachers can and do have a role to play in ensuring students' success, and they are called upon to assume these responsibilities and accommodate the needs of linguistically and culturally different students.

Research has shown that cultural differences influence students' learning styles in many ways. There are differences in regard to perceptual learning styles (*i.e.* visual, auditory, kinaesthetic and tactile). Some ethnic groups prefer group learning to individual learning styles, some prefer analytic tasks with materials void of a social context and others thrive through field-dependent learning contexts in highly social settings (Park, 2002). The importance of culturally responsive teaching (Gay, 2002) and research on different learning styles should be taken seriously. Nevertheless, it might not apply to all groups in the same way: some migrant and minority groups (*e.g.* Punjabis in the United States), who differ significantly in their culture, language and social situation from majority students, show equal or even better educational attainment than their peers, even if schools and teachers make little effort to accommodate these alleged needs (Ogbu, 1995; Nieto, 1995). Thus, teachers have to assess on an individual basis how their students might benefit from using different teaching styles or structural arrangements based on the ethnic composition of their class. Teachers can improve their teaching by acquiring knowledge and expanding their repertoire concerning different styles of learning and teaching and also by learning to assess the individual needs of students in diverse classrooms.

The argument that teaching *about* different ethnic and cultural groups in class is not sufficient does not mean that learning about the histories, experiences and contributions of different groups is not important. All students, whether or not they belong to the majority or a minority group, may benefit from getting to know various cultural ways and specifics. It has the potential to enrich their knowledge, to reduce stereotyping and may allow them to reflect on the particularities of their own culture. Also, if minority students are adequately represented in teaching, in the curriculum and in schoolbooks, they tend to feel included and valued.

It appears to be a challenging task for teachers, on the one hand, to acknowledge and act upon their students' cultural differences and particularities and, on the other, to bear in mind that the cultures of ethnic and migrant groups are multi-faceted and changing. Therefore, teachers must not simply presume that a students' national or ethnic belonging points to a specific culture or indicates a certain way of teaching. Rather, teachers have to get to know their students and base their decisions about teaching on an assessment of the particular situation at hand.

What is the crucial factor for children's school success? Nieto (1992, p. 203) provides an answer to this question by pointing to the interplay of cultural and structural factors and concludes:

> *Structural inequality and cultural incompatibility may be major causes of school failure, but they work differently on different communities, families, and individuals. How these factors are mediated within the school and home settings and their complex interplay probably are ultimately responsible for either the success or failure of students in schools.*

The significance attributed to structural and cultural factors in educational institutions is linked to choices made about school organisation, curricular contents, languages of instruction and teaching styles as well as to attitudes, expectations, judgements and courses of action taken by teachers and school administrators.

Responses to diversity – multicultural and intercultural education

Recognising and addressing diversity in education has taken a unique form in each of the OECD member countries. This has led to manifold educational approaches over time and space, each focusing on diverse target groups.[*] There are different historical circumstances that triggered the development of multicultural and intercultural education, different strands of thought, paradigms and ideologies, and different policies regarding, as well as various forms of, practical applications, curricula and pedagogies. In national contexts, multicultural and intercultural theories, policies and practices do not always correspond with each other, but, also, different and sometimes conflicting theories and practices exist at any given time.

Beginning in the 1970s, multicultural education in English-speaking countries in the OECD (*i.e.* Australia, Canada, New Zealand, the United Kingdom and the United States) began to respond to societal diversity. In the United States, the civil rights movement and the fight against racial inequality can be regarded as the prime driving force for the formation of multicultural education. Subsequently, the emerging ethnic revival movement and ongoing challenges resulting from immigration influenced the advancement of multicultural approaches. In Canada, historical conflicts between English-speaking citizens and Franco-Canadians, the struggle for the rights of their "First Nations" and continuing immigration can be seen as key elements underlying educational responses to diversity. In Australia, multicultural education was originally a reaction to massive immigration but not to the situation of aboriginal people, while current multicultural policy aims to be for all Australians. In the United Kingdom, the onset of educational responses to cultural diversity emerged in relation to the influx of people from former colonies and later of other immigrant groups.

In many other European countries, school systems began responding to increasing diversity in various ways and at various paces. In the wake of de-colonisation, educational approaches to diversity in the Netherlands and France targeted immigrants from former colonies. In several Central and Northern European countries, school systems developed programmes aimed at educating children of migrant workers (the so-called "guest workers").

---

[*] See for example: Banks, 2009; Banks and Banks, 1995; Grant and Portera, forthcoming; Gundara and Jacobs, 2000; Gundara and Portera, 2008; Luciak, 2006; Mecheril, 2004; Ramsey *et al.*, 1989; Sleeter, 1996; Sleeter and Grant, 2007.

Southern European countries that were previously countries of emigration, as well as former communist countries in Eastern Europe that had little experience with immigration, have only recently encountered diverse migrant populations, which include repatriated groups of former emigrants. Despite the existence of large Roma populations as well as other minority groups, multicultural or intercultural approaches to education were not pursued in these countries. In Japan, it was events occurring during the Second World War, in particular the bombings of Hiroshima and Nagasaki, that obliged educators to focus on inter-group relations and peace education. Hirasawa (2009) argues that prior to the 1990s *de facto* approaches to multicultural education can be found in practices that targeted the education of Japanese returnee students, who were socialised abroad, in the educational movement against the discrimination of the Buraku minority (Dowa education) and in anti-discrimination strategies to improve the educational situation of resident Korean students. In general, however, multicultural education in Japan is a rather recent phenomenon and can be seen as a response to new immigration.

Today, many OECD countries experience new forms of labour migration as well as family reunification, repatriation, the admittance of refugees and asylum-seekers and transnational mobility of international communities. While all this fosters the multicultural nature of OECD member countries and thus calls for adequate educational responses, in the wake of the economic crisis there are also reverse trends such as Japan's repatriation of Latin American guest workers, whose Japanese parents and grandparents emigrated to Brazil or Peru a century ago or the slowing emigration from Poland which in recent years clearly outweighed immigration. However, despite these trends, schools, particularly in major cities, will continue to be called upon to develop educational approaches that target increasingly diverse student populations.

Multiple forms of multicultural education were developed over the course of time in different contexts. Sleeter and Grant (1987) distinguished five different types:

1. Teaching the "culturally different", an assimilationist approach.

2. A human relations approach to improve interpersonal relations (but which does not address institutional racism).

3. Single-group studies that teach about a group's experience of oppression and its influence on the group's culture.

4. Multicultural education to enhance pluralism and equality (with a focus on curriculum, pedagogy, parent involvement, and tracking).

5. Education that is multicultural and social reconstructionist (this approach teaches about political and economic oppression and dis-

crimination and is meant to prepare students to apply social action skills [Sleeter, 1996, pp. 6-7]).

Other theorists such as Henry A. Giroux (1992) and Sonia Nieto (1992, 1999) subsequently emphasised the implications of structural inequalities and of oppressive social relationships, arguing for the need for educational transformation in order to achieve societal change and social justice.

James Banks (1995, 2009) identifies different elements of multicultural approaches, many of which have been used simultaneously since the onset of multicultural education. Banks names five key elements:

1. **Content integration**, *i.e.* including content about racial, ethnic, and cultural groups into the curriculum;

2. **Prejudice reduction**, *i.e.* reducing stereotyping, increasing inter-group relations by targeting students' racial attitudes through teaching;

3. **Equity pedagogy**, *i.e.* using appropriate teaching strategies by recognising diverse ways of learning and knowing;

4. **Knowledge construction**, *i.e.* viewing concepts, events and issues from the perspectives and experiences of a range of racial, ethnic and cultural groups, and understanding how different cultural frames of reference influence the construction of knowledge; and

5. **Empowering school culture and social structure**, *i.e.* examining and restructuring school culture and organisation to foster equality and empowerment.

Appelbaum (2002, pp. 6-8) points out that the various approaches to multicultural education have different implications for learners: purely additive approaches, if applied in a superficial way, may reinforce ideas that ethnic minority groups are outside the mainstream and might miss the various inter-relations between majority and minority students. Transformative approaches that enable students to view events and issues from the perspectives of different groups are more likely to highlight and foster the inter-connectedness of multicultural communities. Human relations approaches aiming at more sensitivity towards others and proposing the idea that "being different is what connects all students" are important but not sufficient to demonstrating and dealing with social inequalities. Approaches that look at minority groups as culturally different and call for culturally responsive teaching practices might contribute to raising the academic achievement of certain groups, but they may not benefit all groups in the same way and bear the risk of essentialising minority groups by disregarding within-group differences. Finally, social action or social reconstructionist models that teach about political and economic oppression may promote intergroup coalitions and induce transformative processes and social change.

However, not all approaches are similarly applicable for all groups or students of all ages. While all pupils may benefit from learning about different ways of perceiving the world, from getting to know how various forms of cultural specifics interrelate or from developing mutual respect, older students might be more able to question the dynamics of historical and societal developments that bring about social inequalities and put some groups in society at a disadvantage. Also, by offering culturally responsive teaching or language support, some approaches help to raise academic achievements of particular minority groups in schools that generally favour majority students. Other approaches that foster interrelations, stereotype reduction and mutual understanding are geared towards all students.

In the United States many school systems started with compensatory models that aimed at "teaching the culturally deprived" or "the culturally different". The development of multicultural theories with a stronger focus on enhancing pluralism was not always followed by corresponding applications in schools even though by the 1980s multicultural education had become a topical issue at universities and colleges. In several other countries (*i.e.* Australia, Canada and Great Britain), where the driving force of social movements was lacking or less influential, federal governments took steps to overcome assimilationist models (Sleeter, 1996). It should be noted that racial inequality played a central role in educational approaches in the United States (*i.e.* "racial awareness education") and Great Britain ("anti-racist education"), but racial issues were not as high on the agenda of most other OECD countries. There are at least two possible explanations for this: first, members of so-called "racial minorities" comprise a much smaller percentage of the population of these countries; and second, despite the acknowledgment of the existence of racism, the use of "race" as a category or concept became highly controversial in many European countries after the holocaust, when racist propaganda legitimised the persecution and genocide of members of different ethnic, cultural and religious groups by referring to them as "races" with distinct biological differences.

Since the late 1970s in Europe, *intercultural education* is the term most frequently used when referring to the teaching of culturally diverse groups even though the concepts of multicultural education or anti-racist education are also used (Allemann-Ghionda, 2008). Nowadays, intercultural education is meant to target all students; however, over the course of time and in many ways even today, practical applications of intercultural education focused primarily on the education of migrant communities. Also, school programmes for indigenous, autochthonous or national minorities, which are often termed "minority schooling", generally are not regarded as intercultural programmes.

The initial "dual approach" of intercultural education was meant to preserve students' original language and culture to allow repatriation at any given time while at the same time offering measures to learn the host country's language. This was followed by *assimilatory and compensatory* measures ("pedagogy for foreigners") when it became clear that many migrants were to stay in the host countries. In the 1980s, previously deficit-oriented approaches were critiqued, and the theoretical discourse changed from perceiving only migrants as being different to a mutual recognition of *difference*. Schools were now seen as part of the problem rather than the solution in regard to migrant students' academic under-achievement (Mecheril, 2004).

As a result of this reframing of the situation, intercultural education was aimed at targeting all students rather than just minority students. Theories about intercultural learning or intercultural communication and dialogue began to evolve and to be applied. The educational principle of intercultural education was meant to underlie all forms of teaching and to foster mutual respect and understanding. Starting in the 1990s, discourses on *dominance* (Mecheril, 2004) that highlighted the negative impacts of institutional discrimination and that called for social justice and inclusion began to develop on the European continent. Thus, elements that were previously addressed by anti-racist or non-racist education in Great Britain were now included in the debate in mainland Europe. Hitherto existing intercultural approaches were criticised for using a static and ahistorical concept of culture, for over-emphasising cultural differences and for "culturalising" phenomena induced by social and structural inequalities. Parallel to that, the process of European Union integration heightened awareness that former notions of citizenship needed to be reconsidered and that students had to be prepared to live in societies that were becoming increasingly diverse.

While theoretical conceptions of intercultural education have changed over time, it appears that the main emphasis of policies and school practices continues to lie on fostering migrant students' integration and second language acquisition. Even though throughout much of recent history, students' native languages were perceived as a problem rather than an asset, schools in some countries do offer first-language instruction. However, the controversy about the role that the native language plays in minority students' education continues. For some, native language is seen as a prerequisite for acquiring proficiency in a second language, but also, valuing students' native language is regarded as "an essential component of intercultural education, ensuring that migrant children feel that their cultural and language background is appreciated as much as that of the majority" (Brind *et al.*, 2007, quoted in Nusche, 2009, p. 29).

Aside from language issues, implementing a non-centric curriculum and intercultural pedagogy are regarded as relevant intercultural measures that, on the one hand, target academic underachievement of minority groups and, on the other, are geared towards preparing all students for living in a diverse society. In her comparative study of five European countries that differ in diversity, namely Germany, France, the United Kingdom ("old" immigration countries); Italy ("new" immigration country); and Hungary (little immigration but larger national ethnic minority groups), Allemann-Ghionda (2008, p. viii) points to difficulties regarding the implementation of official policies in daily school practice:

> *In all member states, the implementation of intended policies tends to be difficult. One problem is the successful instruction and integration of migrant and minority pupils from families with low incomes and little education. The other problem is a contradiction between intercultural ideas and the national and mono-cultural thinking as well as cultural prejudice present in societies and schools.*

As described, cultural diversity and difference are conceptualised in various ways and the application of educational approaches – irrespective of being labelled multicultural or intercultural – varies depending on national and local school contexts as well as individual teacher practices. Also, how diversity is perceived, interpreted, and dealt with depends on political considerations and – consciously or unconsciously – is guided by ideological concerns. If we consider how different societies and schools nowadays deal with diversity, we cannot detect a unilinear progressive process. Rather, in many ways diversity is still regarded as a problem much more frequently than it is perceived as a resource or as a right. Thus, teachers need to decide which model best addresses their students' needs, fosters their education, and has the potential to minimise social inequalities.

Implications for policies and practice

Proclamations to work toward equity and inclusion and toward fostering diversity certainly entail noble goals and conform to the current *zeitgeist*. However, educational strategies, policies, and practices intending to make positive contributions must rely on "empirical foundations" rather than "good will" (Dietz, 2007, p. 18) and on "evidence-based work" rather than "hunches" (Gundara and Portera, 2010, p. 465). Not only do we need improved conceptual clarity, *i.e.* a thorough understanding of what diversity means, but we also need a better understanding of the implications of diversity in different national, regional, and local contexts and for institutionalised forms of education therein. Furthermore, there is a need for more informative data in order to better assess the effects of current policies and practices.

The wealth of literature on the perceived underachievement of migrant and ethnic minority groups in schools raises two major concerns: firstly, it points to evidence that students' cultural, social, and linguistic backgrounds could influence academic success or failure in certain educational contexts. Secondly, it frequently obscures the fact that there is variability in school performance of migrant and minority students across different national settings (OECD, 2006). Overall, migrant students in OECD countries have lower academic success than native students, yet there are hardly any differences in performance between migrants and natives in Australia, Canada, and New Zealand, especially when socio-economic background is controlled for. Students with Turkish backgrounds perform better in Switzerland compared to Germany and Austria; and in Canada, Hong Kong-China, Luxembourg, Sweden and Switzerland, the performance gap between immigrant and native students is much smaller than in other OECD countries (OECD, 2006). However, conclusions based on the basis of aggregated data must be interpreted with caution.

Finding adequate responses to diversity is among the most pressing concerns of our time. This goal is supported by initiatives and publications of supranational organisations such as the UNESCO (2006) *Guidelines on Intercultural Education*, the Council of Europe's (2008) *White Paper on Intercultural Dialogue*, European Commission's (2008) *Green Paper on Migration and Mobility* and publications related to tolerance and non-discrimination by the Organization for Security and Co-operation in Europe (OSCE). As outlined above, multicultural and intercultural initiatives have worked towards achieving this goal for decades, and many individual teachers and schools in a variety of countries have made great efforts in this direction. However, the application of diversity policies and practices on a broader scale is still lacking, and there are indications that many teachers do not feel well-enough prepared to teach diverse student populations (Burns, 2009).

Preconceived notions about ethnic and migrant groups' distinctiveness and "recipes" or "tools" offered in teacher education that are meant to be "multicultural" or "intercultural" are likely to have negative effects if they are not suitably adapted to the context and student. Teachers, who are called upon to recognise diverse ways of learning and knowing and to develop culturally responsive teaching strategies, need to engage with all students in their classes and make attempts to understand their cultural backgrounds and the communities to which these students belong. Equity not only presupposes respect for cultural difference but also a recognition of special rights pertaining to minority groups, in particular, disadvantaged and marginalised groups.

Interpretations that attribute school success and failure primarily to cultural differences must be treated with care as they tend to obscure oppressive relations in society as well as the relevance of individual actors. Ng *et al.* (2007, p. 101) have shown that this not only holds true for migrant and minority groups who show comparatively low school success but also for high achieving minorities. For instance, regarding Asian Americans as a distinct and stable cultural group and calling them a "model minority" goes hand in hand with "perpetuating stereotypes about Asian American foreignness and endorsing the goal of assimilation."

It should be noted that recognition of diversity concerns issues that go beyond matters related to educational performance of diverse student populations. On a broader level, it stirs debates about the role of schools as state institutions and about the essence of national culture and citizenship. As pointed out by Dietz (2007, p. 25), "The main obstacle that any strategy directed towards interculturalising and/or diversifying education will have to face is the institution of school and how deeply rooted it is not only in nationalising pedagogy, but in the nation-state itself". There are highly charged controversies about bilingual education, about favouring secular or religious worldviews in public schools, about the canon of great books and curriculum diversification as well as about minority representation and affirmative action. Often, the arguments for or against are motivated more by political rather than by educational concerns.

A lot can be gained if diversity is seen as a resource and as a right. From an educational standpoint, diversity opens opportunities for self-reflection and reflection on one's own cultural background. Engaging with people from different cultures and getting to know other languages fosters personal development, interpersonal understanding, and connectedness. School climates in which diverse cultural identities can be freely expressed support the relationship between schools and the communities they serve. Teachers and teacher educators can make important contributions in helping students prepare for living in a society characterised by rapidly changing cultural, social and economic conditions. The conventional means and aims of education are no longer suited to help students keep up with the demands and challenges of an increasingly globalised world with high international mobility and transfer as well as speedy technological advances. Societies at large are challenged to unite against recurring social divide and inequalities; it is the role of educators to facilitate educational achievement of all groups, intercultural understanding, social justice and solidarity.

References

Albro, R. (2005), *Making Cultural Policy and Confounding Cultural Diversity, www.culturalpolicy.org/commons/comment-print.cfm?ID=26.*

Allemann-Ghionda, C. (2008), *Intercultural Education in Schools*, a comparative study on behalf of the European Parliament's Committee on Culture and Education, Brussels, April 2008, available at*www.europarl.europa. eu/activities/committees/studies.do?language=en.*

Altman, I. and M. M. Chemers (1984), *Culture and Environment*, Cambridge University Press, Cambridge.

Appelbaum, P. M. (2002), *Multicultural and Diversity Education: A Reference Handbook,* ABC-CLIO, Santa Barbara, California.

Banks, J. A. (ed.) (2009), *Routledge International Companion to Multicultural Education*, Routledge, Taylor and Francis, Oxford.

Banks, J. A. (1995), "Multicultural Education: Historical Development, Dimensions, and Practice", in Banks J. A. and C. A. M. Banks (eds.), *Handbook of Research on Multicultural Education,* Macmillan, New York, pp. 3-24.

Banks J. A. and C. A. M. Banks (eds.) (1995), *Handbook of Research on Multicultural Education,* Macmillan, New York.

Bennett, T. (2001), *Differing Diversities Transversal Study on the Theme of Cultural Policy and Cultural Civersity*, Council of Europe, Strasbourg.

Brind, T., C. Harper and K. Moore (2008), *Education for Migrant, Minority and Marginalised Children in Europe*, a report commissioned by the Open Society Institute's Education Support Programme.

Burns, T. (2009), *Teacher Education for Diversity*, Powerpoint presentation delivered at OECD/ CERI Teacher Education for Diversity experts meeting, Genoa, Italy, 29 May 2009. *www.oecd.org/dataoecd/34/7/42945624.pdf.*

Clifford, J. and G. E. Marcus (eds.) (1986), *Writing Culture. The Poetics and Politics of Ethnography,* University of California Press, Berkeley.

Council of Europe (2008), White Paper on Intercultural Dialogue "Living Together as Equals in Dignity", Strasbourg, *www.coe.int/t/dg4/intercultural/ Source/Pub_White_Paper/White%20Paper_final_revised_EN.pdf.*

Dietz, G. (2007), "Keyword: Cultural Diversity, A Guide through the Debate", *Zeitschrift für Erziehungswissenschaft*, Vol. 10, No. 1, pp. 7-30.

European Commission (2008), Green Paper Migration and Mobility: Challenges and Opportunities for EU Education Systems, Brussels, *http:// ec.europa.eu/education/school21/com423_en.pdf.*

Gay, G. (2002), "Preparing for Culturally Responsive Teaching", *Journal of Teacher Education,* Vol. 53, No. 2, pp. 106-116.

Geertz, C. (1986), "The Uses of Diversity. The Tanner Lectures on Human Values", paper delivered at The University of Michigan on 8 November 1985, *www.iwp.uni-linz.ac.at/lxe/sektktf/gg/GeertzTexts/Uses_Diversity.htm.*

Gibson, M. A. (1988), *Accommodation without Assimilation: Punjabi Sikh Immigrants in an American High School,* Cornell University Press, Ithaca, New York.

Gibson, M.A. (1997), "Complicating the Immigrant/Involuntary Minority Typology", *Anthropology and Education Quarterly*, Vol. 28, No. 3, pp. 431-454.

Grant, C. A and A. Portera (eds.) (2010), *Intercultural and Multicultural Education: Enhancing Global Interconnectedness*, Routledge, New York.

Gundara, J.S. (2008), *The Organisation and Structure of Intercultural Teacher Education*, paper delivered at The Copenhagen Conference "Education for Intercultural Understanding and Dialogue" on 21-22 October 2008, Danish Ministry of Foreign Affairs, UNESCO, ISESCO, ALESCO, Council of Europe, The Anna Lindh Centre (unpublished).

Gundara, J.S. and S. Jacobs (eds.) (2000), *Intercultural Europe: Diversity and Social Policy.* Aldershot, Hampshire/ Brookfield, Ashgate, Vermont.

Gundara, J.S. and A. Portera (2008), "Theoretical Reflections on Intercultural Education", *Intercultural Education*, Vol. 19, No. 6, pp. 463-468.

Hall, S. (1996), *Critical Dialogues in Cultural Studies*, eds. D. Morley, C. Kuan-Hsing, Routledge, London.

Hirasawa, Y. (2009), "Multicultural Education in Japan", in Banks, J. A. (ed.), *Routledge International Companion to Multicultural Education*, Routledge, Taylor and Francis, Oxford, p. 159-169.

International Organization for Migration (2005), World Migration Report 2005, *www.iom.int/jahia/Jahia/about-migration/lang/en.*

Knudsen, S. (2006), "Intersectionality: A Theoretical Inspiration in the Analysis of Minority Cultures and Identities in Textbooks", in Bruillard E., B. Aamotsbakken, S.V. Knudsen, and M. Horsley (eds.), *Caught in the Web or Lost in the Textbook*, Caen: IARTEM, pp. 61-76, www.caen.iufm.fr/colloque_iartem/pdf/knudsen.pdf.

Kroeber, A. L. and C. Kluckhohn (eds.) (1952), *Culture: A Critical Review of Concepts and Definitions*, Peabody Museum, Cambridge, Massachusetts.

Luciak, M. (2004), "Minority Status and Schooling – John U. Ogbu's Theory and the Schooling of Ethnic Minorities in Europe", *Intercultural Education*, Vol. 15, No. 4, pp. 359-368.

Luciak, M. (2006), "Minority Schooling and Intercultural Education – a Comparison of Recent Developments in the Old and New EU Member States", *Intercultural Education*, Vol. 17, No. 1, pp. 73-80.

Mecheril, P. (2004), *Einführung in die Migrationspädagogik*, Beltz, Weinheim and Basel.

Ng, J. C., S.S. Lee, and Y.K. Pak (2007), "Contesting the Model Minority and Perpetual Foreigner Stereotypes: A Critical Review of Literature on Asian Americans in Education", in Parker, L. (ed.), *Review of Research in Education: Difference, Diversity, and Distinctiveness in Education and Learning*, Vol. 31, pp. 95-130.

Nieto, S. (1992), *Affirming Diversity: The Sociopolitical Context of Multicultural Education*, White Plains, N.Y., Longman, White Plains, New York.

Nieto, S. (1995), "From Brown Heroes and Holidays to Assimilationist Agendas: Reconsidering the Critiques of Multicultural Education", in Sleeter, C. E. and P. McLaren (eds.), *Multicultural Education, Critical Pedagogy, and the Politics of Difference*, State University of New York Press, Albany, pp. 191-220.

Nusche, D. (2009), "What Works in Migrant Education? A Review of Evidence and Policy Options", *OECD Education Working Paper No. 22*, OECD Publishing, Paris.

OECD (2009), *International Migration Outlook*, OECD annual report, OECD Publishing, Paris, *www.oecd.org/document/51/0,3343 ,en_2649_33931_43009971_1_1_1_1,00.html*.

Ogbu, J. U. (1991), "Immigrant and Involuntary Minorities in Comparative Perspective", in Ogbu, J. U. and Gibson, M. A. (eds.), *Minority Status and Schooling; a Comparative Study of Immigrant and Involuntary Minorities*, Garland, New York, pp. 3-33.

Ogbu, J. U. (1992), "Understanding Cultural Diversity and Learning", *Educational Researcher*, Vol. 21, No. 8, pp. 5-14.

Ogbu, J. U. (1995), "The Influence of Culture on Learning and Behaviour", in Falk J.H. and L.D. Dierking (eds.), *Public Institutions for Personal Learning,* American Association of Museums, Washington, D.C., pp. 79-95.

Park, C. C. (2002), "Cross-cultural Differences in Learning Styles of Secondary English Learners", *Bilingual Research Journal*, Summer 2002.

Peters, B. (1997), "'Multikulturalismus' und 'Differenz'. Zu einigen Kategorien der Zeitdiagnose", in Münkler, H. and B. Ladwig (eds.), *Furcht und Faszination. Facetten der Fremdheit*, Akademie Verlag, Berlin.

Ramsey, P, G., E. Battle, L. R. Williams (1989), *Multicultural Education: a Source Book,* Garland Publishing, New York.

Schütz, A. (1959), *Strukturen der Lebenswelt*, Suhrkamp, Frankfurt.

Sleeter, Christine E. (1996), *Multicultural Education as Social Activism*, SUNY Press Albany, New York.

Sleeter, C. E. and C. A. Grant (1987), "An Analysis of Multicultural Education in the United States", *Harvard Educational Review*, Vol. 57, No. 4, pp. 421-444.

Sleeter, E. and C. A. Grant (2007), *Making Choices for Multicultural Education,* 5th edition, Wiley, New York.

OECD (2006), *Where Immigrant Students Succeed. A Comparative Review of Performance and Engagement in PISA 2003,* OECD, Paris.

UNESCO (2006), *UNESCO Guidelines on Intercultural Education.* Paris, *http://www.unesdoc.unesco.org/images/0014/001478/147878e.pdf.*

UNESCO (2009), "What is Cultural Diversity", *http://portal.unesco. org/culture/en/ev.php-URL_ID=13031&URL_DO=DO_TOPIC&URL_ SECTION=201.html.*

United Nations (2009), *International Migration Report 2006, A Global Assessment.* Department of Economic and Social Affairs. Population Division. New York, *www.un.org/esa/population/publications/2006_ MigrationRep/report.htm.*

Chapter 3

The OECD Teaching and Learning International Survey (TALIS) and teacher education for diversity

Ben Jensen

Grattan Institute, Australia

On average across TALIS countries, 47% of teachers report a high or moderate need for professional development for teaching in a multicultural setting. This level of need was found to vary within schools but not as a function of school types or different types of teachers. Professional development programmes therefore should focus on the needs of individual teachers rather than of schools or regions. It is further shown that there is a need to develop a strong evaluative framework capable of providing feedback on all aspects of teaching, particularly those related to diversity. Teachers report that such evaluation and feedback has a positive impact upon their development and leads to changes in their teaching practices. It is argued that an evaluative framework is an effective mechanism to develop teachers' skills and provides policy makers with a cost-effective tool to prioritise specific aspects of school education and foster school improvements.

> ## *From the OECD online consultation: relevant professional development is key*
>
> **Although sensitivity to diversity issues was considered very important for effective teaching, only half of responding teachers reported receiving professional development which met their needs. What do we know about how schools and systems can respond to the training needs of their teachers?**

Introduction

Expansions in migration in a number of countries have occurred during a period of increasing retention rates and focus of many policy makers upon the proportion and types of students completing their school education (OECD, 2008a). This has placed further demands upon teachers who are required to educate students with a broader array of abilities and, in many cases, a wider range of backgrounds (OECD, 2005). Given these changes there should be greater demand for teachers that are trained for teaching a diverse student population and the extent to which teachers are effective in teaching such populations is of paramount importance.

This chapter utilises the OECD Teaching and Learning International Survey (TALIS) to analyse aspects of teacher development and diversity. It provides much needed data and quantitative analysis on teachers and teaching in the context of these important issues and complements the analysis already undertaken of the TALIS data which is described in the next section (OECD, 2009). Quantitative analysis of teacher development and diversity first requires that the concepts are defined. Teacher development can serve a number of purposes such as (OECD, 1998):

- to update individuals' knowledge of a subject in light of recent advances in the area;

- to update individuals' skills, attitudes and approaches in light of the development of new teaching techniques and objectives, new circumstances and new educational research;

- to enable individuals to apply changes made to curricula or other aspects of teaching practice;

- to enable schools to develop and apply new strategies concerning the curriculum and other aspects of teaching practice;.

- to exchange information and expertise among teachers and others, *e.g.* academics, industrialists;

- to help weaker teachers become more effective.

For the issue of diversity, teacher development will depend upon the initial and the on-the-job training of teachers. This will vary across and within countries as well as within schools. TALIS takes a broad view of teacher development extending the concept past structured courses and programmes to also emphasise the on-the-job training and continual development of teachers. This chapter emphasises the importance of the school as an organisation that evaluates and develops teachers in all areas of their work but especially in regard to diversity.

Diversity is potentially a broad subject. A definitive answer to the question of what is and is not diversity is not attempted here. Instead, it is important to define diversity with respect to the TALIS data that is being analysed in this chapter in which diversity is discussed in the context of *teaching in a multicultural setting.* This is the closest match to diversity available in the TALIS dataset. Although it would also be possible to analyse data regarding *teaching students with special learning needs* (which could be incorporated into a discussion on diversity), the focus here is solely on teaching in a multicultural setting.

This chapter seeks to address two main questions:

1. How much professional development is needed for teaching in a multicultural setting and which teachers need it the most?

2. What is the role of the evaluative structure of education in schools to develop teachers' abilities to teach in a multi-cultural setting?

The second of these research questions moves away from narrow definitions of professional development with structured courses or programmes. It underscores the role of school evaluation and teacher appraisal and feedback in the ongoing development of teachers' abilities. Such an emphasis views teacher development not as a static activity where development occurs at specified periods (*e.g.* after completing a course or short-programme) but as a continual process where ongoing appraisal and feedback allow teachers to develop their skills in the school organisational environment (OECD, 2009).

What is TALIS?

TALIS is the first OECD international survey of teachers and their school principals. It focuses on lower secondary education in both public and private schools. It offers a rich dataset that provides representative samples of teachers across 23 countries (Australia, Austria, Belgium [Flemish Community], Brazil, Bulgaria, Denmark, Estonia, Hungary, Iceland, Ireland, Italy, Korea, Lithuania, Malaysia, Malta, Mexico, Norway, Poland, Portugal, the Slovak Republic, Slovenia, Spain, and Turkey). Data was obtained on a number of issues but concentrated specifically on aspects of teacher professional development; teacher beliefs, attitudes and practices; teacher appraisal and feedback; and school leadership (OECD, 2009).

In each of the 23 participating countries, around 200 schools were randomly selected to participate in the survey. In each school, one questionnaire was completed by the school principal and another by 20 randomly selected teachers. The questionnaires each took about 45 minutes to complete and could be filled in on paper or on-line. In total, TALIS sampled around 90 000 teachers representing more than 2 million teachers in TALIS countries.[1]

Questions pertinent to teaching in a multicultural setting span several areas: teachers' professional development needs, school evaluation, and teacher appraisal and feedback.[2] Each of these are analysed below and the links between them and teacher development are explored. It is important to remember that the TALIS data is not administrative data but is the voice of teachers and school principals. It is their beliefs and reports on themselves, their teaching and work and their school. This makes TALIS a unique and important dataset in shaping public policy and the development of schools and teachers.

Teachers' professional development and their developmental needs

TALIS asked teachers about the professional development they had received and their professional development needs. It was found that most teachers undertake often substantial levels of professional development. Just fewer than 90% of teachers reported that they had undertaken some form of professional development in the preceding 18-month period. On average, these teachers undertook just over 17 days of professional envelopment during this period, just over half of which was compulsory (OECD, 2009). However, the extent of this professional development varied considerably between teachers and also between countries. Many teachers in Australia, Belgium (Flemish Community), Iceland, Malta, the Slovak Republic and Slovenia undertook professional development that amounted to less than 10 days over the 18-month period. While in countries such as Bulgaria,

Italy, Korea and Mexico teachers, on average, undertook more than 30 days of professional development during this 18-month period. The professional development undertaken by teachers most commonly consisted of informal dialogue to improve teaching, specified courses and workshops, and reading professional literature (OECD, 2009).

Within schools, specific programmes focusing on mentoring and induction for teachers who are new to a school have been considered successful in a number of countries (OECD, 2005). TALIS has shown that these programmes are generally common across TALIS countries but with sometimes large country differences. On average across TALIS countries, 45% of teachers worked in schools that had a formal induction process for all teachers new to a school and a further 27% worked in schools that restricted the induction programme to only those teachers for whom it is their first teaching job. On average, 29% worked in schools with no formal induction process. Comparatively, on average among TALIS countries one-quarter of teachers worked in schools with no formal mentoring process. There is a substantial proportion of schools which consider mentoring programmes as an initial rather than an ongoing activity in teachers' careers. On average across TALIS countries, 37% of teachers worked in schools that provided a mentoring programme for all teachers new to the school and a similar proportion (38%) worked in schools that provided mentoring programmes only for those teachers for whom it is their first teaching job (see Chapter 3 of *Creating Effective Teaching and Learning Environments: First Results from TALIS* OECD, for further details). It is argued in this chapter that an evaluative framework within schools should be an ongoing process in the evaluation and development of schools and teachers.

Difficulties exist in many education systems in identifying the best professional development and training for teachers that will increase their effectiveness and have the greatest positive impact upon students. Not only is the most appropriate format of the professional development difficult to determine but also the focus. Administrators and policy makers are often forced to best estimate which professional development would be most effective. Should it focus on new content and performance standards, students with special learning needs or another area? Of importance should also be which teachers undertake different sorts of professional development. Greater information is required to answer these questions and in many education systems this information does not exist to guide decision-making.

A key aspect of the issue of training and developing teachers to teach in diverse classrooms is the extent that current teachers believe they require further professional development in the area. Teachers may believe that they have great professional development needs while others may feel adequately equipped to effectively teach their classes and handle diversity issues.

Teachers' beliefs of the developmental needs would most likely be influenced by a number of factors such as the amount and quality of their initial education and the professional development they have already received, their natural abilities to effectively teach diverse classrooms, and feedback from appraisals of their work.

Developmental needs for teaching in a multicultural setting

TALIS asked teachers about their professional development needs[3] in 11 different areas: content and performance standards in their main subject field(s); student assessment practices; classroom management; knowledge and understanding of their main subject field(s); knowledge and understanding of instructional practices in their main subject field(s); ICT skills for teaching; teaching students with special learning needs; student discipline and behaviour problems; school management and administration; student counselling; and, teaching in a multicultural setting. While the focus here is on this last area, it is interesting to also consider professional development needs in this area relative to other areas.

Over half of teachers reported that they required more professional development than they received during the previous 18 months (OECD, 2009). The extent required in particular areas varies across aspects of teaching with the greatest level evident in teaching students with special learning needs. One third of teachers reported a high need for development in this area. Table 3.1 details the extent to which teachers report they require professional development to teach in a multicultural setting. Just under one-fifth of teachers believe that they need no professional development in this area. This is particularly apparent in Belgium (Flemish Community), Denmark and Slovenia where around one-third of teachers believed they had no need for this type of professional development, and in Poland where this was reported by 45% of teachers. This contrasts sharply with the situation in Brazil, Italy, Korea, Malaysia, Portugal and Spain, where less than 10% of teachers reported having no need for professional development for teaching in a multicultural setting. On average across TALIS countries, just over one-third of teachers reported having a low level of need for professional development in this area and a similar amount reported having a moderate level of professional development needs. Fourteen percent of teachers reported having a high level of need for professional development for teaching in a multicultural setting on average across TALIS countries. Demand for this type of professional development is greatest in Ireland and Italy, where around one-quarter of teachers reported a high need for professional development, and in Brazil and Malaysia, where over 30% of teachers report high professional development needs for teaching in a multicultural setting.

Table 3.1. **Teachers' professional development needs: teaching in a multicultural setting (2007-08)**

Percentage of teachers who reported their level of need for professional development for teaching in a multicultural setting

Countries	No need at all		Low level of need		Moderate level of need		High level of need	
	%	(SE)[a]	%	(SE)	%	(SE)	%	(SE)
Australia	22.2	(1.25)	53.5	(1.46)	20.2	(1.18)	4.0	(0.43)
Austria	27.8	(0.93)	38.6	(0.96)	23.7	(0.88)	10.0	(0.68)
Belgium (Flemish)	32.6	(1.27)	46.6	(1.03)	17.1	(1.08)	3.7	(0.46)
Brazil	7.7	(0.64)	22.9	(1.08)	36.4	(1.13)	33.2	(1.22)
Bulgaria	22.1	(1.59)	31.4	(2.06)	31.0	(1.91)	15.5	(2.35)
Denmark	32.0	(1.86)	38.8	(1.51)	22.1	(1.37)	7.1	(0.98)
Estonia	18.6	(0.91)	40.7	(1.20)	31.1	(1.22)	9.7	(0.77)
Hungary	23.6	(1.48)	35.5	(1.01)	30.2	(1.03)	10.7	(0.68)
Iceland	10.2	(0.90)	35.5	(1.37)	40.3	(1.35)	14.0	(0.92)
Ireland	12.0	(0.87)	28.3	(1.29)	35.4	(1.22)	24.3	(1.31)
Italy	6.1	(0.44)	19.0	(0.84)	49.6	(0.88)	25.3	(0.85)
Korea	4.8	(0.41)	30.3	(0.93)	54.6	(1.03)	10.4	(0.61)
Lithuania	25.7	(1.18)	37.6	(1.07)	27.0	(1.13)	9.8	(0.79)
Malaysia	7.3	(0.89)	17.9	(0.95)	44.5	(1.16)	30.3	(1.35)
Malta	12.8	(1.13)	36.7	(1.64)	36.5	(1.66)	14.0	(1.36)
Mexico	15.0	(0.79)	31.2	(1.02)	35.6	(1.05)	18.2	(0.93)
Norway	19.1	(1.23)	40.2	(1.48)	32.5	(1.36)	8.3	(0.75)
Poland	44.5	(1.35)	30.0	(0.97)	18.9	(0.82)	6.6	(0.58)
Portugal	6.8	(0.52)	28.1	(0.96)	48.2	(1.09)	17.0	(0.73)
Slovak Republic	25.9	(1.62)	40.7	(1.24)	28.8	(1.42)	4.6	(0.52)
Slovenia	30.0	(1.08)	34.7	(1.02)	25.4	(0.96)	9.9	(0.68)
Spain	8.9	(0.58)	29.3	(0.85)	44.3	(1.11)	17.5	(0.73)
Turkey	21.2	(1.74)	35.8	(1.68)	28.8	(2.03)	14.5	(1.10)
TALIS Average	*19.0*	*(0.24)*	*34.0*	*(0.26)*	*33.1*	*(0.26)*	*13.9*	*(0.21)*

Note: a. Standard error.

Source: OECD, TALIS Database.

TALIS did not probe reasons underlying teachers' identification of their developmental needs, so it is not possible to ascertain why they reported high professional development needs for teaching in a multicultural setting. Presumably these teachers believe that their teaching effectiveness would be enhanced with such professional development. This could be because they have difficulties with particular aspects of teaching in a multicultural setting or, alternatively, because they wish to improve what they believe is already an effective level of teaching. Regardless, it sends a clear signal to policy makers and administrators of the need to provide effective professional development in this area.

Given the necessity of training teachers who report having a high need for professional development for teaching in a multicultural setting, it is important for school principals, administrators, stakeholders and policy makers to know which teachers report having these needs, and why. A common assumption may be that these teachers are concentrated in particular schools or geographic locations or perhaps lack the experience to have properly developed these skills. However, data from TALIS shows that this is not the case and that there are no major defining characteristics that separate teachers who report high needs for this kind of training from those who do not. Comparing the populations of these two groups of teachers revealed neither substantial gender differences nor differences stemming from age or experience. Subject differences also revealed no discerning pattern in the need for professional development for teaching in a multicultural setting. In addition, no substantial differences were found between teachers in different types of schools. That is, similar proportions of public school teachers reported having high needs for professional development for teaching in a multicultural setting as teachers from non-government schools.[4]

This issue was further analysed by looking at the linguistic diversity of teachers' classrooms. Comparisons of teachers' reports of the linguistic diversity of the classes they teach[5] did not reveal substantial differences in the proportion reporting high needs for professional development for teaching in a multicultural setting. There was little difference in the percentage of teachers reporting high development needs in this area across teachers who reported different percentages of students in their class with a language background other than the language(s) of instruction. It should be noted however that this is not an ideal proxy for diversity as countries can have large portions of the population who speak languages other than the language of school instruction. Examples would include the French-speaking population in Canada and the Russian-speaking population in Estonia but it should also be noted that in both of these cases French and Russian would be considered the language of instruction in many schools in these two countries. In addition, analysis of the data did not indicate that this was a significant problem in this case.

It is an important finding for those involved in teacher development that *those teachers with relatively few students from different language backgrounds still reported just as high professional development needs for teaching in a multicultural setting.* This has two crucial implications:

- First, professional development programmes aimed at diversity issues should not be concentrated in particular schools or geographic areas. Rather, they should be targeted to teachers who have the greatest need for professional development and training focused on this area. Ideally, teachers' developmental needs would be identified as part of the evaluative structure of school education where various mechanisms such as peer observation, self-assessment and analysis of student progress identify the greatest needs for development. Comprehensive systems do not, unfortunately, exist across education systems and there is relatively little data on teachers' developmental needs considering the resources invested and the potential benefits from effectively targeted development programmes. As shown above, teachers with high professional development needs for teaching in a multicultural setting are likely to come from across the spectrum of the school education system. It is therefore important to not only develop a system that provides teacher professional development and training to teachers in different schools but, in the longer term, develop mechanisms that document teachers' developmental needs and the methods employed to address such needs.

- Second, it highlights the importance of including diversity issues in the continual development of teachers. It needs to be a factor of the feedback and development they receive within schools regarding their teaching and the appraisal of their work. This should also coincide with a focus on diversity issues in the evaluation of the education that schools provide. This second issue is developed further in the following section.

Teacher development in the TALIS context

One of the four main areas covered in TALIS is teacher professional development. This covers a number of issues such as the amount and type of professional development undertaken by teachers, the impact of that development and their professional development needs (OECD, 2009). Yet, teacher development is also a focus of the analysis of school evaluation[6] and teacher appraisal and feedback which are considered important mechanisms for helping teachers improve their work, develop their skills, and improve the effectiveness of schools. This is detailed in the description of the framework for the evaluation of schools which is briefly described below in the context of teacher development (OECD, 2009).

The development of teachers and organisations requires continual evaluation of strengths and weaknesses to identify areas in which development is needed, to assess progress in such development, to further develop and disseminate strengths, and to generally help teachers in their work to enhance job satisfaction and improve their working lives (OECD, 2009). Mechanisms to provide feedback to teachers and school principals need to be established for evaluation and appraisal to be effective and influence people's work. For example, teachers can act to improve their teaching of diverse classrooms after receiving feedback about their teaching from a peer or senior member of a school. Evaluating or appraising teachers' work and providing feedback to develop teachers' skills provides opportunities for continual development. Emphasis on these areas requires a shift from thinking of development as a more static activity whereby teachers develop only in specified development activities such as courses and education programmes. TALIS showed that teachers believe in the positive benefits of ongoing teacher appraisal and feedback reporting that it increases their job satisfaction and improves specific aspects of their teaching (OECD, 2009). This is particularly important given the focus on the opposition from various stakeholders that can occur with a new system of teacher and school evaluation (OECD, 2008; Bethell, 2005). Effective evaluation of, and feedback to teachers and schools provides important personal benefits to teachers, and can further develop the effectiveness of schools and teachers.

Framework for the evaluation of school education

The framework for evaluation of education in schools encompasses both school evaluation and teacher appraisal and feedback which are guided by centralised objectives, policies and programmes to improve school and teacher development. Figure 3.1 depicts the framework and the corresponding data collected in TALIS. A key feature of an effectively operating framework is an alignment of teacher appraisal and feedback and school evaluations not only with each other but with central objectives, policies, programmes and regulations. Such alignment with effective evaluation should create school and teacher development in the areas identified centrally. This is supported by a key finding from TALIS that details that even though the framework is underdeveloped in most TALIS countries, school evaluations can affect the nature and form of teacher appraisal and feedback which can, in turn, affect what teachers do in the classroom (OECD, 2009). A greater focus on the structure for evaluation for education and the ongoing development of teachers and schools may create sustained benefits in the form of teacher and school improvement.

Historically, school evaluation focused upon ensuring that schools adhered to procedures and policies and various administrative requirements

(OECD, 2008a). In several countries, this focus has shifted to using the evaluation of schools to facilitate school choice, elevate school accountability, and increase school and teacher improvement (Plank and Smith, 2008; OECD, 2006). An additional motivating factor in some education systems is the increase in school autonomy that occurred over recent years that have shifted greater decision-making to the school level (OECD, 2008b). As governments have sought to utilise the increased information and knowledge for important decision-making at the school level, a greater need for monitoring has been created. Increased school autonomy can therefore increase the need for greater monitoring of schools which can often lead to a higher emphasis upon standards (Caldwell, 2002).

A focus on school improvement can inform decision-making within schools and offer support for school principals and teachers (van de Grift and Houtveen, 2006) as well as provide evidence of the relationships between resource use, school processes and various outcome measures (Caldwell and Spinks, 1998). Such evaluation would focus on specified policies and education objectives and how schools and teachers act to best meet these (OECD, 2008a; Sammons *et al.*, 1994; Smith and O'Day, 1991). This is depicted in Figure 3.1 which illustrates that the focus of the evaluative stricture of school education originates from a centralised administrative and policy-making body (Webster, 2005; Caldwell, 2002). This then flows to the evaluation and development of schools and teachers.

School evaluations should focus upon the same aspects or standards as the objectives, policies and programmes specified by the central body and should also be aligned with the focus of teacher appraisal and feedback. This implies that the emphasis on student performance standards that has been the target in some education systems (Ladd, 2007) may be too narrow. Several factors can be included in the school education evaluation framework. In fact, TALIS data indicates that the focus varies across a number of areas including teaching in a multicultural setting (OECD, 2009). But it is crucial that school evaluations, teacher appraisal and feedback, and centralised objectives, programmes and policies are aligned. An effective evaluation of a school or organisation should be aligned to the evaluation of teachers and other actors in that organisation (Lazear, 2000).

Inasmuch as evaluations and appraisals create incentives, the incentives for school leaders should be the same as those created for individual teachers (OECD, 2008a). Therefore, a centralised programme or stated objective to, for example, improve teaching in a multicultural setting in schools should be key in school evaluations and also in teacher appraisal and feedback. In this manner, the assessment and development of the main actors in improving school effectiveness (school principals and teachers) are aligned to centralised objectives. This focus may have a flow-on effect on the school and its practices depending upon the process of the school evaluation and the potential impact upon schools (O'Day, 2002; Odden and Busch, 1998; Senge 2000). TALIS indicates that in some cases, a focus on specific criteria in school evaluations occurred with a similar focus on teacher appraisal and feedback. Importantly, a greater focus on a specific aspect in a teachers' appraisal and feedback was found to lead to greater changes in their teaching practices in that area. This is further explored in the following section in regard to teaching in a multicultural setting.

Figure 3.1. **Framework for evaluation of education in schools: data collected in TALIS**

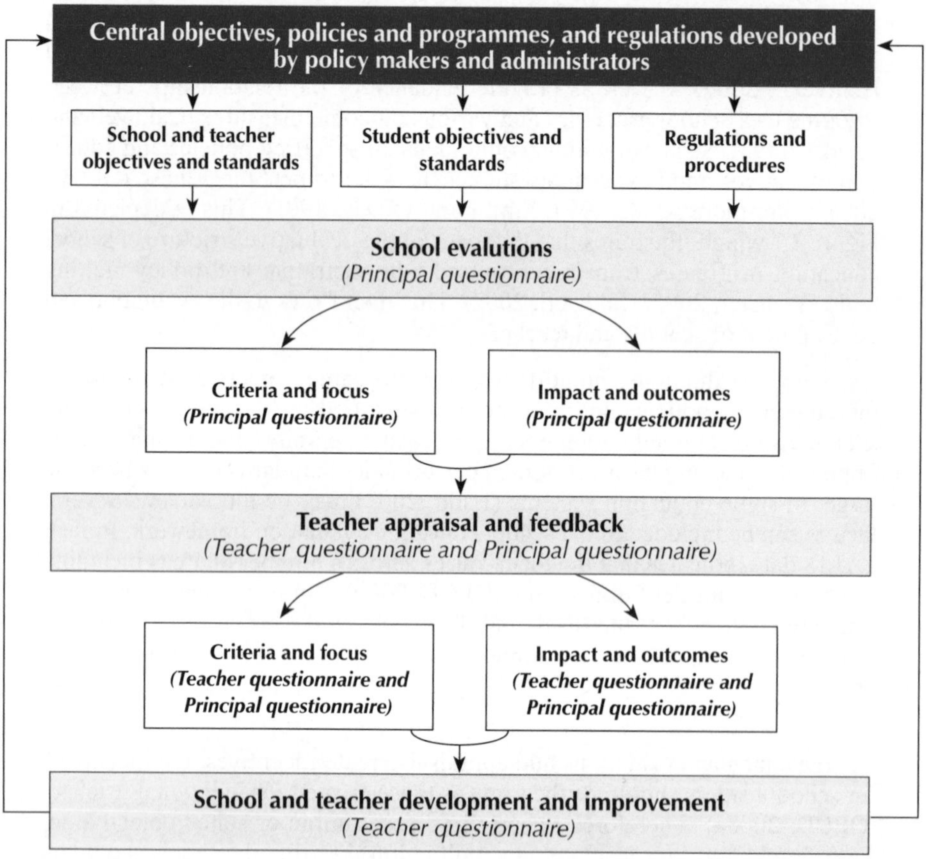

Source: Figure 3.1 (p. 142) *Creating Effective Teaching and Learning Environments: First Results from TALIS*, OECD, Paris.

Importance of teaching in a multicultural setting in the framework for evaluation of education in schools

TALIS obtained data on 17 different criteria for school evaluations (either school self-evaluations or those conducted by an external agent) and teacher appraisal and feedback. Data were analysed from school principals relating to school evaluations and from teachers regarding the appraisal and feedback they received. The criteria encompassed various student performance measures; feedback from parents and students; teaching practices; teachers' knowledge and understanding of their main subject field and instructional practices; relations with students; direct appraisals of classroom teaching; professional development; and, teachers' handling of student discipline and behaviour problems. It also includes teaching in a multicultural setting. Given the importance of all of these issues in school education it was not surprising that all were considered to be of at least some importance in schools (OECD, 2009).

Given the role that school evaluations can play in emphasising issues in schools and providing assistance and incentives to teachers, it is important to consider the importance of teaching in a multicultural setting in school evaluations. As shown in Table 3.2, of the 17 criteria analysed, teaching in a multicultural setting was the lowest rated criteria for school evaluations on average across TALIS countries and specifically in Australia, Belgium (Flemish Community.), Estonia, Hungary, Iceland, Lithuania, Malta, Poland, the Slovak Republic and Slovenia. On average across TALIS countries, just over half of teachers worked in schools where the school principal reported that their school evaluations place either moderate or high importance upon teaching in a multicultural setting. This compares with over 80% of teachers for factors such as relations between teachers and students, working relationships between teachers, and student discipline and behaviour.

Table 3.2. **Criteria of school evaluations (2007-08)**

Percentage of teachers of lower secondary education whose school principal reported that the following criteria were considered with high or moderate importance in school self-evaluations or external evaluations

Countries	Student test scores		Retention and pass rates of students		Other student learning outcomes		Student feedback on the teaching they receive		Feedback from parents		How well teachers work with the principal and their colleagues		Direct appraisal of classroom teaching		Innovative teaching practices		Relations between teachers and students	
	%	(SE)	%	(SE)	%	(SE)	%	(SE)	%	(SE)	%	(SE)	%	(SE)	%	(SE)	%	(SE)
Australia	86.9	(3.12)	81.9	(3.62)	94.8	(2.14)	69.0	(4.13)	88.3	(2.92)	79.5	(4.02)	58.8	(4.50)	78.6	(4.00)	89.7	(2.92)
Austria	57.7	(5.01)	33.3	(4.40)	60.7	(4.24)	81.2	(3.01)	83.4	(2.88)	76.3	(3.65)	68.5	(3.78)	76.5	(3.09)	86.4	(2.79)
Belgium (Fl.)	85.6	(3.03)	93.8	(1.82)	80.4	(3.40)	72.4	(3.97)	71.5	(4.51)	92.3	(2.48)	70.4	(4.09)	78.9	(4.14)	90.9	(2.53)
Brazil	85.7	(2.67)	93.7	(1.70)	90.1	(2.58)	88.0	(2.56)	83.9	(2.87)	95.5	(0.91)	95.4	(1.25)	92.8	(1.62)	95.6	(1.18)
Bulgaria	82.8	(3.25)	64.2	(4.78)	74.3	(7.50)	60.3	(4.74)	45.2	(5.76)	78.0	(4.05)	84.3	(3.75)	78.6	(4.87)	79.3	(4.13)
Denmark	55.8	(5.77)	68.4	(4.59)	78.7	(5.31)	69.6	(3.94)	58.5	(5.58)	65.6	(6.07)	50.8	(5.36)	37.5	(6.04)	83.1	(4.84)
Estonia	86.2	(2.94)	91.9	(2.40)	80.3	(3.58)	80.7	(2.78)	73.7	(4.12)	83.0	(3.27)	60.7	(4.31)	75.7	(4.14)	85.0	(3.10)
Hungary	69.7	(4.26)	73.1	(3.82)	78.3	(3.10)	68.3	(3.88)	83.5	(3.15)	79.9	(3.21)	66.3	(3.96)	69.7	(4.28)	81.5	(3.27)
Iceland	60.5	(0.20)	51.7	(0.23)	68.5	(0.15)	60.2	(0.19)	88.8	(0.12)	87.0	(0.18)	46.1	(0.21)	68.8	(0.20)	78.5	(0.12)
Ireland	80.5	(4.91)	84.2	(4.67)	80.9	(5.07)	55.8	(6.80)	76.1	(5.77)	82.3	(5.17)	75.7	(5.69)	90.3	(3.85)	94.5	(2.89)
Italy	76.3	(3.47)	78.8	(3.11)	78.3	(3.09)	80.0	(3.07)	93.1	(1.99)	91.2	(2.03)	69.5	(3.74)	76.4	(3.20)	92.3	(2.30)
Korea	57.8	(4.27)	23.7	(3.97)	62.6	(3.99)	70.8	(3.64)	80.1	(3.20)	87.3	(2.76)	81.9	(3.50)	82.6	(3.27)	82.5	(3.13)
Lithuania	62.1	(3.75)	74.8	(3.77)	88.2	(2.22)	88.7	(2.25)	87.9	(2.58)	85.7	(2.62)	71.3	(4.15)	88.0	(2.83)	93.7	(2.01)
Malaysia	97.7	(1.10)	47.7	(3.98)	82.6	(2.65)	87.1	(2.54)	86.0	(2.40)	98.7	(0.90)	98.6	(0.82)	96.4	(1.26)	97.3	(1.20)
Malta	84.3	(0.13)	78.4	(0.20)	84.3	(0.20)	68.0	(0.22)	89.8	(0.19)	90.2	(0.14)	81.7	(0.19)	83.1	(0.12)	100.0	(0.00)
Mexico	94.0	(1.80)	97.3	(1.28)	88.6	(3.10)	84.8	(3.05)	74.7	(3.97)	89.2	(2.69)	94.4	(2.14)	86.9	(2.85)	90.9	(2.43)

Table 3.2. **Criteria of school evaluations (2007-08)** *(continued)*

Percentage of teachers of lower secondary education whose school principal reported that the following criteria were considered with high or moderate importance in school self-evaluations or external evaluations

Countries	Student test scores		Retention and pass rates of students		Other student learning outcomes		Student feedback on the teaching they receive		Feedback from parents		How well teachers work with the principal and their colleagues		Direct appraisal of classroom teaching		Innovative teaching practices		Relations between teachers and students	
	%	(SE)	%	(SE)	%	(SE)	%	(SE)	%	(SE)	%	(SE)	%	(SE)	%	(SE)	%	(SE)
Norway	52.0	(4.95)	32.1	(4.90)	51.2	(4.99)	50.3	(4.79)	65.1	(4.55)	64.9	(4.89)	31.7	(4.67)	37.4	(4.95)	69.6	(4.58)
Poland	96.5	(1.40)	89.0	(2.68)	91.0	(2.33)	89.8	(2.29)	93.5	(2.02)	93.6	(2.02)	86.7	(2.85)	80.2	(3.36)	92.7	(2.64)
Portugal	65.9	(4.72)	94.2	(2.19)	85.2	(3.52)	73.5	(4.73)	78.3	(4.45)	79.8	(3.85)	40.8	(5.71)	71.8	(4.56)	88.7	(2.95)
Slovak Republic	87.2	(2.96)	50.5	(4.85)	80.1	(3.68)	65.7	(4.21)	55.6	(4.69)	81.5	(3.70)	80.8	(3.70)	85.7	(2.94)	82.2	(3.62)
Slovenia	74.2	(3.81)	77.8	(3.36)	84.2	(3.03)	67.5	(4.27)	82.5	(3.12)	88.6	(2.49)	68.7	(4.16)	74.8	(3.77)	85.3	(3.17)
Spain	74.1	(4.14)	79.2	(3.84)	73.4	(3.99)	60.4	(4.94)	67.1	(4.50)	69.8	(4.16)	64.4	(4.64)	66.5	(4.34)	75.8	(3.80)
Turkey	80.1	(5.50)	68.0	(6.55)	77.6	(5.45)	81.2	(4.13)	70.7	(4.25)	86.3	(4.16)	88.9	(4.29)	87.8	(4.02)	86.8	(4.03)
TALIS Average	*76.2*	*(0.77)*	*70.8*	*(0.77)*	*78.9*	*(0.79)*	*72.7*	*(0.79)*	*77.3*	*(0.79)*	*83.7*	*(0.70)*	*71.1*	*(0.81)*	*76.7*	*(0.76)*	*87.1*	*(0.63)*

Note: Only includes those teachers that work in schools that had a school evaluation sometime in the previous 5 years.

Source: OECD, TALIS Database (Note: This is a reproduction of Table 5.1a of *Creating Effective Teaching and Learning Environments: First Results from TALIS*).

This could be an issue for the 14% of teachers who reported a high level of need for professional development for teaching in a multicultural setting and for policy makers concerned with diversity issues. Analysis comparing these needs with the reported importance of teaching in a multicultural setting in school evaluations illustrates that there is considerable scope for better focusing school evaluations with respect to diversity. Of the 14% of teachers who reported a high level of need for professional development for teaching in a multicultural setting, one-quarter worked in schools where the school principal reported that teaching in a multicultural setting was either not considered in their school evaluations or had little importance. As shown in Table 3.1, one-third of teachers (in addition to the 14% reporting a high level of need) reported having a moderate level of need for professional development for teaching in a multicultural setting. Of these teachers, 28% worked in schools where teaching in a multicultural setting was either not considered in school evaluations or considered with low importance in school evaluations. This indicates that school evaluations are not focussing on diversity issues in schools where teachers report they need to improve their skills for teaching multi-cultural classrooms. It appears that diversity issues are either being ignored or not given the importance in the evaluative framework that teachers report is needed to improve their teaching. In this sense, the evaluative framework is not as focused as it could be on important and emerging classroom issues.

In discussion of the extent of the focus of school evaluations on teaching in a multicultural setting it is important to consider the linguistic diversity of schools as well as the developmental needs of teachers. On average across TALIS countries, similar proportions of teachers worked in schools where their school principals reported that their school evaluations considered teaching in a multicultural setting to be of no, low, or high importance regardless of the linguistic diversity in teachers' classrooms. However, in school evaluations in Australia, Austria, Belgium (Flemish Community), Denmark, Norway and, to a lesser extent, Portugal, there was a greater emphasis on teaching in a multicultural setting in evaluations of schools with greater linguistic diversity (OECD, 2009).

The low emphasis given to teaching in a multicultural setting in school evaluations is also found in teacher appraisal and feedback. Of the 17 criteria that teachers considered in the appraisal of and feedback on their work, teaching in a multicultural setting was again reported as being given the least emphasis on average across TALIS countries and was the lowest rated criteria in 16 TALIS countries (Australia, Belgium [Flemish Community], Denmark, Estonia, Hungary, Iceland, Ireland, Korea, Lithuania, Malta, Norway, Poland, Portugal, the Slovak Republic, Slovenia, and Turkey). Moreover, a major finding from TALIS was that teachers believe that appraisal and feedback on their work has a positive impact upon their job satisfaction and is helpful for their development as teachers (OECD, 2009). Such development may be stymied when it comes to teaching in a multicultural setting due to lack of emphasis in teacher appraisal and feedback, particularly for teachers who have high developmental needs in this area. In fact, 32% of teachers with moderate or high development needs for professional development for teaching in a multicultural setting received appraisal or feedback which gave little or no importance to this issue. This mismatch between stated development needs of teachers and the appraisal of their work was also found to be greater in a number of countries (OECD, 2009). This reinforces the findings that school evaluations failed to emphasise teaching in a multicultural setting in schools whereas teachers report having high developmental needs in the area. The appraisal and feedback that teachers receive is not focusing sufficiently on diversity issues even for teachers reporting that they need to improve their teaching. Teacher appraisal and feedback are not being used as a developmental tool to address diversity issues. TALIS has shown that when teacher appraisal and feedback pinpoint specific areas to a sufficient degree, teachers then improve their teaching skills in this area (OECD, 2009). This highlights the potential benefits of a strong alignment between school evaluations and teacher appraisal and feedback within the school education evaluation framework.

The links identified in the evaluation framework of education in schools were tested with a number of aspects of school education. Given the data available, path analysis was undertaken to examine the links between various factors in school evaluation, teacher appraisal and feedback, changes in teaching practices, and teachers' professional development needs. This analysis tested the extent to which school evaluations, teacher appraisal and feedback were aligned in schools so that the same issues are emphasised across the evaluative framework. It examined whether this alignment is associated with changes in teaching practices following their teacher appraisal and feedback. The path analysis also reveals whether such changes are associated with increased or decreased professional development needs.[7] Across the areas analysed, it was shown that there is often a link between an emphasis in school evaluations and teacher appraisal and feedback. However, a more significant connection was found between the emphasis on an issue in teacher appraisal and feedback and the extent that teachers report changing their teaching practices following the appraisal and feedback (OECD, 2009). In these cases, the evaluative framework is operating effectively and it provides administrators and policy makers with a lever to influence teaching practices and develop teachers' skills.

As discussed above, teachers have professional development needs for teaching in a multicultural setting although they are given little attention in both school evaluations and teacher appraisal and feedback. However, the analysis shows that even with the relatively little emphasis across schools and teachers overall, there are significant links between school evaluations and teacher appraisal and feedback, and between teacher appraisal and feedback and changes in teaching practices and teachers' work. In addition, there is a significant relationship with the extent of teachers' professional development needs for teaching in a multicultural setting.

Figure 3.2 shows the relationships between:

1. the emphasis given to teaching in a multicultural setting in school evaluation;

2. the emphasis given to teaching in a multicultural setting in teacher appraisal and feedback;

3. changes in teachers' teaching of students in a multicultural a setting following their appraisal and feedback;

4. teachers' professional development needs for teaching in a multicultural setting.

The path model presented in Figure 3.2 shows the associations between these factors. The correlations in Figure 3.2 between each factor represent those for the international model that include all TALIS countries. As a measure of the strength of the relationships, all of the correlations were found to be statistically significant for the international model. Table 3.3 presents the

Figure 3.2. **Path analysis for teaching in a multicultural setting**

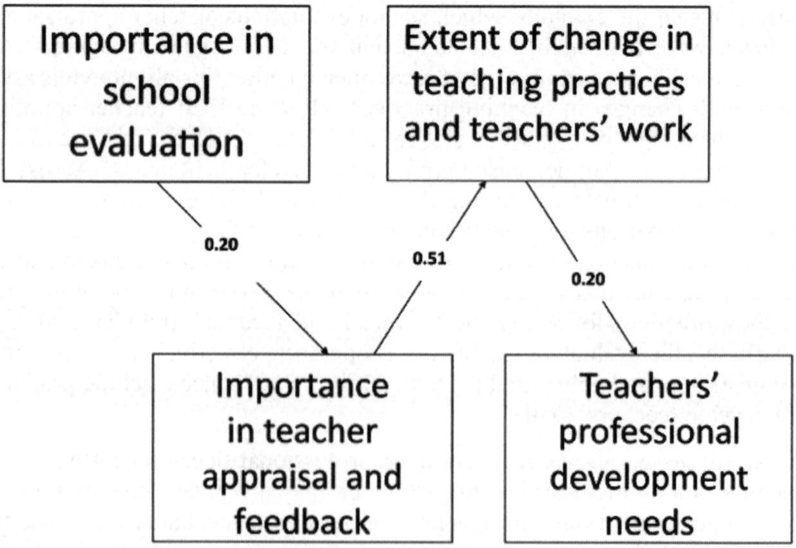

correlation coefficients for each TALIS country. The statistical significance of these relationships shows that even given the low emphasis given to teaching in a multicultural setting in school evaluations and teacher appraisal and feedback, when it is underscored teachers report that it has an impact upon them and their teaching.

There is a statistically significant relationship between the importance placed on teaching in a multicultural setting in a school evaluation and the importance placed upon it in teacher appraisal and feedback in that school. As shown in Table 3.3, the relationship between the importance in school evaluation and in teacher appraisal and feedback is significant in 14 TALIS countries, and greater in Belgium (Flemish Community), Bulgaria, Denmark and Norway. This follows the pattern depicted in Figure 3.1 of the framework for the evaluation of education in schools. There should be a connection between the focus of school evaluation and teacher appraisal and feedback so that school principals and teachers and other school staff are all working towards the same goals, standards and objectives. This link exists to some extent with teaching in a multicultural setting even though the overall emphasis on diversity is relatively low. Efforts to better align the focus of school evaluations and teacher appraisal and feedback would provide a more coherent and potentially effective evaluative framework.

Perhaps the most important aspect of the path analysis depicted in Figure 3.2 is the relationship between the importance placed on teaching in a multicultural setting in teacher appraisal and feedback and the amount of change in teaching practices and teachers' work following that appraisal and feedback. That the strongest correlation found in the path analysis is between these two factors is an encouraging finding for those looking to develop skills in teaching in a multi-cultural setting. It highlights the importance of the evaluative framework in providing ongoing improvements and teacher development. As shown in Table 3.2, the link between the importance of teaching in a multicultural setting in teacher appraisal and feedback and the extent to which it led to changes in teachers' practices is significant for every TALIS country. The evaluative framework is therefore acting as a developmental tool to improve teaching in respect to diversity. Greater focus on diversity issues and a more coherent framework better align the focus and consequences of school evaluations and teacher appraisal and feedback could have a considerable impact on teachers' work and the education students receive.

An interesting finding is the relationship between changes in teaching practices and teachers' reported needs for professional development for teaching in a multicultural setting. As shown in Figure 3.2, the greater the changes in teachers' teaching practices in a multicultural setting, the larger the increase of their professional development needs in this area. Increased emphasis in the evaluative structure therefore leads not only to greater changes in teaching practices, but is also related to a stronger need for professional development for teaching in a multi-cultural setting. This pattern was also found for other issues (*e.g.* teaching students with special learning needs) analysed in the evaluative framework of school education (OECD, 2009).

As shown in Table 3.3, teachers reporting that they have changed their teaching practices in a multicultural setting were found, in all TALIS countries except Malta and Turkey, to have significantly greater professional development needs. Changes in teaching practices as a result of teachers' appraisal and feedback do not appear sufficient to overcome the need for further professional development in these areas. This may be because while teachers are responding positively to appraisal and feedback they may not yet be able to access the required professional development to meet their needs. This may be due to a lack of professional development overall or what is available may not be targeted to meet teachers' needs and expectations. Alternately, the appraisal and feedback may highlight needs that require further training, particularly if previous education and training did not focus on these areas. Teachers' needs and expectations may change with the appraisal and feedback they receive. Ongoing teacher appraisal and feedback should highlight the need for professional development as it is an evaluative exercise that, among other things, highlights strengths and weaknesses for teacher development. This also emphasises the need for cohesive flows of information to assist teachers to develop their skills and identify and then provide the required tools for that development. This is an additional policy or programme implication of this analysis that is further discussed below.

Conclusion and policy implications

TALIS provides an opportunity for much needed quantitative analysis of the reports of teachers and their school principals. This analysis is differentiated from a number of others in this area not just in its quantitative nature, but also because it utilises an international database of the views and reports of teachers and school principals. The data for every country presented were sampled so they are representative of lower secondary teachers and their school principals in that country.

This chapter began with asking two research questions and various data and analyses have been discussed above to respond to these important questions regarding teaching and diversity. These two questions are addressed below along with policy implications.

Table 3.3. **Correlation coefficients for path analysis for teaching in a multi-cultural setting (2007-08)**

Countries	Correlation between importance in school evaluations and teacher appraisal and feedback			Correlation between importance in teacher appraisal and feedback and extent of change in teaching practices and teachers' work			Correlation between extent of change in teaching practices and teachers' work and their professional development needs		
	Corr.	(SE)[a]	P-value[b]	Corr.	(SE)	P-value	Corr.	(SE)	P-value
Australia	0.10	0.03	0.00	0.34	0.02	0.00	0.29	0.03	0.00
Austria	0.11	0.05	0.02	0.28	0.02	0.00	0.47	0.02	0.00
Belgium (Fl.)	0.21	0.04	0.00	0.32	0.02	0.00	0.46	0.02	0.00
Brazil	0.04	0.03	0.17	0.45	0.02	0.00	-0.06	0.03	0.03
Bulgaria	0.16	0.05	0.00	0.49	0.04	0.00	0.26	0.04	0.00
Denmark	0.15	0.04	0.00	0.28	0.03	0.00	0.57	0.04	0.00
Estonia	0.15	0.03	0.00	0.43	0.02	0.00	0.45	0.03	0.00
Hungary	0.01	0.04	0.82	0.34	0.03	0.00	0.29	0.03	0.00
Ireland	0.12	0.04	0.01	0.30	0.02	0.00	0.18	0.03	0.00
Italy	0.12	0.04	0.00	0.37	0.02	0.00	0.21	0.02	0.00
Korea	0.02	0.03	0.59	0.55	0.02	0.00	0.28	0.02	0.00
Lithuania	0.11	0.03	0.00	0.50	0.03	0.00	0.45	0.02	0.00
Malaysia	0.07	0.05	0.12	0.58	0.02	0.00	0.41	0.03	0.00
Malta	0.02	0.04	0.59	0.32	0.03	0.00	0.04	0.05	0.37
Mexico	0.00	0.03	0.87	0.51	0.03	0.00	0.09	0.03	0.00
Norway	0.16	0.04	0.00	0.31	0.03	0.00	0.34	0.03	0.00
Poland	0.05	0.02	0.02	0.36	0.03	0.00	0.38	0.03	0.00
Portugal	0.09	0.03	0.01	0.32	0.02	0.00	0.20	0.03	0.00
Slovak Republic	0.09	0.04	0.03	0.44	0.02	0.00	0.35	0.02	0.00
Slovenia	0.10	0.03	0.00	0.50	0.03	0.00	0.43	0.03	0.00
Spain	0.07	0.04	0.08	0.37	0.03	0.00	0.14	0.03	0.00
Turkey	0.02	0.04	0.64	0.39	0.04	0.00	0.06	0.04	0.16

Notes: a. Standard Error.

b. P-value is a measure of probability that a difference between groups during an experiment happened by chance.

Source: OECD, TALIS Database.

1. How much professional development is needed for teaching in a multicultural setting and which teachers need it the most?

It is clear that there is a need to expand professional development for teachers for teaching in a multicultural setting. On average across TALIS countries, over 80% of teachers reported some level of need for professional development of this kind. Moreover, one in seven teachers reported having a high level of need for professional development to improve their teaching in a multicultural setting. This is particularly apparent in Brazil, Ireland, Italy and Malaysia where this applies to around one-quarter or more of teachers. This offers policy makers and administrators the opportunity to address a clear gap in teachers' training and development.

It would simplify matters if it was possible to identify teachers with particular characteristics or who work in particular schools that require more professional development for teaching in a multicultural setting. It would facilitate the development of policy and facilitate implementation of pro-grammes designed to address these development needs. However, this is not the case. Teachers with these development needs are spread across schools and the teacher population.

Therefore mechanisms are needed to obtain information on teachers' developmental needs and create programmes and implementation strategies that address these needs. Of most benefit would be professional development targeted to those teachers that reported a high level of need for development for teaching in a multicultural setting than others. This reflects a major find-ing of the TALIS analysis of the diversity of teacher practices, needs and teaching beliefs within schools compared to between schools (OECD, 2009). There is often more variation between teachers within schools than between schools and countries. *This implies that education programmes and policies should be targeted to individual teachers rather than formulated at either the school, regional or national level.* This would provide a more efficient system as professional development reaches those teachers that have the most to gain from such development and resources are not wasted on development programmes that do not properly address teachers' needs. It is important to also note that TALIS showed that one-quarter of teachers lose at least one-third of lesson time to factors other than effective teaching and learning. Again, these teachers are not concentrated in particular schools nor have specific characteristics that separate them from the general teacher popula-tion even though there may be country-specific factors that help or hinder teachers in the amount of the effective teaching time they can offer (OECD, 2009). A system that properly identifies teachers with particular developmen-tal needs should begin to address these problems.

2. What is the role of the evaluative structure of education in schools to develop teachers' abilities to teach in a multi-cultural setting?

As depicted in Figure 3.1, the framework for the evaluation of education in schools incorporates a number of areas that influence, and are affected by, school evaluation and teacher appraisal and feedback. An effective framework can help teachers develop and improve their skills and effectiveness. TALIS has shown that, on average, teacher appraisal increases teachers' job satisfaction and, to a lesser extent, their job security. In addition, teachers report that it increases their skills as teachers (OECD, 2009). Unfortunately, the evaluative framework is not as effective as it could be in most TALIS countries. Given teachers' positive reports of its influence, the evaluative framework and the components that lead to teacher development should be improved. This analysis has shown that a better evaluative framework requires a number of changes that can create numerous benefits which are discussed below.

Stronger links across the evaluative framework of school education

It has been shown here that a positive impact upon teachers and their work can be obtained through the evaluative framework, specifically through school evaluations and teacher appraisal and feedback. The focus of these two activities should be aligned for consistency with stated policy objectives and to create aligned incentives throughout schools.

When it comes to teaching in a multicultural setting, it has been shown that an emphasis across aspects of the evaluative framework is linked to teacher practices. Strengthening the focus on diversity issues in policy objectives should be matched by a focus in school evaluations and teacher appraisal and feedback with commensurate teacher development as a broader objective. To maximise the potential gains from such a focus requires that changes not be made only in one area. An emphasis upon diversity issues needs to flow from stated policy objectives through to the evaluation and development of schools and teachers.

A system that learns from itself

While it is clear the evaluative framework should follow policy objectives, it is important to consider the framework as not purely top-down management and information flows. In fact, the system should be generating information to inform decision-making at all levels of school education. It should identify the strengths and weaknesses of students, teachers and schools. It should also identify developmental needs and track progression with such development. Using the examples provided here, a school would be evaluated on their teaching of students from multicultural backgrounds using a variety of assessment methods. This would follow with teacher appraisal and feedback for teachers on their teaching in a multi-cultural setting. Such appraisal and feedback would identify strengths and weaknesses and the needs for teacher development for teaching in a multicultural setting. Continual appraisal and feedback would document progress made and how to improve the developmental process. Such a framework would provide important information for schools and teachers to increase effectiveness and for administrators and policy makers in their decision-making concerning teacher professional development and resource allocation. In fact, a functioning evaluative framework could greatly enhance the effectiveness of choosing the focus and type of professional development and training provided to teachers.

Identification of teachers' ongoing developmental needs

A framework that incorporates teachers' development and developmental needs into teacher appraisal and feedback and school evaluation can properly document and develop the required professional development initiatives and how they can best be implemented in the school education system. For example, a teacher with a high level of need for professional development for teaching in a multicultural setting would document and discuss those needs in their teacher appraisal and feedback and identify how to best develop their skills in this area to improve their effectiveness. While the TALIS data documents such need by asking teachers, an evaluative framework would complement such self-assessments with additional assessments such as peer reviews, analysis of student progress, and repeated evaluative judgements. This would be part of an ongoing process in which teachers would be assisted in developing their effectiveness including assessment of the impact of any professional development and the changes teachers are making to improve their effectiveness. Appraisals of teachers work would be complemented with school-level evaluations including an assessment of the progress made in teachers' development while also documenting the professional development needs of teachers. This would help with planning for the provision of required professional development. Once professional development is made available, teachers with needs in the relevant area could attend such development programmes. But it is important to recognise that such teachers need not come from the same school, district, or geographic area. Rather, teachers with high level of need for such development would attend regardless of their geographic location. Clearly this may prove difficult for some teachers in less densely populated areas and online or additional assistance may be required to assist these teachers. This would provide a considerably more targeted and cost-effective approach to professional development expenditure.

Assessment of the impact of professional development programmes

The impact of professional development programmes (*e.g.* in teaching diverse classrooms) would be assessed as part of the ongoing system of teacher appraisal and feedback as well as school evaluations. This would help alleviate a large problem for many education systems. TALIS shows that teachers report that the current framework for the evaluation of education in schools does not provide the necessary support for the development of teachers and effective teaching or the necessary incentives for teachers to develop and progress through the profession (OECD, 2009). Conversely, as shown above, even with a limited evaluative framework in operation in most schools, teachers report that it has a positive impact on their work and their teaching. Extending this evaluative framework and linking it to the design, implementation and monitoring of teacher professional development would create a more effective and efficient system.

Need for a greater focus on diversity issues in the evaluative framework

An effective evaluative framework would identify many of the professional development needs of teachers. As discussed, these frameworks are not as effective as they could be and the links between the identification of teachers' developmental needs and the professional development and training they receive are not as strong as the evidence suggests they would ideally be. Given this situation, it is important that TALIS has documented teachers' reports of their need for greater training on diversity issues and the lack of focus of this issue in the evaluative framework in virtually all TALIS countries.

Just less than one in seven teachers reported a high need for professional development for teaching in a multicultural setting. Unfortunately, many of these teachers do not receive appraisal and feedback that concentrate sufficiently on these issues, and they also work in schools where this is not a strong focus of school evaluations. Of the 14% of teachers who reported a high level of need for professional development for teaching in a multicultural setting, one-quarter worked in schools where the school principal reported that teaching in a multicultural setting was either not considered in their school evaluations or had little importance in those evaluations. In addition, 32% of teachers with moderate or high development needs for professional development for teaching in a multicultural setting received appraisal or feedback which gave little or no importance to this issue (OECD, 2009).

Given teachers reports that focusing on key issues in the evaluative framework benefits their teaching, there is a strong argument for the usefulness of increasing the emphasis of diversity issues in school evaluations and teacher appraisal and feedback. Aligning the key aspects of the evaluative framework for school education indicates that this could also further emphasise diversity in the objectives and content of school education policies and programmes.

Notes

1. See the *TALIS Technical Report* (forthcoming) for further details of the sampling methodology and data collection.

2. In the TALIS analysis, the data collected from teachers focused on appraisal and feedback. The definitions provided to respondents for these terms were:
   Appraisal was defined as when a teacher's work is reviewed by the principal, an external inspector or by his or her colleagues. This appraisal can be conducted in a range of ways from a more formal, objective approach (*e.g.* as part of a formal performance management system, involving set procedures and criteria) to the more informal, more subjective approach (*e.g.* through informal discussions with the teacher).
   Feedback was defined as the reporting of the results of a review of your work (however formal or informal that review has been) back to the teacher, often with the purpose of noting good performance or identifying areas for development. Again, the feedback may be provided formally (*e.g.* through a written report) or informally (*e.g.* through discussions with the teacher).

3. The level of need was grouped into four categories: 'No level of need'; 'Low level of need'; 'Moderate level of need'; and, 'High level of need'.

4. These findings would benefit from multivariate analysis but a simple comparison of the two populations of teachers (those with high need for professional development for teaching in a multicultural setting and those without) revealed little differences in demographic, job or school characteristics.

5. TALIS asked teachers a series of questions about a randomly selected class that they teach in their school. One question asked for the percentage of students in their class "whose first language is different from the language(s) of instruction or a dialect of this/these". Teachers could choose between five categories: "Less than 10%"; "10% or more but less than 20%"; 20% or more but less than 40%"; 40% or more but less than 60%"; "60% or more" (OECD, 2009). Little difference was found between the percentage of teachers reporting student characteristics in these categories and the percentage of teachers reporting a high level of need for

professional development for teaching in a multicultural setting (Source: *OECD TALIS Dataset*).

6.   TALIS defined school evaluation as an evaluation of the whole school rather than of individual subjects or departments.

7.   For the path analysis undertaken, it was hypothesised that the more important selected aspects were to school evaluations, the more important they would be to teacher appraisal and feedback. Subsequently, it was reasoned that increased importance of select elements in school evaluations and teacher appraisal and feedback would be associated with changes in teaching practices and might also be reflected in teachers' professional development needs (OECD, 2009). The path analysis was analysed in respect to six issues: teaching students with special learning needs; teaching in a multicultural setting; teachers' classroom management; student discipline and behaviour; teachers' knowledge and understanding of their main subject(s); and, teachers' knowledge and understanding of instructional practices in their main subject field(s).

References

Bethell, G. (2005), *Value-Added Indicators of School Performance Anglia Assessment,* Battisford, Suffolk, England, Unpublished report.

Caldwell, B. (2002), "Autonomy and Self-management: Concepts and Evidence",. in T. Bush and L. Bell (eds.), *The Principles and Practice of Educational Management*, Paul Chapman, London, pp. 34-48.

Caldwell, B. and J. Spinks (1998), *Beyond the Self-Managing School,* Falmer Press, London.

Ladd, H.F. (2007), *Holding Schools Accountable Revisited*, 2007 Spencer Foundation Lecture in Education Policy and Management, Association for Public Policy Analysis and Management.

O'Day, J. (2002), "Complexity, Accountability, and School Improvement", *Harvard Educational Review,* Vol. 72, No. 3, pp. 293-329.

Odden, A. and C. Busch (1998), *Financing Schools for High Performance,* San Francisco, Jossey-Bass.

OECD (2009), *Creating Effective Teaching and Learning Environments: First Results from TALIS*, OECD Publishing, Paris.

OECD (2008a), *Measuring Improvements in Learning Outcomes: Best Practices to Assess the Value-Added of Schools*, OECD Publishing, Paris.

OECD (2008b), *Education at a Glance – OECD Indicators 2008*, OECD Publishing, Paris.

OECD (2006), *Demand Sensitive Schooling? Evidence and Issues,* OECD, Paris.

OECD (2005), *Teachers Matter: Attracting, Developing and Retaining Effective Teachers*, OECD, Paris.

OECD (1998), *Staying Ahead: In-Service Training and Teacher Professional Development*, OECD, Paris.

Plank, D.N. and B.A. Smith (2008), "Autonomous Schools: Theory, Evidence and Policy", in H.F. Ladd and E. B. Fiske (eds.), *Handbook of Research in Education Finance and Policy,* Lawrence Erlbaum/ Routledge Press, New Jersey, pp. 402-424.

Sammons, P., S. Thomas, P. Mortimore, C. Owen and H. Pennell (1994), *Assessing School Effectiveness: Developing Measures to put School Performance in Context,* Office for Standards in Education, London.

Senge, P. (2000), *Schools that Learn: A Fifth Discipline Fieldbook for Educators, Parents, and Everyone Who Cares About Education,* Doubleday, New York.

Smith, M.S. and J. O'Day (1991), "Systemic School Reform", in S.H. Fuhrman and B. Malen (eds.), *The Politics of Curriculum and Testing: The 1990 Politics of Education Association Yearbook, Falmer Prero,* New York, pp. 233-267.

Van de Grift, W. and A.A.M. Houtveen (2006), "Underperformance in Primary Schools", *School Effectiveness and School Improvement,* Vol. 17, No. 3, pp. 255-273.

Webster, W. J. (2005), "The Dallas School-Level Accountability Model: The Marriage of Status and Value-Added Approaches", in R. L. (ed.), *Value-added models in education: Theory and Applications,* Maple Grove, JAM Press, Minnesota.

Chapter 4

Diversity in education: the importance of disaggregating data

Bruce Garnett
Surrey School District, British Columbia, Canada

Changes in migration patterns have radically altered the composition of the student body and challenged the personnel of urban schools over the last generation. Unfortunately, due to the paucity of data and the presence of epistemological conflicts in research, teacher-educators have rarely relied on empirical research to guide them in their decision-making about how to prepare practitioners to meet the needs of increasingly diverse populations. This paper marshals empirical data from a cohort of students in British Columbia, Canada, to demonstrate where gaps in equity among identifiable social groups occur. It also suggests how the results might be used to challenge both teacher and teacher-candidates' beliefs about schooling and society, as well as teacher-educators' priorities for preparing teachers for diverse populations.

From the OECD online consultation: importance of language

A lack of fluency in the classroom language was reported as a major challenge by the greatest number of responding teachers, followed by socio-economic differences. But what do we know about the impact of language ability and socio-economic status on academic performance?

Introduction

The Canadian context

As a settler country, Canada has experienced large-scale immigration since even before its Confederation in 1867. According to Statistics Canada, since 1911, immigrants (*i.e.* residents born outside the country) have consistently comprised between 15% to 22% of the country's population. As of 2006, this figure was 20% (2008), a number that does not include the Canadian-born children of immigrants. The presence of children of immigrants in Canadian schools, therefore, is not a new phenomenon.

However, three factors are relatively new. First, the source countries of Canadian immigrants have changed over time. Prior to 1961, due to discriminatory official immigration policies, over 90% of immigrants came from Europe. Between 1962 and 1967 a series of reforms including the "points system", which allows immigrants to enter Canada based on occupational and linguistic skills, curbed racial discrimination, and in 1976 family reunification policies further opened doors. Entrepreneurs and investors have also been welcomed, and the country has continued to accept many refugees. As a result, between 1971 and 1980, over half of all immigrants came from Africa, the Caribbean, Asia and the Middle East. Since 1991, over 70% of Canadian immigrants have come from these regions (Statistics Canada, 2004).

Second, settlement patterns have changed. Whereas immigrants in the early to mid-20th century were mostly dispersed throughout the Prairie Provinces and the West, often in farming communities; recent immigrants have overwhelmingly favoured Canada's three largest provinces: British Columbia,

Ontario and Quebec, which contain 75% of Canada's total population and 87% of its immigrant population. These immigrants overwhelmingly settle in the three major metropolitan centres: Toronto (46% of the local population), Metro Vancouver (40%), and Montreal (20%) (Statistics Canada, 2009). The concentration of non-English or non-French speaking immigrant children in urban schools is relatively new.

Third, Canadian schools are under pressure to increase equity in outcomes among identifiable social groups. This pressure results in part from Canada's official policy of multiculturalism under which citizens are encouraged to retain the values and characteristics of the groups with which they identify; while still enjoying full citizenship based on rights, responsibilities and freedoms. As a mediator of life opportunities, school outcomes are critically important in fulfilling the promise of multiculturalism. The pressure also results from a trend across liberal-democratic countries to increase equity both on moral grounds, as discrimination is decreasingly acceptable, and practical ones, as it has become well-recognised that school failure has multiple social and economic costs to the state.

Over the last two decades, school teachers in urban areas have been tasked to operate within this context of increased expectations of universal success and increased populations of immigrant students from non-Western source countries. While these trends have been common, particularly in the three most urban regions, contexts have differed due to Canada's political structure. A confederation of ten provinces and three very sparsely populated territories, the country has no national ministry of education. Each province or territory has complete jurisdiction in this arena, and develops its own curricula and legislation.

The British Columbia context

This study describes the educational trajectories of students for whom English is a "second" language (ESL)[1] in the province of British Columbia. In British Columbia, the provincial government allocates CAD 5 851 per pupil per year to school boards according to their enrolment numbers. In addition to this base allotment, it provides special purpose grants to school boards, one of which is for the amount of CAD 1 182 per ESL pupil, per year, for up to five years, in order for boards to provide these students with extra services. Administrative data for British Columbia therefore describes "ESL" students, not immigrant students. Indeed, these students may not be immigrants themselves, but rather the children of immigrants. Students to whom this money is allocated have "primary language(s) or language(s) of the home … other than English and … may therefore require additional services in order to develop their individual potential within British Columbia's school system" (British Columbia Ministry of Education, 2009). Boards are also periodically obligated to demonstrate that each student for whom ESL money is allocated is indeed receiving additional services. Beyond these requirements, individual school boards and schools have wide latitude in choosing delivery models for these services. In secondary schools (grades 8-12), the amount of time ESL students spend in ESL classrooms is dependent on their levels of English proficiency, and they enter "mainstream" courses once they are judged to be of a suitable level.

Graduation requirements for this study's cohort included 13 mainstream courses, nine at grade 11 or 12 level, four at grade 12 level.[2] Grade 11 mathematics, science and social studies courses were mandatory, as was a Language Arts 12 course. Students typically fulfilled this latter requirement with English 12. Entrance requirements to British Columbia's three largest universities varied by programme but typically demanded English 12 and at least three other grade 12 courses within one or more of the four foundational areas. Principles of Math 12 has typically been associated with university entrance, and thus indicates future plans (Adamuti-Trache and Andres, 2007). By contrast, English 12 is a *de facto* choice for most students.

Teacher education often occurs at one of British Columbia's four largest universities. While variations in routes to teacher candidacy are available, a typical high school teacher most often completes a bachelor of arts or science followed by a 12-month course of additional teacher education including courses in pedagogy, assessment, foundations of education, and subject-area methods. Teacher education in British Columbia, though fairly rigorous compared to some other North American jurisdictions, suffers from the same lack of evidence-based decision making as the others often do. The curricula of teacher education programmes are rarely influenced by, and teacher-candidates are seldom exposed to, data-driven studies.

Ungerleider (personal communication) argues two reasons may help account for this deficiency. First, teacher educators are often not ideologically predisposed to using data. Often they are sessional teachers; that is, they are graduate students and/or ex-teachers, not professors at the forefront of new research. While their technical experience is valuable, they are not familiar with current research, and indeed in many cases are not themselves educated in how to interpret data-driven studies. This lack of knowledge tends to be excused by the "turn" in the social sciences over the last two decades toward a more qualitative orientation and scepticism as to whether the numbers in evidence-based research have "truth" to offer (see *e.g.* Guba and Lincoln, 1994).

Second, administrative data with which studies might be conducted have been relatively rare and/or inaccessible to researchers across Canadian jurisdictions. While this situation has been changing over the last decade and a half, the scarcity of available data is illustrated by the limited amount of published data-driven research describing the educational trajectories of immigrant youth in Canada. This chapter, however, will describe one of these rare studies and show how data-driven research might offer lessons for teacher education for diversity.

Empirical research

Analysis of PISA 2003 data on performance in mathematics suggests Canadian teachers are succeeding in their instruction of immigrant children. After controlling for parental education and occupation, Canada, along with Hong Kong-China, is one of only two countries where second generation immigrants significantly outperform native students in mathematics, and one out of only three countries, along with Macao China and Australia, where native students do not significantly outperform first generation immigrants (OECD, 2006). Within British Columbia, the Ministry of Education (2009b) also reports that ESL students, our imperfect proxy of immigrant status, indeed graduate more frequently than native English speakers.

Unfortunately, decision-makers will be hard pressed to either support or nuance these findings with further large-scale data-driven studies describing the outcomes of immigrant students in Canada. A recent search of relevant literature from the last two decades revealed only six articles published in peer-reviewed academic journals, four reports published for government or non-governmental agencies, two dissertations, and one book (see Garnett, 2008 for a full review).

Earlier research seemed to indicate that children of immigrants with low English proficiency (*i.e.* ESL students) in high school disproportionately dropped out of high school but children of immigrants who had attended Canadian schools for most or all of their careers, and who were likely to be proficient in English by high school, did very well. Watt and Roessingh (1994 and 2001) (n = 505) and Derwing, deCorby, Ichikawa and Jamieson (1999) (n = 516) all indicated dropout rates from 60-75% for students who required ESL services in high school.

By contrast, Samuel, Krugly-Smolska and Warren's (2001) survey of children (n = 1 954) whose parents had immigrated from four non-Anglophone geographic regions and the Caribbean revealed three of the four non-English groups self-reported higher mean scores and higher proportions of scores over 80% than did the children of Canadian-born parents. All these respondents had English proficiency high enough to respond to the survey. Using secondary analysis, Worswick (2001) similarly reported that children of non-English or non-French speaking immigrants (n = 2 698), whose educational careers began in Canadian kindergartens, equaled or exceeded children of Canadian-born parents in reading, writing and mathematics by age 13.

Overall, disparities in the five studies' results seemed attributable to differences in English (or French) language proficiency, and perhaps acculturation, among the populations.

Three recent Canadian studies have attempted to describe trajectories while accounting for the effects of ethno-cultural background and socio-economic status. All have used ESL data describing students from the Vancouver School Board (Gunderson, 2007 [n = 2 213]; Toohey and Derwing, 2008 [n = 1 554]; Garnett, Adamuti-Trache and Ungerleider, 2008 [n = 2 679]). Across the three, similar patterns emerge. Chinese speaking ESL students' outcomes exceed those of many other ethno-cultural groups on most performance measures, while Tagalog, Spanish and Vietnamese speakers appear to be most at risk (Gunderson, 2007; Toohey and Derwing, 2008; Garnett, Adamuti-Trache, and Ungerleider, 2008). Chinese speakers disproportionately arrive as independent or entrepreneur class immigrants, considered a marker of high socio-economic status (SES); whereas the underperforming ethno-cultural groups disproportionately arrive as refugee or family reunification immigrants, so are considered lower markers of SES (Gunderson, 2007; Toohey and Derwing, 2008). However, the latter two studies neither systematically report the exact proportion of immigration statuses in each group nor control for this imperfect SES indicator statistically. By contrast, Garnett *et al.* (2008) controlled for school and family income and education levels and found that school-level income predicts ESL enrolment in mathematics and science courses, but has little effect on mean scores and does not negate ethno-cultural effects. Family-level SES effects appear negligible, though the indicators are only estimations based on proportions of university degrees and low-income families in the students' neighbourhoods. A final cross-study finding is the preference for science courses among ESL students, as indicated by enrolment rates.

This study employs a more precise indicator of family income than these previous three studies, in an attempt to better understand the role of at least one dimension of SES, and controls for English proficiency and age on arrival to better understand the roles these variables play in predicting achievement among various ethno-cultural groups. As such, it asks:

1. What do the academic trajectories of ESL students look like?

2. To what degree do SES, ethno-cultural background and English proficiency, predict these trajectories, and how might we interpret these results?

3. What are the policy implications of these findings for teacher education *vis-a-vis* ESL students?

In addressing these questions, it illuminates how empirical studies like this one may prove particularly useful to teacher-educators wishing to prepare teacher candidates for classrooms that include immigrant children.

Methods

Data for British Columbia's 1997 grade 8 cohort (n = 48 265) were received from the British Columbia Ministry of Education. This final group of students was selected after cleaning the data of obvious errors (such as the inclusion of students born in 1907), and selecting only those born in 1984, the typical birth year of a grade 8 entrant in 1997. Grade 8 is typically the first year of secondary school in British Columbia.

The target population was all students who had never claimed English as a language spoken at home, and who had received ESL service at some point in their K-12[3] educational careers (n = 7 527). *Ethno-cultural background* was proxied by language spoken at home. The seven most frequently occurring home language groups of the grade 8 cohort were selected (see Table 4.1). The "Chinese" category included students who reported speaking Chinese, Mandarin and Cantonese; "South Asian" included Punjabi, Hindi, Gujarati and Urdu; "Filipino" included Tagalog and Pilipino. The comparison group was native English speakers (NES) (n = 37 612).

Table 4.1. **Numbers of ESL-ever and three subsets: beginner ESL students, low income students and high income students**

	ESL ever	Beginner ESL	Low income	High income	Missing income data
Total ESL	**7527**	**3540**	**3691**	**3675**	**157**
Chinese	3 365	1 865	1 456	1 863	46
South Asian	1 470	549	807	611	52
Vietnamese	373	218	287	79	7
Filipino	323	142	179	134	10
Spanish-speakers	291	116	183	103	5
Persian	284	120	105	175	0
Korean	239	109	80	152	7
Other	1 182	349	594	558	30

English language proficiency was proxied by calculating the sum of years of ESL service required by the student (mean = 4.5; std. dev. = 2.2; range = 10). More years of ESL service correlates with a lower level of English proficiency upon entry to the British Columbia school system and/ or a lower rate of English language acquisition. A *beginner ESL* variable was created by selecting students who received ESL service for two or more years during or after grade 8. Subsequently, a beginner ESL subset was derived from each ethno-cultural group. The complete ESL group from which the beginner ESL subset was derived is labelled "ESL-ever" (see Table 4.1).

Years of ESL service was an unsuitable predictor of graduation and grade 12 enrolment, as students who do not graduate often have fewer years of service, or do not enrol in classes (because they have dropped out). Reading comprehension scores on a province wide grade 10 standardized reading test, the Foundation Skills Assessment (FSA), were thus used to indicate English proficiency in the graduation and enrolment logistic regression models.

Socio-economic status was estimated by matching 2001 student postal codes with 2001 census data describing average family income per postal code according to all six characters. The size of local delivery units' (*i.e.* final three characters of the postal codes) averages 15 households (Edudata, n.d.). These data describe average neighbourhood income. While this is a neighbourhood effect and perhaps should be modeled as such, it is interpreted here as a proxy for individual income because it is the most finely grained SES indicator available. In the multivariate analyses, average family income is a continuous variable divided into deciles. For cross-tabulations, average family income (mean = CAD 60 712; std. dev = CAD 18 233) is divided at the median to create a simple high–low dichotomous variable. Table 4.1 shows the distribution of ethno-cultural group members according to estimated family income.

Further individual level variables include gender, an original database variable and age of entry to the British Columbia system (mean = 8.7; std. dev. = 2.2; range = 7-13). These are included in multivariate models. Similarly, variables derived from the same data-set describing school-level effects are included in multivariate analysis but they are not described here, and indeed exhibit minimal effects.

The dependent variables are graduation within five and six years of grade 8 entry, and enrolment and performance in Mathematics 11 and 12 and English 12. Mean scores were calculated from final marks present in the original dataset. Course enrolment was determined by the presence of a mark in the dataset. Graduation was calculated from graduation dates present in the dataset. Graduation within five years represents a non-delayed progression for a grade 8 cohort. The British Columbia Ministry of Education recognises some students require more time, and reports graduation within six years.

Results

Figure 4.1 represents a cross-tabulation of the five- and six-year graduation rates of NES, ESL-ever, and disaggregated ESL ethno-cultural groups. Although "All ESL" students' graduation rate surpasses that of NES, the large number of Chinese-speaking graduates raises this aggregate ESL average. Other ethno-cultural groups fare slightly worse than NESs and substantially worse than Chinese speakers. The graduation rates for Spanish and Vietnamese speakers are particularly low.

Figure 4.1. **Graduation rates of NES, all ESL and individual ESL ethno-cultural groups**

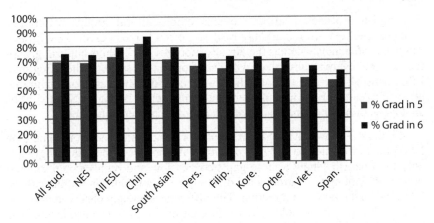

Figure 4.2. **Five and six-year graduation rates of beginner ESL students**

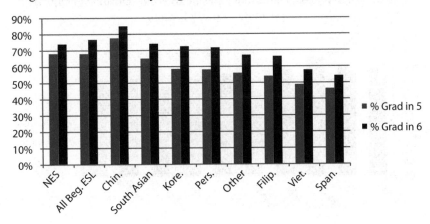

Following Rumberger and Larson (1998) and Watt and Roessingh (1994 and 2001), ESL students at lower levels of English language proficiency at entry to high school might have diminished trajectories. Figure 4.2 shows the five and six-year graduation rates for beginner ESL students.

Although "All beginner ESL" graduation rates remain remarkably high in both Figures 4.1 and 4.2, again the strong performance of Chinese speakers pulls them upwards. When requiring two or more years of high school ESL, the five-year graduation rates of all groups except Chinese and South Asian speakers are below 60%. The lowest outcomes are among speakers of Spanish, Vietnamese and Filipino languages. Fewer than half of beginner ESL Vietnamese and Spanish speakers graduated within five years of beginning grade 8.

English proficiency affects diverse ethno-cultural groups differently. Chinese speakers are remarkably resilient to the barriers erected by limited English proficiency, whereas the already more "at risk" ethno-cultural groups face a more severe disadvantage when confronting the same hurdles. Beginner ESL Spanish-speaking students, already the most disadvantaged group, graduate in six years at rates nine percentage points below ESL-ever Spanish. The analogous drop for Chinese speakers is only two percentage points.

Figure 4.3 shows "All ESL" graduation rates depend less on income than NES graduation rates do (t = 300; p <.001)[4]. Among all ethno-cultural groups, only the Spanish[5] show a large gap between low and high-income graduation rates. Among most groups the difference is negligible, and in the case of Filipinos, in the opposite direction. The differences already observed between ethno-cultural groups hold when this control for SES is introduced. The low-income Chinese graduation rate is still higher than every other group's

Figure 4.3. **Six-year graduation rates of all ethno-cultural groups by estimated family income**

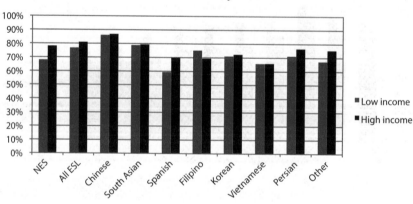

high-income rate. The high-income Spanish-speaker, Filipino and Vietnamese graduation rates are still lower than Chinese, South Asian, Korean and Persian low-income rates. Overall, ESL students' family economic backgrounds minimally affect graduation.

Enrolment and mean scores in Mathematics 12 and English 12

The first two columns of Table 4.2 show Math 12 enrolment and mean scores of NES and ESL-ever students, as do columns five and six for English 12. While the average Math 12 All ESL scores are identical to NES', they hide the performance of Spanish-speaking, Filipino and Vietnamese students who respectively score 11, 10 and 6 points below the NES baseline. Similarly, the two point English 12 gap between NES' and All ESL students mask 4-7 point gaps in the same three groups plus South Asians. In both subjects, the numerous Chinese, and to a lesser degree the smaller numbers of Koreans and Persians raise the All ESL average.

Enrolment rates dramatically illustrate ESL academic effort, more so among certain groups than others. The Math 12 All ESL enrolment rate is nearly double that of NES'. This owes largely to the Chinese students who enrol in Math 12 at 2.5 times the rate of NES'. Korean and Persian enrolment is also very high. In fact, despite differences among ethno-cultural

Table 4.2. **Enrolment and performance in Mathematics 12 and English 12 among NES, ESL, and individual ESL ethno-cultural groups: ESL-ever *versus* beginner ESL**

	Math 12				English 12			
	Enrolment	Mean score	Enrolment	Mean score	Enrolment	Mean score	Enrolment	Mean score
NES	23%	69	--	--	67%	70	--	--
	ESL-ever		Beginner ESL		ESL-ever		Beginner ESL	
All ESL	43%	69	44%	69	77%	68	75%	65
Chinese	57%	72	60%	71	87%	70	86%	67
South Asian	32%	65	21%	62	74%	66	66%	64
Spanish-speakers	18%	58	8%	47	58%	63	46%	58
Filipino	30%	59	17%	58	72%	65	63%	59
Korean	45%	73	54%	73	74%	68	72%	63
Vietnamese	32%	63	24%	57	62%	66	55%	63
Persian	43%	69	47%	66	75%	68	75%	64
Other	28%	64	27%	64	67%	68	61%	64

subgroups, all except Spanish-speakers enrol in Math 12 at rates higher than NES'. Similarly, all ethno-cultural groups except Spanish-speaking and Vietnamese enrol in English 12, the typical graduation requirement, more frequently than NES'. Chinese enrolment rates are extremely high.

Table 4.3 shows the enrolment rates in Mathematics 12 and English 12 of all groups, cross-tabulated by their estimated family income. Unlike graduation, estimated family income predicts Mathematics 12 enrolment more strongly for all subgroups of ESL students than NES'. This gap is more pronounced in some ethno-cultural groups than others. Chinese have only a 6 percentage point gap, while all other groups except Filipinos have 9 to 12 percentage point gaps. English 12 enrolment is not predicted as strongly by estimated family income for any of the ESL subgroups as it is for NES'. In five of the subgroups, the difference is three percentage points or fewer. The largest gaps are among the Spanish-speakers and South Asians. Income is also a stronger predictor of ESL mean scores in mathematics than in English, particularly among the Spanish, Filipino and Vietnamese speakers. Also, the

Table 4.3. **Mathematics 12 and English 12 enrolment and mean scores by estimated family income among NES, ESL and individual ethno-cultural groups**

| | Math 12 | | | | English 12 | | | |
| | Mean score | | Enrolment | | Mean score | | Enrolment | |
	Low income	High income	Low income	High income	Low income	High income	Low income	High income
NES	68	71	21%	25%	69	71	60%	72%
All ESL	66	73	37%	48%	68	69	74%	80%
Chinese	69	73	53%	59%	70	70	86%	87%
South Asian	66	64	27%	39%	66	66	71%	77%
Spanish-speakers	52	65	14%	24%	60	67	56%	64%
Filipino	56	62	32%	26%	66	63	73%	72%
Korean	75	72	38%	49%	68	68	71%	74%
Vietnamese	61	68	30%	39%	66	67	62%	63%
Persian	68	69	35%	47%	65	70	73%	76%
Other	60	67	22%	34%	67	69	63%	71%

Notes:

NES Math enrolment: sample n = 3 752; chi square p = .02

NES Math 12 mean score: F = 6.056, p = .014

NES English enrolment sample n = 3 752; chi square p = .000

NES English 12 mean score: F = 15.666, p<.001

low-income – high-income gap is seven points among all ESL students, compared to three points among NES'. In English 12, only the Spanish-speakers and Persians appear substantially advantaged at the high-income level, and only one point separates the low and high-income All ESL group. While income generally has a slightly larger effect on enrolment than mean scores in most subgroups, overall, the income variable does not suppress the previously established patterns of ethno-cultural variation.

Multivariate models

Logistic regression models were built to control for all possible variables when predicting graduation within six years, and Math 12 and English 12 enrolment. Appropriate statistical assumptions were met according to Garson (n.d.). Only the statistically significant odds ratios are shown in Figure 4.4. Scores of one indicate even odds. Males are the reference group for gender; "all other ESL students" are the reference group for each ethno-cultural group. For the continuous variables, odds describe the average advantage or disadvantage attributable to each unit of increase. The units for family income and FSA reading scores are deciles; for age of entry they are years. The four school level variables, education index, income index, academic climate and proportion ESL, were included in the models, but are not the subject of this report; their effects were exceedingly weak as evidenced by their proximity to the score of 1.0. Each model is strong.[6]

Females have moderately better chances of graduating and enrolling in English than males, but the opposite is true for mathematics. The ethno-cultural patterns previously observed hold in many cases. The Chinese advantage remains strong across outcomes, as does a Persian and smaller South Asian advantage. Koreans are advantaged in odds of enrolment in both

Figure 4.4. **Odds ratios of logistic regression models predicting graduation in 6 years, and enrolment in Mathematics 12 and English 12**

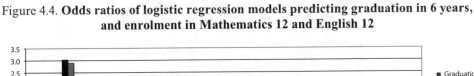
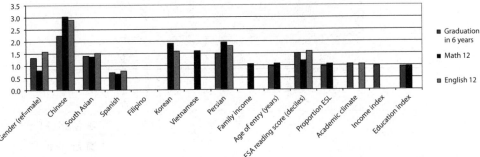

subjects. The Spanish-speakers remain significantly disadvantaged in all outcomes with all other variables controlled. A difference is the Vietnamese and Filipino students are no longer disadvantaged across any of the outcomes once all other factors, notably English proficiency, are controlled.

Family income provides a statistically significant but trivial boost only in mathematics enrolment. Interestingly, reading scores are a robust predictor of graduation and academic enrolment. Age of entry, by contrast, though statistically significant in predicting mathematics enrolment and graduation, is a trivial predictor. It appears as long as students have English proficiency, their ages entering the system do not matter. This suggests subject matter learned in the first language is transferable to the second language context.

Multiple regression models were built to predict mean scores in mathematics and English. Mathematics 11 was the dependent variable as enrolment in Mathematics 12 among some subgroups were too low to produce significant results (math n = 4 536; English n = 5 813). Appropriate statistical assumptions were met according to Garson (n.d.b). Figure 4.5 shows statistically significant standardised beta weights, the proportion of a standard deviation of variation attributable to each variable.

Results are again consistent with the descriptive cross-tabulations[7]. Females have a slight advantage in mathematics and a large one in English. Across the ethno-cultural groups, the Chinese clearly have performance advantages over

Figure 4.5. **Standardised beta weights of multiple regression models predicting mean scores in Mathematics 11 and English 12**

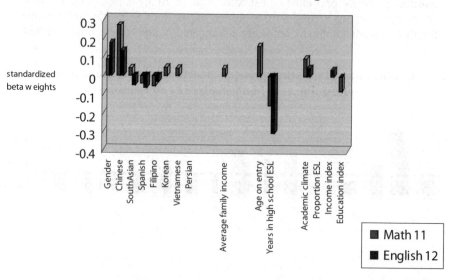

their ESL peers, particularly in mathematics. South Asian, Spanish-speakers and Filipino have small disadvantages. Again the Vietnamese disadvantage in the descriptive results is attenuated when all factors are controlled. Family income contributes a trivial advantage in mathematics and nothing in English. Later ages of entry actually increase mathematics scores among ESL students, a fact further analysis revealed was largely attributable to the large proportion of Chinese students (not shown). Low English proficiency, as indicated by years spent in ESL classes, is very problematic. It contributes a substantial disadvantage in mathematics – home country education is beneficial in mathematics but harmful if it comes at the expense of English proficiency – and a very large disadvantage in English 12.

Discussion and relevance for teacher education

The results suggest a number of implications for teacher education. First, decision-makers must be careful to disaggregate data and use them critically when making judgments. Specifically, "immigrant" or "ESL" labels mask tremendous variation among the groups they subsume. In this study, Chinese-speaking students performed extraordinarily well, and generally inflated the apparent achievement of other ESL ethno-cultural groups. Indeed, three of these ethno-cultural groups attained significantly lower outcomes than native English speakers. Teacher-educators are encouraged to make their teacher-candidates aware of such variation, and that the challenges and advantages of one immigrant group may be far different than those experienced by another.

A troubling finding was that among most ethno-cultural groups, achievement did not match their apparent aspirations. All but one ethno-cultural group exceeded native English speakers in mathematics enrolment, as did all but two in English 12. These enrolment rates speak to the high degree of investment immigrant families place in schools. Unfortunately, in the former subject, four of the seven groups were unable to equal NES mean scores; and in the latter class none were.

These results are disconcerting first in that our schools do not seem to be capitalising on the aspirations of large segments of our immigrant communities. It may seem unsurprising that students for whom English is not a first language are not able to match the outcomes of native English speakers in an English medium school system; however, as a grade 8 cohort, all students had been in British Columbia schools for a minimum of five years at the time they received these marks. Most had been in much longer; the mean age of entry was 8.7 years (roughly grade 3). That schools were unable to offer equity of outcomes to subgroups that had been so long in the system suggests a need for teacher education to prepare teacher-candidates more adequately to serve immigrant populations.

Adequate preparation of teacher-candidates has two strands, technical and attitudinal. ESL students in British Columbia spend the greatest amount of time with content-area teachers. Although they may receive ESL special- ist support in the form of classes or pull-out tutorials, like most students, the bulk of their subject-matter learning occurs in mainstream classes. It is imperative that mainstream teachers in immigrant-serving schools be trained in the pedagogical techniques that most effectively serve English language learners. Although, there are no magic solutions, much literature over the last two decades has suggested how content-teachers might *(a)* integrate language instruction with their content teaching, and *(b)* adapt their teaching techniques to render content more accessible to second language learners (*e.g.* Chamot and O'Malley, 1994; Mohan 1986; Brinton, Snow and Wesche, 2003).

Generally, the "authenticity" of learning English through subject matter content is motivating for students; and more importantly, ESL students do not have the time to wait until they have mastered English before they can begin their content area studies. This latter point is critical, as the variation in mathematics outcomes was likely partially attributable to variation in first- language-content knowledge. Namely, Chinese students from countries with extremely competitive, highly-developed educational infrastructures likely had a "head start" in mathematics not shared by the lower achieving ethno- cultural groups. Indeed these subgroups may have been behind native English speaking grade-level peers in mathematics when entering school. It is critical therefore that they be able to begin their content learning as soon as possible, rather than "wait until they learn English" before beginning their subject- matter instruction. Under this latter approach these students simply do not have time to catch up (see Cummins, 2000). Predictably, when examining the perceptions of secondary ESL students and teachers of ESL navigation of high school, Derwing *et al.* (1999) note, a "stronger link between ESL and content curricula is necessary" (p. 545) to promote success. Teacher-candidates in urban Canadian jurisdictions need to be able to do so effectively.

A related point is that student success appears bolstered by well-devel- oped first language content knowledge. Age of entry was not a disadvantage when English proficiency was controlled. In some cases it was an advantage. The Chinese resilience to low English proficiency probably owed in part to their first language content knowledge. Teacher candidates and in-service teachers should be made aware of the value of the students' prior school expe- riences. Practically, this may involve allowing generous use of the student's first language, in order to access this knowledge. The evidence implies teach- ers will be harming students by not allowing the use of their first languages in classrooms (see also Cummins, 2000).

Universities more consistently attend to a second strand of teacher education for immigrant students, trying to instill positive attitudes toward diversity from a social justice perspective. The moral push for more equity in democratic societies demands teachers not be satisfied with underachievement, particularly among those from identifiable social subgroups, many of which have and may continue, to suffer discrimination.

Such courses are necessary components of teacher education. In this study, although estimated family income was often not a particularly good predictor of outcomes, the three most disadvantaged immigrant groups were those most over-represented at lower levels of income. And the three highest achieving groups were indeed over-represented at higher levels of income (see Table 4.1). So while income did not always predict outcomes very well within these groups, there is little doubt the ethno-cultural groups disproportionately observed at higher levels of income were, on average, higher achievers. Therefore, it seems likely that the disadvantaged social status of the groups most represented in the low-income column can partially account for their lower than average outcomes.

Ogbu, when discussing minorities (*e.g.* 1992), and Willis (1977) when discussing the British working class, developed analogous theories that dominant behavioural patterns among socially disadvantaged students and their families were to fail in school if school were not seen as a legitimate vehicle of upward social mobility. Ogbu theorised colonised minorities like African-Americans or indigenous peoples were unlikely to believe schooling credentials would be rewarded in a racist society. Willis similarly showed that the "lads" in his study were uninterested in school success as they realised their destinies were in blue collar labour that did not require academic training. A similar mindset may be present in the disadvantaged ethno-cultural groups in this study. Gunderson, who researched Vancouver, interviewed a Vietnamese girl who said:

> *Even if you do really well you just get an ordinary job ... I have a few cousins, they all drop out. There's no future, so what's the point* (Gunderson, 2007, p. 207).

Indeed, Cummins (1997), building on Ogbu's theory, hypothesised that broader social power relations (*e.g.* media representations of minorities produced by dominant groups) filter into schooling, particularly in teacher perceptions of students, and can oppress students according to *any* category of difference (language, class, ethnicity, sexuality, gender, etc.). Students from oppressed groups may be sceptical of the rewards offered by schooling credentials; teachers may – even subconsciously – doubt the aptitude of the same students. If this is the case, social justice education is clearly a critical part of teacher education. Teacher-educators ought to find data-driven studies like this one invaluable in demonstrating empirically that these kinds of inequities are really occurring, given that teacher-candidates, generally from the dominant social groups themselves, are often sceptical that oppression and discrimination still occur in our liberal societies (*e.g.* Gay and Kirkland, 2003).

Regrettably, in most Canadian teacher-education programmes, ESL methods education – the technical skills of teaching subject matter content to ESL students – is not mandatory for teacher-candidates of mainstream subjects. At the University of British Columbia, teacher-candidates may enroll in ESL methods courses, but they are not required to, even though the great majority will teach in Metro Vancouver. This gap is particularly ironic since some of the leading language and content research in Canada has taken place in the same faculty at that institution.

While teacher-education programmes in British Columbia, and throughout Canada, prioritise social justice education, they appear to assume that the technical skills needed to teach ESL students can be learned on-the-job. This is flawed thinking in that *(a)* teachers on the job in British Columbia typically have little opportunity to learn from their colleagues, and *(b)* moreover, their colleagues in most cases will not have any training in ESL education. But perhaps more critically, this thinking assumes actions always follow attitudes, when there may be good reason to believe attitudes also follow actions. In other words, teachers who feel confident in their ability to teach English language learners are more likely to accept these students as their responsibilities, and work to raise their outcomes. Some research shows mainstream teachers are indeed sympathetic to, and admiring of, immigrant students, but do not feel they have the expertise to give them the instruction they need; therefore they believe the ESL teacher, not themselves, must be responsible for ESL students' education (Reeves, 2006; Garnett, 1999; Penfield, 1987). Teacher-education programmes ought to attend to these technical skills. School boards, the employers of British Columbia public school teachers, could probably ensure that they do simply by making such training a prerequisite for hire.

Conclusion

This chapter reported on one data-driven study conducted in British Columbia, Canada. Readers are strongly cautioned against generalising the specific findings to their local contexts, and in assuming that the limited data available in this study can completely account for the trajectories of immigrant students through school; they cannot. To do so would require analysis of a range of personal and contextual variables, more sensitive and numerous than those reported here, and indeed well beyond the scope of any single piece of quantitative research. One should be particularly careful not to make misguided assumptions about the role of genetics when looking at the ethnocultural variables. They owe their power to the interplay of the knowledge, skills and dispositions more commonly brought by ethno-cultural groups from some countries – with competitive and well-developed education systems – than others, and the reception provided to the groups in the host society.

What this study can do, is show how even with relatively limited data, patterns of inequities in achievement emerge which may be amenable to policy interventions. In this case, decision-makers in the arena of teacher-education have seen how data can:

1. show where under- and over-achievement is occurring and how it varies underneath labels;

2. demonstrate if schools are meeting the apparent aspirations of immigrant populations;

3. provide a rationale for better technical education of teachers who serve diverse populations;

4. allow inferences about how social power relations filter into schooling, thereby;

5. providing an empirical rationale for social justice education that is sometimes met with scepticism; and

6. demonstrate to teacher-candidates how immigrant student success depends on both second language proficiency and first language content knowledge, thereby encouraging them to make appropriate classroom level decisions.

Decision-makers are therefore encouraged to collect and use data in the interests of creating more equitable and just societies through education.

Notes

1. "ESL" is provincial terminology. Many of these students have learned more than one language before English.

2. Grade 12 is the final grade of high school in the province of British Columbia and most other Canadian provinces.

3. Kindergarten to grade 12. This comprises the full spectrum of the basic education system in most Canadian provinces.

4. Unlike every other analysis, the NES income analyses are based on a 10% random sample generated by SPSS.

5. Note that this refers to Spanish-speakers (and thus includes students from Mexico and Central and South America as well as Spain).

6. Nagelkerke r-squares and reductions in error produced by each are as follows: graduation, r sq =.357, reduction in error = 26%; mathematics 12, r sq. = .191, reduction in error = 20%; English 12 r sq = .398, reduction in error = 31%.

7. Multiple regression model strengths were: Mathematics 11 r-squared = .115; English 12 r-squared = .146.

References

Adamuti-Trache, M., Andres, L. (2007), "Embarking on and Persisting in Scientific Fields of Study: Social Class, Gender and Curriculum Along the Science Pipeline", *International Journal of Science Education*, pp. 1-28.

Brinton, D, M. Snow and M. Wesche (2003), *Content-based Second Language Instruction*, Newbury House Publishers, New York.

British Columbia Ministry of Education (2009), *English as a Second Language: Policy and Guidelines, 2009. http://www.bced.gov.bc.ca/esl/ policy/guidelines.pdf.*

British Columbia Ministry of Education (2009b), Edufacts: The Facts About ESL in British Columbia. *http://www.bced.gov.bc.ca/news/edu-facts/2009/0903_esl.pdf.*

Chamot, A. and M. O'Malley (1994), *The Calla Handbook,* Addison Wesley, New York.

Cummins, J. (1997), "Minority Status and Schooling in Canada", *Anthropology and Education Quarterly*, Vol. 28, No. 3, pp. 411-430.

Cummins, J. (2000), *Language, Power and Pedagogy: Bilingual Children Caught in the Crossfire,* Multilingual Matters, Toronto.

Derwing, T.M., E. DeCorby, J. Ichikawa, and K. Jamieson (1999), "Some Factors that Affect the Success of ESL High School Students", *The Canadian Modern Language Review*, Vol. 55, No. 4, pp. 532-547.

Edudata Canada (n.d.). *Socio-economic Status Indicators, http://edu-data.educ.ubc.ca/Data_Pages/StatCan/SES_Indicators.htm*, accessed 2 September 2007.

Garnett, B. (1999), "The Effects of ESL: A Case Study of Mainstream Teachers' Perceptions of ESL Students and the ESL Program at a Junior Secondary School", MA Thesis, University of British Columbia, Vancouver, Canada.

Garnett, B, M. Adamuti-Trache and C. Ungerleider (2008), "The Academic Mobility of Students for whom English is not a First Language: The Roles of Ethnicity Language and Class", *Alberta Journal of Education Research*, Vol. 54, No. 3, pp. 309-326.

Garson, D. G. (n.d.), *Logistic Regression. Statnotes: Topics in Multivariate Analysis http://www2.chass.ncsu.edu/garson/pa765/statnote.htm*, accessed 4 August 2007.

Garson, D. G. (n.d.), *Multiple Regression. Statnotes: Topics in Multivariate Analysis, http://www2.chass.ncsu.edu/garson/pa765/statnote.htm*, accessed 10 August 2007.

Gay, G. and K. Kirkland (2003), "Developing Cultural Critical Consciousness and Self-Reflection in Preservice Teacher Education", *Theory into Practice*, Vol. 42, No. 3, pp. 181-187.

Guba, E. and Y. Lincoln (1994), "Competing Paradigms in Qualitative Research", in Denzin and Lincoln (eds.), *Handbook of Qualitative Research*, Sage Publishing, Thousand Oaks, California, pp. 105-117.

Gunderson, L. (2007), *English Only Instruction and Immigrant Students in Secondary Schools: A Critical Examination*, Lawrence Erlbaum Associates, Mahwah, New Jersey.

Mohan, B. (1986), *Language and Content*, Addison-Wesley, Reading, Massachusetts.

Ogbu, J. (1992), "Adaptation to Minority Status and Impact on School Success", *Theory into Practice*, Vol. 31, No. 4, pp. 287-295.

Penfield, J. (1987), "ESL: The Regular Classroom Teacher's Perspective", *TESOL Quarterly*, Vol. 21, No. 1, pp. 21-39.

Reeves, J. (2006), "Secondary Teacher Attitudes toward Including English-language Learners in Mainstream Classrooms", *The Journal of Educational Research*, Vol. 99, No. 3, pp. 131-142.

Rumberger, R. and K. Larson (1998). "Toward Explaining Differences in Educational Achievement among Mexican-American Language-Minority Students", *Sociology of Education*, Vol. 71, No. 1, pp. 69-93.

Samuel, E., E. Krugly-Smolska, and W. Warren (2001), "Academic Achievement of Adolescents from Selected Ethnocultural Groups in Canada: A Study Consistent with John Ogbu's Theory", *McGill Journal of Education*, Vol. 36, No. 1, pp. 61-73.

Schleicher, A. (2006), "Where Immigrant Students Succeed: A Comparative Review of Performance and Engagement in PISA 2003", *Intercultural Education*, Vol. 17, No. 5, pp. 507-516.

Statistics Canada (2004), "Immigrant Population by Place of Birth and Period of Immigration, 2001 Census", *http://www40.statcan.ca/l01/cst01/demo24a-eng.htm*.

Statistics Canada (2008), "Immigrant Status (4) for the Population of Canada, Provinces and Territories, 1911 to 2006 Censuses", *http://www12.statcan.gc.ca/english/census06/data/topics*.

Statistics Canda (2009), "Population by Immigrant Status and Period of Immigration, 2006 Counts, for Canada, Provinces and Territories", *http://www12.statcan.ca/census-recensement/2006/dp-pd/hlt/97-557/T403-eng.cfm?Lang=E&T=403&GH=8&SC=1&S=0&O=A*.

Toohey, K and T. Derwing (2008), "Hidden Losses: How Demographics Can Encourage Incorrect Assumptions about ESL High School Students' Success", *Alberta Journal of Educational Research*, Vol. 54, No. 2, pp. 178-193.

Watt, D. and H. Roessingh (1994), "ESL Dropout: The Myth of Educational Equity", *The Alberta Journal of Educational Research*, Vol. 40, No. 3, pp. 283-296.

Watt, D. and H. Roessingh (2001), "The Dynamics of ESL Dropout: Plus ca Change...", *Canadian Modern Language Review*, Vol. 58, No. 2, pp. 203-222.

Worswick, C. (2001), *School Performance of the Children of Immigrants in Canada*, Statistics Canada, Ottawa.

Part II

Preparing teachers for diverse classrooms

Chapter 5

Diversity and educational disparities: the role of teacher education

Russell Bishop
University of Waikato, New Zealand

The most pressing problem facing education today is the persistent pattern of edu-cational disparity which disproportionately affects indigenous peoples, populations of colour, those with lower socio-economic status, and new migrants. This disparity is exacerbated by a continuing lack of diversity among the teaching force, which tends to engage in pedagogic practices more appropriate to monocultural popula-tions. This chapter suggests solutions drawn from "Te Kotahitanga: Improving the Educational Achievement of Māori students in Mainstream Schools", a govern-ment-funded professional development and research project underway in 50 sec-ondary schools in New Zealand. Six main challenges identified include: (i) the hegemony of the status quo, (ii) the primacy of teachers' positioning, (iii) the need for evidence, (iv) the role of power in knowledge construction, (v) the disconnect between pre-service and in-service education, and (vi) the fundamental importance of research in the areas of teaching and teacher education.

> *From the OECD online consultation: importance of connecting with community*
>
> **Practitioners overwhelmingly reported that they did not receive preparation or tools to help include parents or community members in their work. But this type of outreach can help improve student achievement and allow practitioners to better understand their students' diversity.**

Introduction: diversity and educational disparities[1]

Educators are increasingly identifying the most pressing problem facing education today as the interaction between the ever more diverse student population and the associated persistence of educational disparities affecting indigenous peoples and populations of colour, poverty, various abilities and new migrants. This problem is exacerbated by the continuing lack of diversity among the teaching force who demonstrate discursive positionings and pedagogic practices more appropriate to monocultural populations.

For example, Villegas and Lucas (2002) indicate that the United States is becoming more racially, ethnically and linguistically diverse than ever due to higher birth rates among minority groups, the differing age structures (fertility *versus* death rates) of minority *versus* the majority white population, and net immigration of non-white peoples. In Europe, the migrations of people from previous colonies and other sending countries with their different age structures and birth rates has also created a similar pattern of diversity among the school-age population where now sizable groups of ethnic and religious minorities are evident in most towns and cities.

This increasing diversity is coupled with persistent and increasing educational disparities, primarily between those from dominant cultural groups and those of marginalised and minoritised[2] children. As Villegas and Lucas (2002, p. xi) pointed out, in the United States, "[h]istorically, members of economically poor and minority groups have not succeeded in schools at rates comparable to those of their white, middle-class, standard English-speaking peers". The same could be said of many other countries where there are significant and growing multicultural populations (OECD, 2002).

However, while the student population is becoming increasingly diverse, and disparities in student achievement persist or in many cases are increasing, the teaching population is remaining homogeneous, or in the case of the United States, according to Villegas (1998), is becoming more homogeneous as the proportional representation of minorities drops. Problems thus arise due to teachers' limited range of cultural experiences and understandings as well as their possible unawareness of the "funds of knowledge" that children of different backgrounds can call upon in classrooms. They also may not understand the cultural cues that people use to indicate their willingness to enter into the dialogue that is fundamental to the conversation of learning such as eye contact or standing in the presence of older people (Clay, 1985; Cazden, 1990; Grumet, 1995). In addition, the lack of role models and advocates for students of colour in schools is also of considerable concern.

Together these factors exacerbate the problems presented by a largely monocultural workforce who draw upon deficit discourses to explain educational disparities while trying to address the needs of a multicultural/multi-ethnic student population from education models developed more to suit children of the majority cultures. As Sleeter (2005, p. 2) suggests, "[i]t is true that low expectations for students of colour and students from poverty communities, buttressed by taken-for-granted acceptance of the deficit ideology, has been a rampant and persistent problem for a long time ... therefore, empowering teachers without addressing the deficit ideology may well aggravate the problem".

With this problem in mind, this chapter looks at how educators might address this situation. *Te Kotahitanga: Improving the Educational Achievement of Māori students in Mainstream Schools* (Bishop *et al.,* 2003), is a Kaupapa Māori[3] research and professional development project that aims to improve the educational achievement of Māori students in mainstream classrooms. While this analysis is based on a case study of an intervention study undertaken in New Zealand, it is suggested that the messages drawn are applicable beyond the shores of this country.

The current educational context

The major challenge facing education in New Zealand today is that the *status quo* is one of ongoing social, economic and political disparities, primarily between the descendents of the British colonisers (*Pakeha*) and the indigenous Māori people. The Māori have higher levels of unemployment, are more likely to be employed in low paying jobs, have much higher levels of incarceration, illness and poverty than do the rest of the population and are generally under-represented in positive social and economic indicators

(Education Counts, n.d.). These disparities are also reflected at all levels of the education system.

In comparison to majority culture students (in New Zealand, these students are primarily of European descent), the overall academic achievement levels of Māori students is low; their rate of suspension from school is three times higher; they are over-represented in special education programmes; they enrol in pre-school programmes in lower proportions than other groups; they tend to be over-represented in low stream education classes; they are more likely than other students to be found in vocational curriculum streams; and they leave school earlier with fewer formal qualifications and enrol in tertiary education in lower proportions.

Despite the choice provided by Māori medium education in New Zealand, and decades of educational reforms and policies such as those promoting "multiculturalism" and "biculturalism" that have sought to address these problems, for the 90% of Māori students (Ministry of Education, 2001) who attend mainstream schools, there has been little if any shift in these disparities since they were first statistically identified over forty years ago (New Zealand Department of Māori Affairs, 1962).

Six challenges for practice and practitioners

This problematic situation raises a number of challenges for teachers and teacher educators both in New Zealand and overseas.

Challenge number 1: the status quo is one where ongoing educational disparities are ethnically based

The major challenge that faces educators today is the continuing disparities of outcomes within the education system. In New Zealand, this is seen where Māori children and those of other minoritised groups are consistently over-represented in negative education indicators and under-represented in the positive as detailed above. In terms of qualifications, Māori students in mainstream schools are not achieving at the same levels as other students, and this situation has remained constant for some time. For example, in 1993, 4% of Maori gained an A or a B Bursary and 33% of Maori left school without qualifications. Yet, some 10 years later, in 2002, 4% of Maori gained an A or a B Bursary and 35% of Maori left school without qualifications. In effect, despite the implementation of large scale numeracy and literacy projects little changed over that decade.

Similarly, in 1998, 74.1% of candidates gained university entrance, of whom 6.1% were Māori (1 247). In 2002, 87.2% of candidates gained university entrance, of whom 6.3% were Māori (1 511). That is, despite an absolute increase in numbers, there was a relative decline in the proportion of Maori students gaining university entrance. Exacerbating this situation was the decrease in retention rates for Māori students: from 1994 to 2003, school retention rates for Māori boys to age 16 fell by 12.4% and those for Māori girls by 7.1%. For the same period, retention rates for non Māori boys fell by 0.7%, whereas, the rate for non Māori girls increased by 1.4%. In addition to these statistics of disparity over time, statistics also show that Māori children are referred to specialist services for behavioural problems at far greater rates then other students, and comprise 47% of those suspended from school while only making up 21% of the national school population (this figure is far higher in some regions) (Ministry of Education, 2004). Despite many attempts to address these disparities, these patterns have remained relatively unchanged throughout the current decade.

The ongoing nature of these problems suggests two major implications. *(1)* The *status quo* in New Zealand education has ethnically-based educational disparities, and despite many protests to the contrary, this has been case for over 40 years. This pattern is also found among non-European migrant children in New Zealand. *(2)* Despite the best intentions of educators from schools, colleges of education and policy agencies, New Zealand does not currently seem to have a means of systematically addressing these disparities.

How are teacher educators going to assist and educate student teachers to be able to produce equitable outcomes for children of different ethnic, racial, cultural, class and language groups when they become practicing teachers faced with these long-term and seemingly immutable disparities? The first thing they need to do, I maintain, is to examine their own discursive positioning and those of their students and the impact that this might be having on student achievement. Discursive positioning refers to how teachers construe the complex historical phenomena experienced by Māori youth and where they stand as educators in the situation. In other words, which sets of ideas and actions, *i.e.* discourses, do educators draw upon to explain their experiences.

Challenge number 2: teacher positioning

All educators hold a variety of discursive positions on the challenge posed by minoritised students. Bishop *et al.* (2003) found that teachers tend to draw upon three major discourses when explaining their experiences with the education of Māori students: *(i)* the child and their home, *(ii)* school structures, and *(iii)* relationships. The first two tend to locate the problem outside of the classroom and often blame the child and/or the child's home or the school systems and structures for the seemingly immutable nature of the ongoing disparities. The outcome of teachers' theorising from within these discourses is that change is seen to be beyond the power of the teacher to act or to produce an effect, that is, to have agency (freedom to act). In contrast, the discursive position of relationships tends to promote the agency of the teacher in that it acknowledges that ongoing power imbalances within classrooms create educational disparities and power imbalances that can be altered through changes in pedagogy. Such a position is agentic, as in being one of a change agent, and thus enables teachers to examine how they themselves might participate in the systematic marginalisation of Māori students in their own classrooms through their discursive positioning.

To Māori theorists (Bishop, 1996; Smith, 1997), it is clear that unless teachers openly address how dominance manifests itself in the lives of Māori students (and their *whänau*[4]), how the dominant culture maintains control over the various aspects of education, and the part they themselves might play in unwittingly perpetuating this pattern of domination, they will not understand how they and the way they relate to and interact with Māori students may affect learning. An appreciation of relational dynamics without an analysis of power balances can result in professional development that promotes ways of "relating to" and "connecting with" students of other cultures that do not actually require teachers to understand, internalise and work towards changing the power imbalances of which they are a part. In particular, teachers need an opportunity to challenge those power imbalances that are manifested as cultural deficit theorising in the classroom, which, in turn, support the retention of traditional classroom interaction patterns that perpetuate marginalisation.

To this end, Valencia and others (1997), traced the origins of deficit thinking, including various manifestations such as intelligence testing, constructs of "at-riskness" and "blaming the victim" (see also McLaren, 2003). More recently, Shields, Bishop and Mazawi (2005) have detailed how educators and policy makers continue to pathologise the experiences of children through the examination of American Navajo, Israeli Bedouin, and New Zealand Māori children's schooling. In general, they detailed the common practice of attributing school failure to individuals because of their affiliation with a minoritised group within society by a process termed pathologising. According to Shields, Bishop and Mazawi (2005, p. 120) this is a process in which perceived structural-functional, cultural or epistemological deviation from an assumed normal state is ascribed to another group as a product of power relationships, whereby the less powerful group is deemed to be abnormal in some way.

Pathologising represents a challenge for educational reformers, teacher educators and teachers alike in that, as Bruner (1996) identified, it is not just a matter of intervening in part of the system. There is need to challenge whole discourses and move beyond current ways of thinking. The end goal would be to create alternative discourses that offer educators an opportunity to act as change agents.

In *Te Kotahitanga*, we have identified that when teachers draw upon deficit positions, they blame others for educational disparities, they exhibit feelings of helplessness, and they reject their personal and professional responsibilities and agency. In contrast, when teachers actively reject blaming explanations, they accept personal and professional responsibility for their part in the learning relationships. This entails that they believe that they are powerful change agents, they know how and what to do in their classrooms to bring about such change, and they report being reinvigorated as teachers. The majority of teachers still position themselves within these outmoded deficit discourses, thus limiting their agency and, hence, their students' achievement. This is problematic for education, in general, and needs to be addressed by schools and teacher educators specifically.

Identifying discursive positioning involves teacher education students, staff and teachers engaging in ongoing reflection of the impact of these positions on student learning. Therefore, critical questions such as "how do we provide our students/teachers with these opportunities for reflection?" are important. This reflection needs to involve those outside of the current reference groups because consultation within a closed set of people tends to reinforce the range of discourses used rather than challenge them. Widening the range of discourses open to student teachers is vital, as is increasing the numbers of student teachers from minority populations.

Ryan (1999) identifies a number of strategies by which this could be achieved. These include: challenging racist discourses; critically analysing mass media as well as contemporary and historical curriculum resources; fostering cultural identities and community relations; and valuing different languages, knowledge, and alternative discourses. One effective means of employing this latter strategy has been used in Te Kotahitanga (Bishop *et al.,* 2003), whereby narratives of the experiences (Connelly and Clandinin, 1990) of a number of Māori students have been used at the commencement of a professional development programme with teachers and school leaders. This is done to challenge the audience to reflect upon their own positionings *vis-à-vis* the lived realities of these students and to examine the discourses within which they and the students position themselves.

The major finding of this aspect of *Te Kotahitanga* reveals that education professionals who do not challenge their positions or assumptions about the experiences of minoritised students are actually disempowering themselves from achieving their goals for their students' academic achievement. Teacher educators, teachers and student teachers need to be supported and to encourage one another to accept an active role as agents of change and the responsibility for their actions that such a position entails. In order to bring about change in student outcomes, teacher educators should create contexts for learning which emphasise a culture of agency rather than reinforcing the unwitting perpetuation of blame. Once this has been achieved, teachers can then learn how to develop and change their practice through the use of a wide range of evidence, and to take responsibility for any required changes. For example, student teachers will be able to learn how to set and measure appropriate achievement goals for minoritised students and know what to do with the information if and when they get it. This latter expectation, of course, raises the issue of how are pre-service and in-service teachers going to undertake this activity?

Challenge number 3: the call for evidence

Among educators there is an increasing demand that teachers understand how to engage in critical reflection on student learning that is evidence-based rather than assumption-based. That is, there is an expectation that evidence will inform educators' problem-solving in a manner that enables them to change their practice in response to student learning.

The implications of this position for teacher educators is that they need to ascertain if they and their students are able to use data to identify how minoritised students' participation and learning is improving; data such as students' experiences of being minoritised, student participation, absenteeism, suspensions, on-task engagement and student achievement. Such data is then able to be used in a formative manner so that appropriate changes can be made to teachers' practice in response to students' schooling experiences and progress with respect to learning.

In their recent research on developing and sustaining a programme to improve the teaching of reading to five and six-year-olds, Timperley, Philips and Wiseman (2003) found that when achievement information (ranging from teachers classroom tests to national standardised, norm-referenced tests) was used by classroom teachers to inform their teaching practice, they were able to constantly monitor the effectiveness of their practice. When necessary, teachers were then able to adjust their teaching methods to ensure that the learning needs of the child were being addressed. In this way, by using both formative (which is crucial) and summative assessment to guide the single objective – improving Māori children's achievement – teachers received timely and regular information on the effect of their efforts. "Successful actions are reinforcing and likely to be repeated … practices that are new and unfamiliar will be accepted and retained when they are perceived as increasing one's competence and effectiveness" (Timperley, et. al. (2003), p. 130).

In such an approach, one pedagogic style cannot be preferred over another because achievement in its widest sense is the sole criterion for the determination of teaching method. In Timperley et al.'s study, the data were used to prompt change in teaching practice where it was found that a particular teaching method was not working for a specific child. It therefore became possible for "the main measure of the effectiveness of professional development [to be] the extent to which it results in improved student learning and achievement" (Timperley, *et. al.* (2003), p. 131).

Standardised tests were used in this case and can provide schools with data that are critical to sustaining and maximising the benefit of the practice, albeit where there is a degree of match between what is being taught and what is being tested. The tests potentially measure children's collective progress and thus the efficacy of pedagogy, the knowledge and skill gaps to which teachers must attend, and the areas of strength exhibited by children. By way of caution, however, Goldberg and Morrison (2002, p. 73) warn that these potential benefits do "not come automatically" and that "harmful effects of the tests can offset them, if these are not managed appropriately". They advocate that teachers be supported through professional development to understand the statistical concepts necessary to interpret test results, to be able to interpret results within the context of other data, and to work in an environment in which such results are taken seriously. They argue that the judicious use of standardised testing is more likely to occur when there is a strong professional community examining data with a good mix of curiosity and scepticism.

Therefore, it is suggested that such activities are best not undertaken in isolation. Timperley *et al.* (2003) also found that schools which were making a difference to children's achievement held regular meetings to focus on teaching strategies for children whose progress was not at the expected rate. These meetings were held with a sense of urgency and were supported by senior teachers working with other teachers in their classrooms to assist in developing new strategies for these children. School-wide commitment to the urgency and centrality of structured and focused meetings of the professional learning community was also found to be essential.

The Timperley *et al.* (2003) study identified that when teachers were organised into groups and worked together as a professional learning community, with regular meetings within which they considered the evidence of student progress and achievement so as to inform their collective progress, they were able to update their professional knowledge and skills within the context of an organised, school-wide system for improving teaching practices. In addition, teachers' efforts, individually and collectively, "are focused on improving student learning and achievement and making the school as a whole become a high-performing organisation" (Timperley *et al.* (2003), p. 132).

Therefore, teacher educators need to be creating contexts for learning in which their students are able to participate in professional learning communities focusing on problem-solving conversations. Through this approach, student teachers will learn and practice how to set, measure and re-set achievement goals for minoritised students. Furthermore, they will learn what to do with the information they obtain.

Challenge number 4: realisations about learning

There is an increasing realisation that learning involves constructing knowledge individually and socially rather than receiving it from others. There is also an increasing realisation that knowledge is situational and not gender or culture-free. It is always created and promoted for a specific defined purpose. Often these purposes (either explicitly or inadvertently) promote the language, culture and values of those in power.

Teachers retain power and control over what knowledge is legitimate in their classrooms by constructing what Australian educationalist Robert Young (1991, p. 78) terms the traditional classroom as a learning context for children. Young states:

> The [traditional] method [classroom] is one in which teachers objec-
> tify learners and reify knowledge, drawing on a body of objectifying
> knowledge and pedagogy constructed by the behavioural sciences for
> the former, and empiricist and related understandings of knowledge
> for the latter.

To Young (1991), in the traditional classroom teachers see their function "as to 'cover' the set curriculum, to achieve sufficient 'control' to make students do this, and to ensure that students achieve a sufficient level of 'mastery' of the set curriculum as revealed by evaluation" (p. 79). The learning context these teachers create aims to promote these outcomes. In these classrooms teachers are "active" and do most of the "official" talk (classroom language). Technical mastery of this language and the language of the curriculum (which is generally one and the same) are pre-requisites for pupil participation with the official "knowledge" of the classroom.

The learning context that is created in traditional classrooms is such that there is a distinct power difference between teacher and learner which, as Smith (1997, p. 178) suggests, may be reinforced ideologically and spatially. Ideologically, the teacher is seen as the "font of all knowledge"; the students (in Locke's terms) as the "*tabula rasa*" – the empty slate; where the teacher is the objective arbiter and transmitter of knowledge. Knowledge, however, is selected by the teacher, guided by curriculum documents and possibly texts that are created from within and by the dominant discourse. In colonial and neo-colonial contexts, it is knowledge often from outside the experiences and interests of the very people one is purporting to educate. Far from being neutral, these documents actively reproduce the cultural and social hegemony of the dominant groups at the expense of marginalised groups. The spatial manifestation of difference can be seen in "the furniture arrangements within the classroom, in the organisation of staff meetings, and by holding assemblies with teachers sitting on the stage and so forth" (Smith, 1997, p. 179). Children who are unable or who do not want to participate in this pattern are marginalised and fail. Teachers will then explain the children's lack of participation in terms of pupil inabilities, disabilities, dysfunctions or deficiencies, rather than considering that it may well be the very structure of the classroom that mitigates against the creation of a relationship that will promote satisfactory participation by students.

In contrast, in what Young (1991) terms a "discursive classroom", new images and their constituent metaphors are present to inform and guide the development of educational principles and pedagogies in order to help create power-sharing relationships and classroom interaction patterns within which young Māori and other minoritised peoples can successfully participate and engage in learning.

Discursive classrooms that are created by teachers who are working within Kaupapa Māori reform projects, such as *Te Kotahitanga*, suggest new approaches to interpersonal and group interactions that have the potential to improve Aotearoa/New Zealand educational experiences for many children of diverse cultural backgrounds. *Te Kotahitanga* practices suggest that where the images and the metaphors used to express these images are holistic, inter-actional and focus on power-sharing relationships, the resultant classroom practices and educational experiences for children of other than the dominant group will be entirely different.

New metaphors are needed in teaching and teacher education that are holistic, flexible and determined by or understood within cultural contexts to which young people of diverse backgrounds can relate. Teaching and learning strategies that flow from these metaphors should be flexible and allow the diverse voices of young people to be heard. In such a pedagogy, the partici-pants in the learning interaction become involved in the collaboration proc-ess, in mutual story-telling and re-storying (Connelly and Clandinin, 1990), so that a relationship can emerge in which *both* stories are heard, or indeed a process in which a new story is created by all the participants. Such pedagogy addresses Māori people's concerns that current traditional pedagogic prac-tices being fundamentally monocultural and epistemologically racist. This new pedagogy recognises that all people involved in the learning and teach-ing processes are participants with meaningful experiences, valid concerns and legitimate questions.

For teaching and teacher education, this implies an increasing realisation that teachers can construct contexts wherein students are able to bring their cultural experiences to the learning conversation, even when these experi-ences and ways of making sense of the world are unfamiliar to the teacher. At the same time, teacher educators need to create learning contexts in which their student teachers can experience such relationships and interactions.

Challenge number 5: relationship between pre-service and in-service education

There is an increasing demand from various sectors of the profession for increased relevance between pre-service education and in-service education, professional development, teaching practice and research. This is further exacerbated by international research strongly suggesting that there is little if any linkage between pre-service teacher education and in-service practice and the perceived hierarchies within the education sector (Cochran-Smith and Zeichner, 2005).

From the experiences of *Te Kotahitanga*, there is an added problem as teacher educators, teacher support staff, school teachers, and educational researchers tend to suggest that what they are doing is sufficient, necessary and adequate, in contrast to the functioning of those people in every other sector. In other words, what is happening in their patch is fine; it is all those other people who are not doing a good enough job. Similar findings have been demonstrated by Prochnow and Kearney (2002) in a study they conducted regarding the effect of suspensions on student learning. They found that all groups involved with the students tended to blame others for the problems the students faced and were less likely to implicate themselves in the problem identification process.

To make matters worse, these notions are supported by the peer review process that teacher educators have devised to review their programmes. These reviews do not usually include their client groups; or, if they do, it is in a prescribed manner that limits the type of critique that could be useful in reforming teacher education programmes for their graduates to be able to address the learning needs of minoritised peoples.

People from different sectors expressed other issues in teacher education. These include increasing concern regarding the frailty of the "silo" model in which pre-service teachers are taught subjects separately rather than in a holistic fashion, and the continued criticism of tertiary teacher education providers by their graduates, their profession, the public and the media, or at least in media that are not part of the formal review process. A means of addressing these criticisms is urgently needed.

However, this type of criticism is not always welcome. One example of the problematic response to criticism is found in a survey of teacher preparedness that was conducted by the Education Review Office (ERO) (2004). The report, which was critical of the preparedness of beginning secondary and primary teachers, was met with criticism by teacher educators and researchers alike regarding the process whereby this finding was attained, rather than the finding itself, or at least the problems that the survey indicated could be present. This reaction did not re-energise the debate but rather killed the conversation, despite many teachers and schools voicing concern about the preparedness of their beginning teachers. Yet, recent observations of 360 teachers in *Te Kotahitanga*, 60% of whom had been to teacher education institutions in the past five years, showed that while they wanted to teach in ways they had learnt while at their college of education, they were in fact teaching in a very traditional manner in their first year of teaching.

When surveyed, they stated that they were keen to implement a wide and effective range of interaction types. This would mean actively engaging their students in the lessons, capitalising on the prior knowledge of students, using group learning processes, providing academic feedback, involving students in planning lessons, demonstrating their high expectations, stimulating critical questioning, recognising the culture of students, etc. However, detailed, measured observations of their classrooms showed that 86% of their interactions were of a traditional nature where they were engaging in the transmission of pre-determined knowledge, monitoring to see if this knowledge had been passed on and giving behavioural feedback in order to control the class. Only 14% of their classroom interactions allowed them an opportunity to create learning relationships to which they initially aspired. In short, despite their aspirations to the contrary, the dominant classroom interaction remained active teacher and passive students. This might signal the pervasiveness of transmission education, the schools could be blamed for their insistence on transmitting a pre-set curriculum. However, this may also indicate the lack of student teacher preparedness and the reliance upon the school for practical training, in which case teacher educators could take notice of the survey and *Te Kotahitanga* results as a warning that their graduates may be facing problems implementing interactive approaches in the classroom. In other words, these findings might signal the need for pre-service teachers to integrate the theory and practice of teaching and learning (using evidence of behaviour as teachers and student achievement for formative purposes) in a systematic manner so that they can practice what they learn.

Pre-service teachers could receive objective analysis of and feedback on their classroom interactions in an ongoing manner upon which they could critically reflect in a collaborative, problem-solving setting. This means that pre-service teachers will need to learn to use evidence of student participation and achievement to inform their practice (to change classroom interaction patterns for instance), and the relationship between teacher education institutions and schools will need to change dramatically.

Challenge number 6: the challenge of research

The Performance Based Research Fund (PBRF) report (Alcorn *et al.,* 2005) states that 75% of staff involved in teaching degree-level courses in education are not involved in research. Furthermore, teacher education is the area with the lowest quality of research and the lowest assessed research performance in education. Therefore, if change is necessary to address disparities, and research is the most common way of informing and promoting change through the systematic production of evidence to inform our practice, and if teacher educators are not involved in research, what mechanisms are they using to inform their practice? This may mean that despite their avowed aspirations to address what Fullan (2005) terms the moral dimension of education, that is, the reduction of disparities, teacher educators may not have a means of addressing the *status quo* that is maintaining the disparities they say they want to reduce.

Conclusion

This chapter has suggested that reducing the seemingly immutable educational disparities in the education system in Aotearoa/New Zealand is possible, and the answer lies in a critical examination of the discourses within which teachers position themselves. Commonly, discourses that promote deficit notions that pathologise the lived experiences of Māori students, together with the schooling systems, limit the agency of teachers to make the difference for their students to which they ironically aspire; whereas, positioning within change-agent discourses allows teachers to take responsibility for their student's learning and reflect upon evidence thereof so as to revise their teaching approaches and enjoy teaching.

When teachers are (re)positioned within relational discourses, and promote what Sidorkin (2002) calls a "Pedagogy of Relations", teachers are able to address power imbalances in their classrooms, within their schools and between various sectors of education which are currently critical of one another. In addition, research becomes part of teachers' everyday lives and proves its usefulness in both formative and summative manners. Powerful accountability will arise in the midst of complex situations and discourses formed around the nexus of relationships.

Above all, in terms of student achievement, this chapter suggests that the classroom should be a place where young people's sense-making processes (culture with a small "c") are incorporated and enhanced, where the existing knowledges of young people are seen as "acceptable", in such a way that their stories provide the learning base from whence they can branch out into new fields of knowledge. In this process, the teacher interacts with students in such a way that new knowledge is co-created. Such a classroom will generate different patterns of interaction, and educational outcomes from those generated by a classroom where knowledge is seen as simply something of which the teacher makes sense and then passes onto students.

Notes

1. This chapter was adapted from a keynote address, "Messages from Te Kotahitanga for Teacher Education", presented at the P.R.I.D.E. Workshop held at the National University of Samoa, Apia, Samoa, 28 November to 2 December, 2005.

2. "Minoritised" is a term used in Shields, Bishop and Mazawi, (2005) to refer to a people who have been ascribed characteristics of a minority. To be minoritised, one does not need to be in the numerical minority, only to be treated as if one's position and perspective is of less worth, to be silenced or to be marginalised.

3. Kaupapa Māori is a discourse of proactive theory and practice that emerged from within the wider revitalisation of Māori communities that developed in New Zealand following the rapid Māori urbanisation in the 1950s and 1960s. This movement grew further in the 1970s, and by the late 1980s it had developed as a political consciousness among Māori people that promoted the revitalisation of Māori cultural aspirations, preferences and practices as a philosophical and productive educational stance and resistance to the hegemony of the dominant discourse.

4. Extended family.

References

Alcorn, N., R. Bishop, C. Cardno, T. Crooks *et al.* (2004), "Enhancing Education Research in New Zealand: Experiences and Recommendations from the PBRF Education Peer Review Panel", *New Zealand Journal of Education Studies,* Vol. 39, No. 2, pp. 275-302.

Bishop, R. (1996), *Collaborative Research Stories: Whakawhanaungatanga,* Dunmore Press, Palmerston North.

Bishop, R. and S.Tiakiwai (2003), *Improving the Educational Achievement of Māori Students in Mainstream Classrooms,* Conference Papers, Ministry of Education, Wellington.

Bishop, R., M. Berryman, S. Tiakiwai and C. Richards (2003), *Te Kotahitanga: The Experiences of Year 9 and 10 Māori Students in Mainstream Classrooms,* Ministry of Education, Wellington.

Bruner, J. (1996), *The Culture of Education,* Harvard University Press, Cambridge, Massachusetts.

Cochran-Smith, M. and K.M. Zeichner (2005), *Studying Teacher Education: The Report of the AERA Panel on Research and Teacher Education,* Lawrence Erlbaum Associates Inc, Mahwah NJ.

Connelly, M. and J. Clandinin (1990), "Stories of Experience and Narrative Inquiry", *Educational Researcher,* June-July, pp. 2-14.

Education Counts (n.d.), *www.educationcounts.govt.nz.*

Education Review Office (2004), *The Quality of Year 2 Beginning Teachers,* Education Evaluation Reports, Ministry of Education, Wellington.

Foucault. M (1980), *Power/knowledge: Selected Interviews and Other Writings 1972-1977,* C. Gordon (ed.), Pantheon, New York.

Fullan, M. (2005), "Resiliency and Sustainability", *School Administrator,* February, Vol. 62, No. 2, pp. 16-18.

Goldberg, B. and D.M. Morrison (2003), "Con-nect: Purpose, Accountability, and School Leadership", in J. Murphy., and Datnow, A. (eds.), *Leadership*

Lessons from Comprehensive School Reforms, Corwin Press, Thousand Oaks, California.

McLaren, P. (2003), *Life in Schools: An Introduction to Critical Pedagogy in the Foundations of Education* (4th Edition), Pearson Education, Boston, MA.

Ministry of Education (2001), "Nga Haeata Matauranga: Annual Report on Māori Education 1999/2000 and Directions for 2001", *www.minedu.govt. nz/web/document/,* accessed 25 May 2001.

Ministry of Education (2004), Nga Haeata Matauranga, "Annual Report on Māori Education 1999/2000 and Directions for 2004"; *www.minedu.govt. nz/web/document/.*

New Zealand Department of Māori Affairs (1962), J.M. Booth and J.K. Hunn, *Integration of Māori and Pakeha,* Wellington.

OECD (2002), *Education at a Glance: OECD Indicators,* OECD, Paris.

Prochnow, J. and A. Kearney (2002), *Barriers to Including Students with Difficult Behaviour: What are We Really Saying?,* Paper presented to the New Zealand Association for Research in Education, Palmerston North, 5-7 December.

Ryan, J. (1999), *Race and Ethnicity in Multi-ethnic Schools: A Critical Case Study,* Multilingual Matters, Clevedon.

Sidorkin, A.M. (2002), *Learning Relations,* Peter Lang, New York.

Shields, C.M., R. Bishop, and A.E. Mazawi (2005), *Pathologising Practices: The Impact of Deficit Thinking on Education,* Peter Lang, New York.

Smith, G.H. (1997), "Kaupapa Māori as Transformative Praxis", Unpublished PhD Thesis, University of Auckland, Auckland.

Timperley, H, G. Phillips and J. Wiseman (2003), *The Sustainability of Professional Development in Literacy – Parts One and Two,* University of Auckland, Auckland.

Valencia, R. R. and D.G. Solórzano (1997), "Contemporary Deficit Thinking", in R.R. Valencia (ed.), *The Evolution of Deficit Thinking,* Falmer, Washington, D.C.

Young, R. (1991), *Critical Theory and Classroom Talk,* Multilingual Matters, Clevedon.

Chapter 6

Attracting and retaining diverse student teachers

Rick Wolff, Sabine Severiens and Marieke Meeuwisse
Rotterdam Institute for Social Science Policy Research, Erasmus University
the Netherlands

This chapter examines the role that programmes play in the success of students from ethnic minorities by comparing the learning environments of three urban teacher training programmes. Although ethnic diversity of children in the Netherlands has dramatically increased as a result of several post-war waves of migration, this is not reflected in the composition of the teaching staff. In addition, the policy aim to train more students from ethnic minorities as teachers has proven far from simple. Students from minority backgrounds who attend teacher training programmes for primary education are far more likely than native Dutch students to leave before graduation. The research presented here suggests that an open atmosphere in a programme, the presence of career counsellors and internship co-ordinators specifically attuned to diversity issues, and the relative ease of finding internships all serve to increase the educational success of these students. The chapter concludes with recommendations for programme climate, guidance and internships.

From the OECD online consultation: diversity in the teaching force

Student teacher, teacher, and teacher educator respondents were less diverse than their student populations. Why is the teaching force not more diverse, and what can be done about it?

Introduction

Ethnic diversity among children and young adults in the Netherlands has increased spectacularly as a result of several post-war waves of migration (decolonisation, labour migration and asylum-seeking).[1] The larger cities have been particularly affected. In Amsterdam, Rotterdam and The Hague, the group of young people aged 0-20 years from ethnic minorities (primarily Antillean, Moroccan, Surinamese and Turkish) is nearly 17% larger than the native Dutch city residents in the same age group. This figure is as much as 25% greater in the group aged 0-10 years (Statistics Netherlands, StatLine).

These demographic developments have a major impact on education. In the larger cities, nearly all the primary and secondary schools have a student body which represents a wide diversity of ethnic backgrounds. Some schools consist almost entirely of children from migrant families. This is due to two concurrent mechanisms, in which *(a)* migrant children live nearby and so attend their local school, and *(b)* white Dutch parents in the neighbourhood tend to enrol their children in schools in other areas that have less minority presence. This new situation raises different questions. How should an ethnically diverse class be handled? Should the lesson materials and methods be changed or updated? What approaches could be used to increase parent involvement in schools, particularly among migrant parents? And last but not least, how do we make the composition of the teaching staff reflect the student population? Teachers from ethnic minorities could serve as role models for pupils from migrant communities and help to build bridges between the school and the parents.

Before more teachers from ethnic minorities can be brought into the classroom, more students from ethnic minorities will have to be trained as teachers. This aim has proven far from simple. More often than their native Dutch counterparts, many of these students attending the teacher training programme for primary education (PABO) leave before completing the programme. In the student cohorts from 2002 to 2005, an average of 35.3% of the PABO students from non-Western ethnic minorities stopped after three years of study without earning a diploma, compared with 20.6% of the native Dutch students. The 14.7% PABO drop-out rate is more than two and a half times greater than the average difference in the entire higher professional education system.[2]

Are there specific reasons why students from non-Western ethnic minorities do not complete PABO? To what extent are teacher training programmes for primary school teachers in a position to offer students from ethnic minorities the same opportunities for successful completion as the native Dutch students? How can programmes improve in this respect? This chapter examines these questions, focusing primarily on the role that programmes play (programme factors) in the completion rates of non-Western students from ethnic minorities and of native Dutch students. We present the results of a case study comparing the learning environments at three PABO teacher training programmes in large cities.

Completion rates of students from non-Western ethnic minorities and native Dutch students: how much influence does a degree programme have?

A degree programme can influence students in various ways. The learning environment affects students simply because a programme is an environment in which people interact with each other, behave according to certain codes of conduct and deal with mutual expectations. A learning environment is understood to be the entire range of *(a)* written and unwritten principles of education and the details of such principles (educational concept, curriculum, guidance structure, etc.); and *(b)* formal and informal contacts (with fellow students, lecturers, tutors, student counsellors, etc.) related to a programme that students encounter.

In other words, success (graduation) and failure (leaving before graduation) depend in part on aspects of the programme. These factors could involve various aspects of quality such as the quality of the lecturers in a degree programme, the quality of the organisation or the quality of guidance and counselling. Research on differences between students from non-Western ethnic minorities and native Dutch students shows that the extent to which a programme is small-scale or considered to be a learning community can be important (see Severiens, Wolff and Rezai, 2006). Other concepts such as social and academic integration, the culture and degree of inequality in the degree programme and practice shock are also linked to the learning environment and student performance.

Small-scale structure and learning environments

Various educational innovations have been launched in recent years that aim to introduce student-centred learning to a greater or lesser extent (Boekaerts, Pintrich and Zeidner, 2000; Schelfhout, 2002). The underlying concept is that student-centred learning has a positive effect on student learning and motivation, and therefore also on the completion rate for the degree programme. The question is whether this significant development in education has the same consequences for students from ethnic minorities as for native Dutch students.

Previous research (Severiens *et al.*, 2006) showed that learning environments involving a high degree of social engagement result in lecturers playing an important guiding role, balanced attention to diversity, and a central focus on the student, all of which are favourable for students from ethnic minorities. These results point to a learning environment known as a learning community (Lave and Wenger, 1991). Research (Zhao and Kuh, 2006) on the effects of learning communities shows that learning communities are powerful practical teaching tools; besides the sound theoretical basis for such educational practices, there is clear empirical evidence to support their positive impact.

Social and academic integration

Study progress and completion rate is also related to the extent to which students have integrated into the community, both socially and academically. The model proposed by Tinto (1994, 1997) is a study progress model in which various factors are used to explain how students progress through a degree programme and whether they leave before completion or stay to graduation. The two main components in the model are the concepts of academic and social integration. *Academic integration refers to the extent to which students feel at home in the study programme in regard to the field of study and the lecturers and students who represent that field.* Effective academic integration means that students identify with the field in a positive way and that the lecturers engage with them regarding their integration, inviting their students to take part in the profession, in a manner of speaking. *Social integration refers to good social contact with lecturers and fellow students.* For most students, a group where they feel at home is an important defining factor in the enjoyment they derive from the degree programme, ultimately also determining the likelihood that they will complete the programme.

Various studies have shown that students from ethnic minorities and majority students differ in the degree to which they are socially and academically integrated, and that this difference is related to study success. For example, in our own qualitative research (Severiens *et al.*, 2006), carried out among students at institutes for higher professional education and at research universities, we saw that certain experiences of ethnic-minority students, like being treated "differently" by fellow students and teachers and feeling less at home in the programme, had an influence on their social and academic integration and their study progress. Conversely, more equality in the programme and more attention to diversity issues seem to lead to an equal degree of social and academic integration and study progress for ethnic-minority and majority students (see also: Gloria *et al.,* 2005; Braxton, Milem and Sullivan, 2000; Nora and Cabrera, 1996; see also Severiens, Wolff and Rezai, 2006).

Culture and inequality

One of the most important findings from the study by Severiens, Wolff and Rezai (2006) is that students from ethnic minorities are more dependent on the quality of the education, whereas native Dutch students rely on their more favourable starting point (on their social and cultural capital). This means that the quality of the educational structure and the quality of the lecturers can play an important role in the drop-out rate for students from ethnic minorities. It also confirms other studies which show that a poor fit with the programme is an important explanation for drop-out, especially for students from ethnic minorities (Just 1999, Hurtado *et al.,* 1999; Swail *et al.,* 2003, Nora and Cabrera, 1996; Thomas, 2002).

Research linking the culture of an educational institution or degree programme to the ethnic background of the students is primarily found in the United States. An overview of studies in this field shows that African-American students studying at "historically black colleges and universities" (HBCUs) have a perception of receiving more social and psychological support, are more satisfied, feel more a part of a community and have a higher chance of continuing and successfully completing their studies than African-American students studying at "white" universities (Fleming, 2002; Hurtado, Milem, Clayton-Pedersen and Allen, 1998).

We would like to pay particular attention to a study by Hobson-Horton and Owens (2004) which looks at successful methods for keeping students from ethnic minorities in a degree programme. They show that it is about motivation, interaction with peers and lecturers, the contents of the programme, challenging experiences, and perceptions and expectations. Results from their study show that support is very important: mentoring programmes seem to achieve good results (see also Harper, 1994; Stolworthy, 2001). Another important factor is that the degree programme needs to have meaning and relevance for the students. From a student's perspective, this should include a good balance between theory and practice. Finally, they show that it is important to make good use of the cultural diversity at hand by organising productive social activities and offering student support and counselling.

Practice shock

Based on their evaluation of educational innovation in the role of internships as part of degree programmes in the mid-1990s, Stokking *et al.* (2003) identify three important reasons for student drop-out:

- The profession is too demanding; a British study by Day (1999) for example shows that 23% of teachers suffer from a stress-related disorder or illness;

- Student expectations are too idealistic, based on their experiences as a pupil in combination with their experiences during theoretical training. These expectations are often inaccurate which can lead to drop-out;

- Insufficient preparation for the actual experience: "practice shock".

Britzman (1986) writes that the first experiences in the classroom can be very emotional experiences for new teachers. Support during these initial practical experiences is crucially important. Practice shock also plays a key role in the study by Brouwer and Korthagen (2005). They describe the concept of "professional socialisation": a process in which people adopt the values and attitudes and acquire the interests, skills and knowledge of a specific profession that they want to join. Many studies show that professional socialisation has a negative impact on the innovative competencies of new teachers (such as stimulating pupils to be active participants in the learning process) in the specific context of teacher training schools and the school system. The impact of actually teaching a class (practice shock) seems stronger than the impact of learning the theory in teacher training school. Students experience a discrepancy between what they learn in the degree programme (ideal educational contexts and innovative methods of instruction) and the actual practice of teaching, in which they are primarily occupied with survival and are forced to fall back on traditional methods. To our knowledge, there has been no research specifically trying to find out whether students from different backgrounds experience practice shock in a different way. In this study we will examine the issue.

The model and the research question

Figure 6.1 summarises the explanations provided for the high drop-out rate among students from ethnic minorities at teaching training school.

Two contexts must be distinguished with regard to programme factors: the teacher training school itself and the schools to which the students go on work placement. The transitions between these two contexts are related to "practice shock". This model aims to answer the following research question:

Do students from non-Western ethnic minorities and native Dutch students have different perceptions of the programme due to culture and inequality, social and academic integration, the small scale, and practice shock? To what extent can these concepts offer an explanation for the decision to leave the programme?

Figure 6.1. **Explanations for high drop-out rate of students from ethnic minorities**

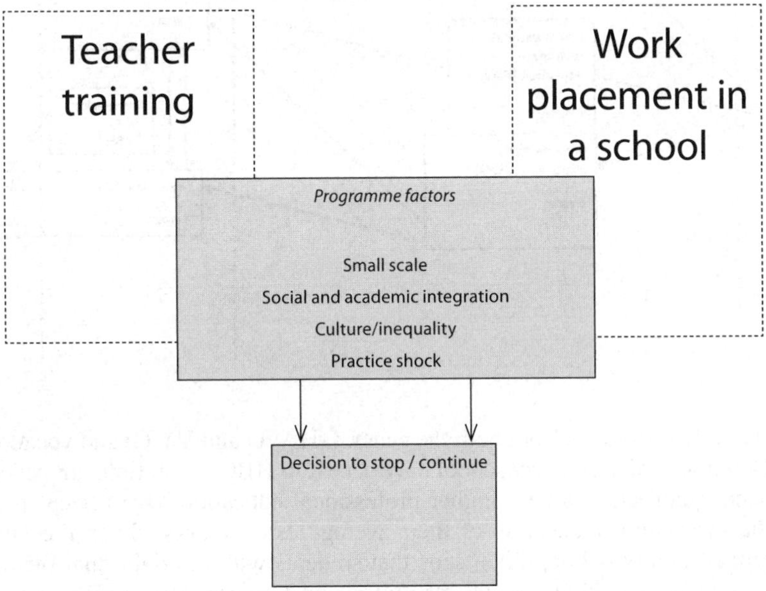

The Dutch school system and the road to higher education

Before we look at the case study, this chapter provides a brief explanation of the Dutch school system in order to clarify the position of the PABO teacher training schools within this system, as well as the learning track that leads to the PABO teacher training school.

The Netherlands has a binary higher education system consisting of research universities and universities of applied science; the latter institutions offer higher professional education (HBO) (Figure 6.2). The PABO teacher training programmes are offered at the universities of applied science. Admission to higher professional education is more open, or less selective, than admission to university.

Figure 6.2. **The road to Dutch higher education**

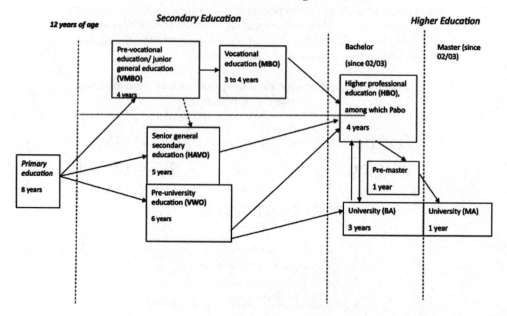

Qualified students from both the general (HAVO and VWO) and vocational (MBO) tracks of secondary school have access to HBO institutions. In general, students qualified to attend higher professional education have access to any public institution, regardless of their average exam marks. Since the Dutch system is mainly public, this means that students with the right qualifications are eligible to attend almost all institutions for higher professional education. The vocational track takes the longest time (seven to eight years without year repitition) to get from secondary education into HBO. HAVO is the shortest road to HBO: five years without year repitition. Admission to universities requires higher secondary education qualifications than admission to HBO institutions. Only students with a pre-university diploma (VWO) are eligible for admission to university. The pre-university track takes six years without year repitition.

Student tracking starts after eight years of primary education, when pupils are twelve years old. Pupils are essentially tracked on the basis of two criteria: *(i)* scores on national tests (entry and/or Cito testing); and *(ii)* a recommendation from the primary school. On the basis of the national test scores and the school recommendation, pupils are directed to either the vocational track (VMBO) or the general track (HAVO/VWO), which is an important decision. Firstly, it determines the learning environment for the coming years: is a student's education focused more on academic theory or practical application? Secondly, it determines the number of years before a pupil is qualified for higher education.

In principle, it is possible to switch from the vocational to the general secondary education track (HAVO), which is a promotion in the pupil's educational career, but national education reforms have made track-switching more difficult. Most vocational pupils remain in their track. Pupils who continue in the general track after primary school can go directly to senior general secondary school (HAVO) or to pre-university school (VWO). However, there is also the opportunity for a transitional first year of secondary school, after which the decision is made as to whether a pupil will go to HAVO or VWO.

Relatively many students from ethnic minorities are tracked into the vocational system and have to take the long route to higher education. As a consequence, the average age for a first-year student from an ethnic minority entering higher education is above the average age of native Dutch students (Wolff, 2007).

Method: three case studies

Our current research examined three PABO teacher training programmes at three different institutions of higher professional education. These three degree programmes, referred here to as programme A, programme B and programme C, were selected on the basis of the differences in drop-out rates for each programme comparing native Dutch and non-Western ethnic minority students, according to the Netherlands Association of Universities of Applied Science (*HBO-raad*). The three programmes display variations in the comparison between drop-out rates which we attempt to explain by comparing the programmes' different learning environments. The emphasis is on the first two years of study because the drop-out rate is highest during that phase (see *HBO-raadcijfers*, Wolff, 2007).

The combination of the data from the *HBO-raad*, of the Dutch universities of applied science, shows that programme A is the most successful at keeping students from ethnic minorities in the programme. During the 2000-04 period, the drop-out rate of 8% was by far the lowest between students from non-Western ethnic minorities and native Dutch students after 3 years of study.[3] Programme B is average in this respect; with a difference in drop-out rate of 19%. Programme C yields the least positive result on the basis of these figures. The difference in drop-out rates between students from ethnic minorities and native Dutch students is greatest at 26%.

For a clear impression of the learning environment in the first two years of study, ten[4] respondents were interviewed from each programme (in total 30 respondents). One group consisted of respondents from the programme and one group consisted of students. The people from the programme who provided information were the programme director (or programme manager), two lecturers and the internship co-ordinator. The students who provided information were second-year students, three from non-Western ethnic minorities and three from native Dutch origins. The study guide for the first and second years was also reviewed.

The respondents were interviewed in-depth about the learning environment. The interview questions were categorised into various interview themes: "diversity policy and equality", "atmosphere/culture in the programme", "social integration" (contact with students), "academic integration" (contact with lecturers and student counsellors), "quality of education", "structure of the internship", "experiences on work placement" and the pedagogical/teaching structure of the programme. Separate questions were also asked about drop-out rates in general and drop-out among students from non-Western ethnic minorities in particular.

The interview themes varied depending on the group of respondents. Interviews with students primarily addressed the day-to-day practical aspects of the programme, while the interviews with programme directors (more than with other groups of respondents) covered the principles of education and the policies of the programme.

Results from the case studies

Before presenting the results of the three case studies, it should be noted that we differentiate between specific and general factors. In relation to the specific factors, the respondents were explicitly asked about an aspect of ethnicity or diversity, or an aspect of ethnicity or diversity was mentioned spontaneously during the interviews. We emphasise specific factors in order to gain a better understanding of the extent to which risk factors for drop-out and study progress occur specifically among students from non-Western minorities. Factors which do not involve an ethnic element – the "general factors" – are also included, but only where they display clear differences between programmes.

This section compares the programmes on the basis of the following aspects:

1. The educational concept and structure

2. Feeling at home

3. Risk factors for student drop-out

4. Academic integration

5. Social integration

6. Internships

7. General factors

Item 1 concerns the programme as it is described "on paper", for example in the study guide, and offers information about its policies. Items 2 through 6 involve the programme in practice. Item 7 deals with the educational concept and structure and about the programme in practice, but from a more general perspective.

The educational concept and structure: diversity policy and activities

Diversity constitutes an explicit focus in the educational vision of programme B. Programmes A and C do not have an explicit diversity policy. The focus on diversity in these programmes is expressed implicitly at the conceptual level. It emerges *e.g.* in phrasing that shows an awareness of the programme's position in an urban context in which people from various cultural backgrounds live. This can be seen clearly in the schools, and students should be prepared for that.

However, there seems to be little connection between incorporating "diversity" into the educational concept and maintaining a focus on diversity at the level of practice. Diversity is addressed in some way in all three programmes, not just in programme B. For example, courses are offered in intercultural education or philosophies of life centred on ethnic, cultural and religious diversity. Thematic meetings on "identity" and "diversity" are held for students and lecturers alike. It is stressed that students undertake internships at as many different types of schools as possible (black, white and mixed). The programmes also take part in projects to promote the teaching profession within migrant communities, projects to develop talent among students who are the first person in their family to attend higher education (including many students from non-Western ethnic minorities) or projects to facilitate a better quality of progression from senior secondary vocational schools, which are attended by many pupils from non-Western ethnic minorities. In programme A, study career counsellors receive training in intercultural communications, and internship tutors have taken a course on dealing with an ethnically diverse group of students. In programmes B and C, "diversity" is among the range of responsibilities of some lecturers whereby they co-ordinate and develop diversity activities. Programme staff also conduct institutional drop-out studies to determine why students drop out. Finally, efforts are also being made to recruit more lecturers from non-Western ethnic minorities for the teaching training schools, but that has proven difficult (*e.g.* complicated recruitment, halt on advertising for job openings).

Feeling at home

In all three programmes, the student respondents from non-Western ethnic minorities feel less at home than the native Dutch students. Dutch students said they more frequently enjoyed their studies and perceived the atmosphere in the programme as pleasant and fun. However, differences were observed between programme A, on the one hand, and programmes B and C, on the other. First, students in programme A have little social engagement with the programme. Neither students from non-Western ethnic minorities nor native Dutch students linger outside their scheduled class times; this is probably related to the temporary accommodations currently provided by the programme. The student respondents from non-Western ethnic minorities associate their sense of feeling less at home with the individualistic attitude of their classmates, rather than with a division between ethnic groups. As two students explain:

> It is not a situation where you feel immediately at home. It is more like everyone is there for him or herself. You only see students when you have to work together on assignments, and then it's simply a requirement, because you have to work together. But it's not the case that you have some sort of bond with your fellow students. (a non-Western ethnic minority student attending programme A)

> I don't really hang around after class – just to do homework with other students, but not much other than that. (a native Dutch student attending programme A)

In programmes B and C, we see that native Dutch students have a stronger sense of social engagement than their fellow students from ethnic minorities. They more frequently spend time at the programme facilities after class, whereas non-Western minority students leave much more quickly. Moreover, a number of student respondents from non-Western ethnic minorities attending these programmes feel less at home because of the division between native Dutch and ethnic minorities, and have a sense that they are not accepted. The following quotes from two students from programme C illustrate this:

> Sometimes there are other students who make discouraging comments. For instance if they see things at their work: "Yes, it was someone from an ethnic minority group again, who just had to yell at me. Always those minorities..." I come from an ethnic minority group too, of course, and when I hear that, it does not motivate me to strike up a conversation with them and sit around chatting and laughing. (a non-Western ethnic minority student attending programme C)

> Everyone knows each other a bit here, that kind of feeling. Like a village, really. (a native Dutch student attending programme C)

Risk factors for student drop-out

The respondents from the programmes mentioned several risk factors that cause students from ethnic minorities to drop out more often than native

Dutch students. The three cases demonstrate significant similarity. A number of factors are general in nature, but appear to occur more frequently among students from ethnic minorities because they are more numerously represented in specific risk groups. This includes students from senior secondary vocational education (MBO) who lack sufficient basic skills (language and arithmetic) as well as study skills (planning and organisation) and students who have a home situation which is difficult to combine with the course of study. The programme manager from programme B explains it as follows:

> You see that students from this city (where the programme and the university of applied science are situated – RISBO) drop out more. They have a different attitude towards study; there is less social cohesion in their home situation. These are students for whom studying is not a normal thing, whose parents did not go to university and cannot keep them on track; they do not know what studying involves. ... Many of them come from senior secondary vocational schools, for example after being trained as a teacher's assistant. There are no jobs available for that. So they continue their studies, which results in drop-out and causes frustrations. (programme manager from programme B)

The opinion of student respondents from non-Western minorities reveals specific drop-out factors for this particular group. First, students from programmes B and C primarily associate drop-out of students from ethnic minorities with the programme, mainly due to the dynamics between students. Comments from programme B refer to exclusion of non-Western students:

> I do think it's a pity that students stop because they feel pestered just because they wear a headscarf or are Moroccan. Things often went wrong in the classroom, and the teacher just continued the lesson. (student from a non-Western ethnic minority attending programme B)

Secondly, we do not hear anything from the student respondents from non-Western ethnic minorities in programme A about specific causes for why students from ethnic minorities drop out. Apparently, the students from this programme who took part in the case study consider general risk factors to play the primary role.

It can be concluded that students from ethnic minorities are probably more sensitive to the climate in the classroom than native Dutch students, who may be more individualistic. We also see a difference in the perception of the respondents from the programme staff, who mainly discuss drop-out of students from ethnic minorities in terms of the individual characteristics of students, whereas students from ethnic minorities focus more on programme-related factors.

Academic integration

In the context of academic integration, specifically looking at whether lecturers treat students from ethnic minorities differently than native Dutch students, the most positive reports came from programme A. This was the only programme where the growing influx of first-year students from ethnic minorities was described by participating lecturers in positive terms: the environment is first and foremost viewed as enriching. Nearly all the student respondents from programme A stated that they saw no difference in how their teachers dealt with students from ethnic minorities and native Dutch students. The programme director of programme A did note that some lecturers perceived a mental distance between themselves and several of their students from ethnic minorities, a distance which they found difficult to bridge.

In contrast to the situation in programme A, we have programme B. Lecturers see that students from ethnic minorities are less assertive, but also less capable of accepting and responding constructively to feedback. Among the student respondents, there are the native Dutch students on the one hand, who do not see that lecturers treat students from ethnic minorities differently, and there are the students from ethnic minorities on the other hand, who feel that some of their teachers are prejudiced and biased and do treat students from ethnic minorities differently:

> *Sometimes you do notice that lecturers differentiate. Like with spelling and grammar, she says that we should pay close attention, and then she says to me, "You especially." As if everyone from an ethnic minority has a problem with language. And in another class, one of the lecturers had some kind of Turkish doll and she said to me, "You must recognise this." First of all, I'm not Turkish; secondly, it wasn't familiar to me.*
> (student from a non-Western ethnic minority attending programme B)

With diversity and contacts between students and lecturers as a backdrop, it is interesting to see whether students from ethnic minorities would also want to have lecturers from ethnic minorities. It is primarily the students from non-Western ethnic minorities who express a preference for more lecturers from ethnic minorities. This could be because these students have a more understanding working relationship with the few lecturers from ethnic minorities than with native Dutch lecturers, or because of the programme's image. However, quality is the main priority for students, regardless of a lecturer's origin. It should be noted that within the three programmes combined, there are few teachers from ethnic minorities. It is striking that the student respondents from non-Western ethnic minorities in programme C know that there are lecturers from non-Western ethnic minorities teaching in the programme, while the native Dutch student respondents were unaware of this. Students from ethnic minorities could be more attentive to this aspect, and native Dutch students less so.

Social integration

Groups form in all the programmes along the lines of ethnic origin. It is not entirely possible to describe the situation as separate worlds, since student groups intermingle to some extent, especially in formal class situations. However, in the end, native Dutch students and students from ethnic minorities tend to be drawn more towards their own group. A similar process is seen within the ethnic minority group, among *e.g.* Moroccan, Surinamese and Turkish students. In programmes B and C, a division between the two groups is intensified from the very start of the programme, when students attend orientation week before actual classes begin. In actual practice, the students that do not attend are usually from non-Western ethnic minorities. The programme staff who took part in the case study are eager to see students from different backgrounds interact more with each other. Attempts are made to achieve this goal by not leaving project group combinations up to students (programme A) and by encouraging students to talk with each other within the classroom context (programmes B and C). The traditional structure of orientation week is also up for discussion. Programmes are considering not requiring students to stay overnight and/or to move this type of combined activity week to a later in the year, when students already know each other better.

Looking at actual interaction between students from ethnic minorities and native Dutch students, we see clear differences between programme A, on the one hand, and programmes B and C, on the other. In programme A, the division between students from ethnic minorities and native Dutch students is considered a less loaded topic. Regardless of their own ethnic origins, the respondents see differences in how they interact with their fellow students from various ethnic backgrounds, but do not make much of an issue of it. More so than in other programmes, students from programme A seem to be open to each other, which is best illustrated by one of the native Dutch student respondents who, out of interest and engagement, spent a day observing Ramadan with their Muslim fellow students from ethnic minorities.

A non-Muslim girlfriend of mine and I spent one day observing Ramadan with Muslims from our class. They said, "No, you'll never be able to keep it up for a day!" We said, "Of course we will. We'll fast that day and then come eat with you in the evening." They were fine with that. I didn't eat or drink anything all day. I only noticed that I was hungry and thirsty in the evening, but that was because her mother had made all sorts of extra things because we were coming. Then there was suddenly this whole table full of food in front of me, and that was when I noticed it. It went very well. They hadn't expected that. I'll do it again next year. (native Dutch student from programme A)

Most of the student respondents from programme A also spend time with fellow students from other ethnic backgrounds outside school hours. In programmes B and C, native Dutch and student respondents from ethnic minorities perceive interaction with their fellow students differently. For example, the native Dutch student respondents see no difference in interaction. The difference is definitely present for respondents from ethnic minorities: they are more familiar with other students from ethnic minorities and therefore have more contact with them.

Moreover, students from ethnic minorities have the perception that they are not accepted or taken seriously by their fellow students in a number of situations, for example during presentations or in discussions on multicultural themes.

I noticed last year (the first year – RISBO) that there were groups. In the classroom, a native Dutch student would simply never sit next to you. As if you had a scary disease. That was the case in every class. Or if you did sit next to someone, that person would just get up and sit somewhere else." (student from a non-Western ethnic minority attending programme B)

You aren't really accepted by them (native Dutch students – RISBO). Last year, for example, I was giving a presentation that went very well. I didn't see it at all myself, but another student noticed that the other students were pulling a face because they couldn't handle the fact that it was going so well. It comes out somewhere. In groups, you often know in advance who will be left over. (student from a non-Western ethnic minority attending programme C)

In the context of social integration, it can be concluded that students from different ethnic groups get along best in programme A. This is less the case in programme C, and even less so in programme B, particularly in the perceptions of students from non-Western ethnic minorities.

Internships

All the programmes encourage their students to do work placement at as many different primary schools as possible with the aim of broadening their horizons. This means, for example, that students need to gain experience in so-called white, black and mixed schools. In programmes B and C, internship co-ordinators see that a small number of schools do not want interns who wear a headscarf. For protective reasons, the programmes therefore prefer not to send these students to intern at those schools. Two strategies are mentioned for addressing this problem. They explain that it may be possible to send students who are very good and very self-confident. They could be viewed as paving the way for the next groups of students. Alternatively, discussion could be initiated with school boards. This approach is used by the Christian programme C, for example, to convince the Christian school boards that the identity of the programme is not jeopardised by the changed composition of the new student body. The issue of having difficulty placing students who wear a headscarf also occurs in programme A, but to a lesser extent, as it seems to be more incidental here. A majority of the student respondents from ethnic minorities in programmes A and B report that they are treated differently and feel less at ease at the school where they do their internship than if they were to have been a native Dutch intern. Among the student respondents from programme A, this impression is primarily based on a feeling; in programme B, the feeling is supported by concrete examples, such as unwelcome comments about pupils and other interns from ethnic minorities or about ethnic minorities in general:

> *I have difficulty with my colleagues. They don't have any difficulty with me, but they do with another student who wears a headscarf, who speaks the language less well. That shocked me. That I heard how they wanted to get rid of her. They aren't used to it; there is simply a very negative impression of foreign interns. Maybe they had bad experiences in the past. I'm glad that I am not dependent on them. I mentioned it to my mentor at the time, who said that they talked about me the same way when I walked away.* (student from a non-Western ethnic minority attending programme B)

These problems do not seem to occur in programme C.

General factors

Besides specific factors as discussed above, a number of general factors related to the programme overall can affect completion success. The general factors that show the distinctions between programmes most are:

- The emphasis on self-regulated study
- Study career counselling
- Extra skill-building programmes
- Social integration
- Internships

Emphasis on self-regulated study is strongest in programme C, the same programme that displays the greatest differences in drop-out rate between native Dutch students and students from non-Western ethnic minorities. Students in this programme are responsible for how they study for the vast majority of the programme. One concrete example is that the attendance of lectures and seminars is not compulsory. This can have a negative influence for students from non-Western ethnic minorities and confirms findings from previous research, which noted excessive independence in the curriculum as a specific risk factor (Severiens *et al.*, 2006). It is also confirmed by actual practice, in which programme C is characterised by a lack of clarity and guidance, and where students from non-Western ethnic minorities in particular are dissatisfied with the guidance provided. Another characteristic is that the lecturers from programme C indicate that they have little insight into how their students work. It would appear that the emphasis on independence in programme C also means that students pursue their studies in relative separation from the programme, with little supervision and guidance.

A second general factor concerns student counselling, particularly study career counselling. A student is assigned a study career counsellor for the entire year; this is often a lecturer who also handles some study career counselling. Throughout the year, a study career counsellor is a regular contact person for students, discussing the student's progress in his or her studies and possibly looking for solutions if the student has fallen behind. Individual talks take place, but students who have the same study career counsellor also meet in groups, for example to discuss improving certain general study skills. The study career counselling groups in programme A are smaller than in the other programmes (eight students *versus* twelve to fifteen students). In addition, programmes A and C offer (standard) training for study career counselling in practice. Finally, programme B has the most individual study career counselling meetings. Four individual meetings per year are scheduled for each student, compared to two in programmes A and C. It is striking that in programme A, where nearly all the student respondents were very dissatisfied with how their programme is organised, the relatively small study career counselling groups and the good quality of the study career counsellors appeared to contribute to the relatively low differences in drop-out rates. An example is presented below:

> *I had a lot of problems at school. I have a lot of problems in my personal life, and I had one mentor who was always there for me.* (student from a non-Western ethnic minority attending programme A)

Thirdly, the organisation of the programmes designed to bring students up to standard, such as courses to improve language skills, also seems to play a role. Programme A is the only programme where students earn credits for such courses. Skill improvement programmes have been incorporated into the curriculum in programme A. Students from programmes B and C have to take such courses outside the official curriculum and do not earn credits for them. This offers no incentive to take part in the programme, which could have a particularly negative impact for students from non-Western ethnic minorities, who more frequently come to the programme from senior secondary vocational school, and more often would benefit from taking part in these programmes. Students from ethnic minorities in particular seem to benefit more from guidance within the programme, as is the case in programme A.

A fourth general factor involves social integration. In programme A, the students from non-Western ethnic minorities perceive their classmates of any ethnic origin as individuals, and in programme B, they view their classmates as assertive, yet in programme C they see their classmates as irritating. Social integration in programme C seems to take place in a "problematic" atmosphere.

> *I find it very disappointing. There is no enthusiasm here, no initiative. We had to make a presentation on art. I worked on it for three days, and even enjoyed it, without the other members of my group knowing about it, because it had been the holidays and no one had done anything about it. So I arranged it all and the only thing I asked was to rehearse it once with the whole group. But no one responded. Why should I still pursue this?* (student from a non-Western ethnic minority attending programme C)

This quote illustrates how students (from a non-Western ethnic minority) attending programme C perceive co-operation within the programme. These students from non-Western ethnic minorities prefer to leave division into groups up to the programme, whereas native Dutch students from programme C prefer to form groups themselves. This situation is completely unlike the situation in programmes A and B. The problematic social integration could accordingly offer an explanation for the major difference in dropout rates in programme C.

Finally, we will consider internships. For many students internship is the first time they practice their future profession. This can be very difficult (a non-Western ethnic minority student from programme B: "My first lesson was a disaster"). Generally speaking, most students are satisfied with their internship, especially in the longer term when students are more accustomed to standing in front of their class, and appreciate their time spent working with children. In their contacts with their internship school supervisors or the team of teachers, students have various experiences. While some supervisors and teachers are very helpful and constructive, others are not. One student explains:

> *One internship was not much fun. Everybody was busy with themselves and teachers never left their classrooms. And if, by accident, you bumped into somebody the response was: "Hi" and nothing else. At my current internship teachers are interested in me and say: "You're the new internship student? Just ask if you need any help."* (student from a non-Western ethnic minority attending programme A)

This example illustrates that personal contacts between students and teachers/supervisors are an important condition for the quality of the internship. These differences exist among individuals, but the example also shows differences in working climate within schools.

In order to have more uniformity in supervision, programme C promotes learning in the workplace, in which the primary school (the internship school) is responsible for much of the guidance and supervision provided to interns. Despite promotion working and reducing the gap between theory and practice, insufficient involvement by the programme seems to be a negative side effect (according to both white majority and ethnic minority students). Combined with the relatively great difficulty it takes for this programme to arrange an internship for students from non-Western ethnic minorities, in particular, this could be an indication that these practices explain the significant differences in drop-out rates. Programme A differs from programmes B and C prior to the internship: the students do their work placement at a later point in programme A. Despite all the placement problems and dissatisfaction in programme A, it does appear to ensure that the students from ethnic minorities from programme A complete their internship successfully and do not see it as a reason to abandon their studies.

Conclusions and recommendations

This final section sets out the most important conclusions. Based on the conclusions, we make a number of recommendations that could contribute to a reduction in the drop-out rate among students from non-Western ethnic minorities attending the PABO teacher training programme to become primary school teachers. We start with the research question formulated earlier:

Do students from non-Western ethnic minorities and native Dutch students have different perceptions of the programme due to culture and inequality, social and academic integration, the small scale, and practice shock? To what extent can these concepts offer an explanation for the decision to leave the programme?

When we compare the educational concepts and structures of the three PABO programmes in the context of diversity policy, there are no indications for variations in drop-out rate differences between students from ethnic minorities and native Dutch students. Programme B is the only programme that has an explicit diversity policy, but an average drop-out rate difference of 19% was observed here. The most that can be said is that the extra attention focussed at this level contributed to the fact that the differences did not increase. All the programmes make concrete efforts to address diversity. The cases do not differ much in this respect. There is a difference in personnel professionalisation. In programme A, study career counsellors receive training in intercultural communications, and internship tutors have taken a course on dealing with an ethnically diverse group of students. In programmes B and C, a number of lecturers have the theme of "diversity" in their range of responsibilities. They co-ordinate and develop diversity activities.

In practice, we see a number of potential causes for the differences in drop-out rates. Programme A exhibits the smallest differences in drop-out rates and is simultaneously also the programme in which ethnic origin is less of a loaded issue, between students and between students (from ethnic minorities) and lecturers. Ethnic origin is not associated with an increased risk of student drop-out, according to the student respondents from programme A. Programme B seems to be the opposite of programme A. The relations between students from ethnic minorities and native Dutch students are more strained, and this is where we hear the most comments about students from ethnic minorities who feel that lecturers do not give them equal treatment. Programme C occupies a middle ground in this area.

As far as finding an internship is related to ethnic diversity issues, first-year and second-year students from ethnic minorities from programme A seem to encounter fewer problems. Programmes B and C have somewhat more difficulty in finding work placement for their internship students from ethnic minorities. During the internship, the student respondents from ethnic minorities from programme C feel the most comfortable on ethnic diversity issues, followed by the student respondents from programme A. The student respondents from ethnic minorities from programme B end up in unfortunate situations most frequently. In general, students do experience practice shock, but in the longer term they are satisfied with their internship. The quality of internship supervision as well as the fitting into the team depends both on the quality of personal contacts and the overall working climate at internship schools.

Based on these findings, the smallest difference in the drop-out rate exhibited in programme A can be explained by the open atmosphere in the programme in which ethnicity is less of a loaded issue (better social and academic integration, more equality), the professionalisation of study career counsellors and internship co-ordinators specifically in relation to working in a multicultural setting, and the relative ease with which the programme finds internships for students from ethnic minorities. In comparing programmes B and C, programme B would be expected to display a greater difference in drop-out rate than programme C. However, programme C's drop-out rate is greater. Two possible explanations can be offered. First, the explicit diversity policy maintained in programme B may keep underlying conflicts contained. This is not to say that there are no conflicts, but they do not escalate to the extent that, for example, many students from ethnic minorities feel so unwelcome that they leave the programme. Second, factors other than the processes related to diversity may also play a role, making the difference in drop-out rate in programme C relatively high. General factors should be considered here, related to the balance between supervising versus self-regulated study, the position of extra skill-building programmes compared to the programme curriculum (Are the courses integral or not? Do the students receive credits for these courses?), social integration of students and the internships and how they are carried out. Programme C does less well in these general areas than programmes A and B.

The results show that the climate in the programme is crucially important. The concept of "climate" here encompasses the results related to culture and inequality, but also includes social and academic integration. It is about an overall sense of feeling at home, about social integration; it is about congruence between the home culture and the PABO culture, and it is about inequality and discrimination. Our study confirms earlier findings (Fleming, 2002; Hurtado *et al.*, 1998; Hobson, Horton and Owens, 2004). On the basis of the case studies, we conclude that students from ethnic minorities appear to be more sensitive to the atmosphere in PABO teacher training. Whereas the native Dutch students primarily emphasise how "nice and friendly" everything is, the students from ethnic minorities talk about the limited social cohesion and incidents in which ethnicity plays a role. In some ways, it is almost as if minority and majority students of the same course programmes take part in different course programmes.

In general, PABO teacher training programmes appear to use a small-scale model. Because there are no large-scale training programmes for primary school teachers to compare to similar programmes with small-scale approaches, we could not confirm or deny the possible effect of scale on differences in dropout rates.

Practice shock is relevant (Stokking *et al.,* 2003), but applies equally to students from ethnic minorities and to native Dutch students. However, if we focus on the experiences related to finding an internship and doing an internship, we do see differences that may also offer an explanation for the relatively high drop-out rate among students from ethnic minorities. Students from non-Western ethnic minorities have a harder time finding an internship in a number of programmes, and we note that students from non-Western minorities regularly face less than pleasant encounters regarding their background or religion during their internship.

Based on the results, we provide recommendations in a number of areas with the aim of increasing the completion success of students from non-Western ethnic minorities attending primary school teacher training, with the ultimate goal of increasing the richness of ethnic diversity among teachers.

Recommendation for climate

- Diversity skills should be an explicit part of the current professional competencies for primary school teachers (and as such, they should also be assessed, for instance in the portfolio). Students should demonstrate an ability to work well in a culturally diverse setting (both at an internship school and in the PABO programme).

Recommendations for guidance

- The talks with the study career counsellor should be intensified, not only with regard to frequency but also to depth. The current emphasis on reflection in the study career counselling talks is an example of this aspect. Research could be done to assess the effect of reflection techniques on students and how guidance in reflection could be tailored to a student's needs.

- Study career counselling is provided on an individual and group basis. We recommend keeping these study career counselling groups as small as possible, to ensure that the guidance is as personal as possible.

- Deliberate and explicit guarantees should be provided to ensure the quality of study career counselling and the quality of teaching in a diverse student population, through training sessions, peer review and/or coaching. Among other things, this involves measures to eliminate and instructions on how to deal with prejudice and discrimination.

Recommendation for internships

- Based on an idea mentioned by a student respondent, PABO programmes for training primary school teachers could offer a course on "forms of interaction", so the students have some preparation for interaction with internship mentors and the teaching team. Such a course could be important, because students indicate that they sometimes have no idea how to handle social interaction with teachers working at the internship school or in the PABO programme.

- Internships would be easier for students from ethnic minorities if primary schools were able to present differences as a resource and explicitly seek to increase the ethnic diversity of the teaching teams. This would require a (much) stronger focus on diversity as a positive aspect in various teams.

Notes

1.   In the Netherlands, a member of an ethnic minority group is categorised by a layered definition. The main criterion is the country in which the parents were born (definition by Statistics Netherlands).

   i. 'A person is a migrant or a person of migrant descent when at least one parent is born outside the Netherlands.'

   ii. A person of migrant descent born in a foreign country is referred to as 'first generation'. If born in the Netherlands, this person is referred to as 'second generation'. Historically, some ethnic groups were target groups of ethnic minority policies by the Dutch national government, although official national policies on ethnic minorities no longer exist and have been replaced by integration policies. The four largest separate ethnic minority groups in the Netherlands are from Surinam, Morocco, Turkey and Antilles/Aruba. A fifth ethnic minority group are persons of 'other non-Western origin'. This is a combined group of people originating from Central and South America, Africa or Asia.

2.   See the website of the Netherlands Association of Universities of Applied Sciences: *www.hbo-raad.nl* "facts and figures".

3.   Compared to the other teacher training programme in the Netherlands, the drop-out rate among students from non-Western ethnic minorities in programme A is the second lowest.

4.   The data collection was focused on generating qualitative data in order to gain in-depth information (from different angles) about the teaching practice and social interaction and dynamics at different teacher training programmes and internship schools. Generalisation, which requires a far greater number of respondents, was not the purpose of the study.

References

Boekaerts, M., P.R. Pintrich and M. Zeidner (2000), *Handbook of Self-Regulated Learning*, Academic Press, San Diego, California.

Braxton, J.M., J.F. Milemand and A.S. Sullivan (2000), "The Influence of Active Learning on the College Student Departure Process: Toward a Revision of Tinto's Theory", *The Journal of Higher Education*, Vol. 71, No. 5, pp. 569-590.

Britzman, D.P. (1986), "Cultural Myths in the Making of a Teacher: Biography and Social Structure in Teacher Education", *Harvard Educational Review*, Vol. 56, pp. 442–456.

Brouwer, N. and F. Korthagen (2005), "Can Teacher Education Make a Difference?", *American Educational Research Journal*, Vol. 42, No. 1, pp. 153-224.

Day, C. (1999), "Professional Development and Reflective Practice: Purposes, Processes and Partnerships", *Pedagogy, Culture and Society*, Vol. 7, No. 2, pp. 221-233.

Fleming, J. (2002), "Who Will Succeed in College? When the SAT Predicts Black Students' Performance", *The Review of Higher Education*, Vol. 25, No. 3, 281-296.

Gloria, A.M., J. Castellanos, A.G. Lopez, and R. Rosales (2005), "An Examination of Academic Nonpersistence Decisions of Latino Undergraduates", *Hispanic Journal of Behavorial Sciences*, Vol. 27, No. 2, pp. 202-223.

Harper, V. (1994), "Multicultural Perspectives in the Classroom: Professional Preparation for Educational Paraprofessionals", *Action in Teacher Education,* Vol. 25, No. 4, pp. 61-66.

Hobson-Horton, L.D. and L. Owens (2004), "From Freshman to Graduate: Recruiting and Retaining Minority Students", *Journal of Hispanic Higher Education*, Vol. 3, No. 1, pp. 86-107.

Hurtado, S., J. Milem, A. Clayton-Pedersen and W. Allen (1999), "Enacting Diverse Learning Environments: Improving the Climate for Racial/Ethnic Diversity in Higher Education", *ASHE-ERIC Higher Education Report*, Vol. 26, No. 8, pp. 1-140.

Just, H.D. (1999), "Minority Retention in Predominantly White Universities and Colleges: The Importance of Creating a Good 'Fit'", *ASHE-ERIC Higher Education Report*, ED 439641.

Lave, J. and E. Wenger (1991), *Situated learning: Legitimate peripheral participation,* Cambridge University Press, New York.

Nora, A and A.F. Cabrera (1996), "The Role of Perceptions of Prejudice and Discrimination on the Adjustment of Minority Students to College", *Journal of Higher Education,* Vol. 67, No. 2, pp. 119-148.

Schelfhout, L.W. (2002), "Kritische beschouwingen bij het constructivisme [Critical reflections on constructivism]", *Tijdschrift voor Hoger Onderwijs,* Vol. 20, No. 2, pp. 94-124.

Severiens, S., R. P Wolff and S. Rezai (2006), *Diversiteit in leergemeenschappen: Een onderzoek naar stimulerende factoren in de leeromgeving voor allochtone studenten in het hoger onderwijs,* ECHO, Utrecht.

Stokking, K., F. Leenders, J. de Jong and J. van Tartwijk (2003), "From Student to Teacher: Reducing Practice Shock and Early Dropout in the Teaching Profession", *European Journal of Teacher Education,* Vol. 26, No. 3, pp. 329-350.

Stolworthy, R. L. (2001), "Preservice Teacher Education Programs: Review of Standards, Practices, and Evaluative Efforts", *Education,* Vol. 107, No. 3, pp. 300-304.

Swail, W.S., K.E. Redd and L.W. Perna (2003), "Retaining Minority Students in Higher Education: A Framework for Success", *ASHE-ERIC Higher Education Report,* Vol. 30, No. 2, 152-187.

Tinto, V. (1994), *Leaving College: Rethinking the Causes and Cures of Student Attrition,* University of Chicago Press, Chicago.

Tinto, V. (1997), "Classrooms as Communities: Exploring the Educational Character of Student Persistence", *Journal of Higher Education,* Vol. 68, No. 6, pp. 599-623.

Thomas, L. (2002), "Student Retention in Higher Education: the Role of Institutional Habitus", *Journal of Education Policy,* Vol. 17, No. 4, pp. 423-442.

Wolff, R.P. (2007), *Met vallen en opstaan: Een analyse van instroom, uitval en rendementen van niet-westers allochtone studenten in het Nederlandse hoger onderwijs 1997-2005,* ECHO, Utrecht.

Zhao, C. and G.D. Kuh (2006), "Adding Value: Learning Communities and Student Engagement", *Research in Higher Education,* Vol. 45, pp. 115-138.

Chapter 7

Curriculum planning and development: implications for a new generation of teacher educators

H. Richard Milner IV and F. Blake Tenore
Vanderbilt University, United States

While doctoral students in education are taught research skills in their programmes, they are rarely explicitly taught how to plan and develop effective curricula, the types of guiding questions which are important to consider or how to study this process in order to improve practices. In an attempt to address this, the authors use Jackson's (1968) framework for reflecting on teacher planning. The following questions are addressed: how does a teacher educator plan and develop a curriculum for student teachers? How do teacher educators critically examine their curriculum planning and development practices? What are the central questions, areas of focus and principles essential for consideration in such planning and development? For each phase of the planning process, a series of questions is presented. The principles derived from these questions may serve as a useful heuristic to guide the work of new teacher educators.

From the OECD online consultation : educating the teacher educators

Teacher educator respondents reported using various strategies to prepare their student teachers for diversity in the classroom. But how are teacher educators themselves prepared and educated?

Introduction

Teacher educators are faced with the demanding task of planning and developing a curriculum for teacher candidates who will eventually plan and develop a meaningful curriculum for diverse P-12 school students.[*] Cochran-Smith (1995) demonstrated how complex planning and developing meaningful teacher education curricula can be in her work focused on preparing teacher candidates to be successful with diverse learners. It is well-documented that doctoral students in education and related disciplines, some of whom will accept and assume roles as university professors, are taught research skills but rarely how to plan and develop a meaningful, relevant, responsive and effective curriculum that can meet the needs of their students once they have graduated (Lieberg, 2005; Moore, 2005). Implicitly, teacher education graduate students may be taught that they should just "figure out" the complex task of curriculum planning and development when programmes do not explicitly provide a set of experiences to assist teachers in curriculum planning and development. This implicit and deleterious lesson – the lack of importance of curriculum planning and development – can create a void in the knowledge base of graduate students who will become teacher educators expected to prepare teachers to perform just such tasks.

This chapter provides insight into important features of curriculum planning and development for teacher education. The aim of this chapter is to offer a heuristic – mainly a set of reflection questions and principles – that may guide the thinking and decision making of (both new and experienced) teacher educators to help graduate students and others in teacher education think through the complexities and multifaceted nature of the curriculum

---

[*] P-12 schools are schools in the United States that serve students from pre-kindergarten through grade 12. Grade 12 is the final year of compulsory schooling.

planning and development process. In this sense, teacher educators, similar to teacher education students, are also learners who must be mindful of their decision making in curriculum planning and development. There are at least two interrelated reasons that a discussion of teacher educators' curriculum planning and development is essential:

- The curriculum planning and development of teacher educators can shape how their teacher education students (who will eventually become P-12 school teachers) plan and develop their own curriculum.

- Focusing on curriculum planning and development can provide insight into some of the necessary complexities and tensions inherent in the process for teacher educators.

Figure 7.1 provides a picture of the complex interplay between and among teacher educators, teacher education students, P-12 students and the many factors that mediate the teaching and learning exchange. In addition to teacher educators having to address the needs of teacher education students and P-12 students, the curriculum must also attend to the many contextual factors that teacher education students may face such as diversity, subject matter, institutional support and barriers, and parental support or lack thereof. Some of the most salient contextual factors in diversity education and teacher preparation are outlined in the next sections.

Figure 7.1. **Complexities of curriculum planning and development**

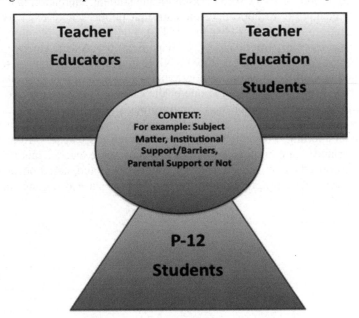

The task of preparing teachers for the diversity they will face in P-12 schools is shaped and grounded in a range of complex realities in United States society and in education. Preparing teachers for diversity is perhaps the most challenging and daunting task facing teacher education in the United States. Ladson-Billings (2001) provided a profound picture of the diversity teachers may encounter in P-12 schools asserting that:

> ... not only [will teachers encounter] ... multiracial or multiethnic [students] but they [students] are also likely to be diverse along linguistic, religious, ability, and economic lines ...Today teachers walk into ... classrooms with children who represent an incredible range of diversity. Not only are students of different races and eth-nicities, but there are students whose parents are incarcerated or drug-addicted, whose parents have never held a steady job, whose parents are themselves children (at least chronologically), and who are bounced from one foster home to the next. And there are children who have no homes or parents (p. 14).

Thus, the idea that teachers will need to be prepared to address such a range of diversity in P-12 classrooms suggests how difficult yet important teacher preparation can be in equipping teachers with the tools they need. A demographic divide rationale is present in much of the literature that makes a case for the preparation of teachers for diversity in United States society (See for instance Gay and Howard, 2000; Zumwalt and Craig, 2005). Zumwalt and Craig (2005, p. 114) wrote, "Although the student population is increas-ingly diverse, 1999 to 2000 data indicate that public school teachers were predominantly White, non-Hispanic (84%). Of the remaining proportion, 7.8% were African American, 5.7% Hispanic, 1.6% Asian American, and 0.8% Native American (NCES, 2003)". While much of the diversity discourse is framed around P-12 teacher demographics in comparison to P-12 students, Merryfield (2000) explained that one of the essential reasons some teachers graduate from teacher education programmes under-prepared to teach in diverse contexts is due to the lack of knowledge, experience, commitment and understanding of faculty members who teach the teachers. In addition to the variability among faculty members who prepare teacher candidates in multicultural education, the structures, organisation and stated purposes of teacher preparation programmes in the United States are also quite variable, as described below.

Teacher education in the United States

The settings and contexts in which teachers are prepared in the United States have a long and hotly debated history. From the early 19th century when teacher education was formalised in academies, normal schools and teacher institutes (Zeichner, 2008), the form, setting and nature of teacher preparation has been thought and re-thought, and always contested. Similarly, the contexts for and goals of teacher preparation for diverse students have taken multiple forms and served varying functions throughout its history (Milner, Laughter and Tenore, 2008). Among the points of contention have been the setting (university-based or "alternative" preparation) and the length of preparation (from two weeks in some community or school-based alternative programmes to four or five years in university-based course work). Sites of teacher preparation also vary in terms of their stated missions or goals, the organisation of coursework and field experiences, admission criteria, experiences and credentials of the teacher educators, and the degree to which institutions use data to drive decision-making about the future of their programmes (Zeichner and Conklin, 2008). The National Council for Accreditation of Teacher Education (NCATE) has established standards in these areas with which teacher preparation programmes must demonstrate compliance in order to be accredited, but the specific nature and characteristics of exactly what teacher candidates have the opportunity to learn, how they are taught, and what the influence of the variety of ways to become a teacher might be on P-12 pupil learning are as yet largely unknown (Zeichner, 2005).

In spite of the variability across forms and contexts of teacher preparation, this constant remains: teacher educators are charged with preparing candidates to skilfully, thoughtfully and responsibly educate *all* P-12 learners. The principles, reflective questions and examples used in this chapter to illustrate promising practices for teacher educators have emerged from our research and teaching in a four-year undergraduate teacher education programme and a master's level alternative certification programme. While this work has been developed in a specific context, we believe it is readily transferable to teacher preparation in any model or form. Indeed, that teacher educators should prepare teachers to offer exemplary learning opportunities to pupils from diverse backgrounds is necessary in any setting. To do so, thoughtful curriculum planning and development in teacher education should be a constant across contexts. The discussion shifts now to one that defines and clarifies what is meant by curriculum throughout this chapter and why it is imperative that graduate students who will become teacher educators have the knowledge and skills to plan and develop meaningful curricula.

Curriculum planning and development

The curriculum can be defined as what students (or teacher education students) have the opportunity to learn. According to Eisner (1994), there are several forms of the curriculum: (a) the *explicit curriculum* concerns student-learning opportunities that are overtly taught and stated or printed in documents, policies, and guidelines, such as in course syllabi or on a web-site; (b) the *implicit curriculum* is intended or unintended but is not stated or written down and can also be considered the hidden curriculum; and (c) the *null curriculum*, which deals with what students do not have the opportunity to learn. Therefore, information and knowledge that are not available for student learning is also a form of the curriculum. Thus, w*hat is absent or not included in the curriculum is actually present in what students are learning. For example, the omission of overt opportunities to study curriculum theory and learn how to plan and develop curricula may imply to graduate students that this is an unimportant aspect of their work.*

This discussion is grounded in the research on P-12 teacher curriculum planning (see for instance, Clark and Peterson, 1986; McCutcheon, 1980; Sardo-Brown, 1988) and development (see for instance, Eisner, 1994; McCutcheon, 2002). The focus is on some of what is known in the P-12 literature regarding teacher planning and development because significant amounts of research in this field have resulted in robust perspectives and a sound knowledge base. In contrast, the teacher education planning and development literature provides a thinner layer of information, although this does not suggest that no studies have focused on curriculum planning and development in teacher education (see for instance, Cochran-Smith, 1995; Ladson-Billings, 1996; Milner and Smithey, 2003); rather, this work has not explicitly addressed the particular aspects and challenges of curriculum planning and development taken up here.

Jackson (1968), McCutcheon (2002) and other researchers and theorists have conceived of at least three essential phases of teachers' curriculum planning and development: a preactive phase, an interactive phase, and a postactive or reflective phase. The **preactive phase** is the curriculum planning that takes place before the actual lesson. The planning of teachers before they actually teach is based on their projections about what may, should, and will actually occur during a lesson. Teachers, for instance, consider the amount of time they will have to complete the lesson, what has been covered in the past, the levels of experience and knowledge base of their students prior to the lesson, and possible challenges that students may face during a particular lesson (see, for example, Milner and Smithey (2003) for a description of such a process in teacher education).

Building on the work of Jackson (1968) and McCutcheon (2002), teachers also plan while they are actually teaching. This planning is what researchers have come to call the **interactive phase** of planning. Although teachers may not even realise it, they mentally plan (Clark and Peterson, 1986; McCutcheon, 1980), (de)construct, and (re)direct their preactive plans in order to attend to the realities of their students in a context as they unfold. Much of their interactive planning has to do with the idiosyncrasies inherent in classroom life and experiences. Thus, if a student in the back corner of the room is not "getting it," the teacher, in interactive planning, recognises this and could (and actually should) alter what she or he had previously planned. The interactive phase of curriculum planning and development requires teachers to be responsive to student needs that emerge during classroom lessons. If teachers or teacher educators are taught to be "responsive" to their students, then the interactive phase may indeed be an implicit aspect of their preparation. However, interactive planning is a vital feature of curriculum planning and development, and thus should occupy a visible place in the "explicit curriculum" of teacher education graduate students. While the importance of making the interactive phase more explicit is recognised, it is difficult to incorporate this implicit phase in teacher preparation because it is sometimes deeply hidden and ingrained in the work of teaching.

The **postactive** phase of teacher planning and development occurs after teaching (and after the interactive phase) has occurred. For instance, teachers reflect on the successes and struggles of a lesson and the extent to which their instruction influenced students' learning or not. The postactive phase lays the foundation for and is the first step in the next preactive phase. It is important to note that the postactive and preactive phases of curriculum planning and development are very much interconnected. For example, as an African American, female teacher educator, Ladson-Billings (1996) was challenged to develop a curriculum that would simultaneously spark deep thinking, reflection and the urge to speak openly about multicultural issues among her mostly white students. As a teacher educator she preactively designed lessons intended to promote dialogue among and between students and herself, but she found that her attempts were too often met with silence from her teacher education students. The postactive phase of her planning revealed the need to (1) uncover the causes of her students' silence, and (2) implement instructional supports to help her students engage in oral discussion in her class. The instructional supports employed to understand her students' thinking and help break the pervasive silences were journaling, small group discussions, and enabling students to ask questions anonymously. Re-designing her curriculum planning in response to students' attitudes and behaviours in her classes enabled her to create learning opportunities (again, through journaling, small-group discussions, and anonymous question asking) that took into account students' diverse backgrounds, communication styles, and experiences (or lack thereof) with people from different races and socio-economic backgrounds. During the postactive phase of planning and development,

Ladson-Billings reflected critically on the silences in her classroom and asked herself what possible causes and solutions might be underlying this particular issue. She used the thinking from her postactive phase to guide her work in the next preactive phase of planning.

For the purposes of this discussion, Jackson's (1968) conceptions of curriculum planning and development, namely employing the preactive, interactive, and postactive framework are used as tools to explicate and analyse the work of curriculum planning and development. Without extensive preparation in the complex tasks of curriculum planning and development, graduate students will be without the ability to interrogate their own teaching, carefully examine their students' learning, and make appropriate modifications when necessary. In the following sections we present three principles of curriculum planning and development conceptualised in the course of our own research and experiences as teacher educators. The principles may be used by new faculty and experienced teacher educators alike to help guide their own course development and professional growth.

Preactive curriculum planning and development

Curriculum planning and development principle 1: Teacher educators think not only about whom their teacher education students are, but also about the identities of P-12 school students the teacher education students will teach.

New teacher educators and teacher education graduate students, when planning and developing curricula, must learn to consider their students' identities not only in relation to the present course material, but also in terms of how teacher candidates' identifications may influence their work with P-12 students. Teacher educators must gauge the multiple and varied identities of the teacher education students as a precursor to planning and developing the curriculum. However, one of the particular complexities of teacher education is that to think only about the teacher education students' identities is insufficient. Teacher educators should also think about the P-12 students whom teacher candidates are and will someday teach, particularly if teacher education students intend to work in schools that serve a diverse student population. This important area of consideration is indeed complex: teacher educators find themselves considering an enormously large range of students and different learning contexts – especially if the teacher education programme is not mission-driven. An example of a specific mission-driven programme would be an urban teacher education programme in the United States. While there is no static definition of "urban education" or of "urban teacher education programme" in the United States, teachers enrolled in urban teacher education programmes may be prepared to work and practice thoughtfully in schools with a high enrolment of racially and/or linguistically diverse learners or learners from lower socio-economic backgrounds, for instance. Ideally, teachers are prepared to develop the mindsets and practices to recognise the rich and powerful assets of those in urban spaces and to use the assets and resources in their practices to create optimal learning opportunities for students (Milner, 2010).

In summary, the preactive phase of planning has to do with the preparation of teachers before a lesson or prior to the planning of an entire course. Unlike teachers in P-12 school contexts, teacher educators are not necessarily privy to a wide range of information about teacher education students' interests, knowledge-base, areas of experience and demographics. For instance, Milner and Smithey (2003) describe how an initial phenotype for working with one class of teacher education students (mostly female and white, with one Asian) was actually inaccurate. After engaging the teacher education students and learning from them, a wide range of diversity was noted. Of the 14 teacher education students (interns) from across the United States enrolled in the course, twelve were from outside the state. Given their age range from 23 to 48 years, these master's-level teacher education students brought diverse experiences to the course. For instance, one female teacher education student had taught microbiology in a university medical school for 16 years, another had eight years of international business experience, two had taught previously in Europe or Asia, and one male had retired from the technology business sector. Because of the varied socio-economic, educational and professional experiences of these teacher education students, there were varied beliefs, opinions and convictions that emerged throughout the course – areas from which, as the teacher educator, he attempted to learn to shape curriculum planning and development during the preactive, interactive and postactive phases. For teacher educators, similarly to P-12 teachers, ideas about the teacher education students' background and experiences growing up, for instance, can be critical to their curriculum planning and development in the preactive phase. A nuanced knowledge of the diversity of learners in a class, at any level, can benefit the instructor and enable him or her to connect new learning more directly to students' experiences in the world as well as help him or her create learning opportunities that draw on the diverse knowledge students bring with them into the course. Teacher educators and P-12 teachers alike benefit from the diversity – that is, the varying perspectives, experiences, worldviews and overall contributions that manifest in the classroom. In short, diversity, from our perspective, should be seen as an asset not a liability.

Gaining a sense of how teacher education students were raised and what they and their parents thought about complex matters such as race, social justice and equity can be considerably important for teacher educators in their preactive phase of planning. In essence, teacher educators have to consider, to the extent possible, all the needs of students in P-12 schools across the country. While there are common characteristics and needs across all students, there are other areas that are much more contextual, dynamic, inconsistent, and uncommon, such as issues of funding and resources, parental involvement or the lack thereof, administrative support, opportunities to collaborate with colleagues, student motivation, and so forth. Therefore, it is not only important for a teacher educator to know his or her students well, he or she has to also think about how to prepare teacher education students to teach P-12 students with particular experiences, needs and strengths. In the preactive phase of planning, there is such a wide range of issues to consider that encompassing the range of obstacles teacher education students may encounter as they plan and develop the curriculum is an impossible task. However, they still should attempt to consider the range of issues and concerns that teacher education students may encounter in P-12 schools. Thus, in curriculum planning and development, teacher educators have to ask themselves several questions about the needs of P-12 school students with whom the teacher education students will work and also questions about the teacher education students themselves. These questions include, but are not limited to:

- What characteristics, demographics and needs might P-12 school students have and of which teacher education students should be aware?

- What characteristics, demographics and needs might teacher education students have and of which teacher educators should be aware?

- In what types of contexts (*i.e.* suburban, urban, rural) might the teacher education students teach after they have graduated and how should curricula and related experiences reflect these different contexts?

- From what types of contexts (*i.e.* suburban, urban, rural) do the teacher education students come and how should the curriculum reflect this?

- What relationships or potential influences exist among the characteristics of teacher candidates' backgrounds and those of their potential P-12 students?

- How do teacher educators plan and develop a curriculum that deepens the teacher education students' knowledge and understanding about themselves and their prospective P-12 school students, and does NOT reinforce stereotypes?

- What are some of the systemic and institutional barriers and supports that teacher education students may encounter that are beyond their control and are unpredictable, and how can the curriculum be structured to adjust to these "out of control" matters?

- How do teacher educators develop curricula heuristics for teacher education students to gauge what their P-12 school students will know about the subject matter, their learning, and other important features of the teaching and learning encounter?

- What content should teacher educators omit in curriculum planning and development, and why?

In his work with preservice secondary English teachers, for example, Tenore taught in a reading and writing methods course. Among the above questions, he considered the potential relationships between his teacher education students' backgrounds and experiences and those of their potential P-12 students with respect to their experiences as readers and writers. Because the university at which he teaches is among the most academically competitive in the United States, he conjectured that, with few exceptions, the teacher education students with whom he worked would generally have had experienced relatively few struggles as readers and writers in their school lives. Based on this conjecture, preactively, it became important to plan course readings, lessons and experiences that might help the teacher education students understand the nature of reading and writing difficulties faced by some P-12 students. Teacher education students who had never experienced serious difficulty learning to read or write would need to understand potential causes of reading and writing difficulty and how such struggles can impact students' learning, and they would need to develop appropriate dispositions and skills to be able to teach struggling readers and writers effectively.

These preactive guiding questions seem important to the overall curriculum planning and development of teacher educators, regardless of the subject matter being taught. In addition to the above preactive guiding questions, new teacher educators and teacher education graduate students should be aware of several important considerations for self-study (Baszile, 2003; Cochran-Smith, 2000; Cochran-Smith and Zeichner, 2005; Ladson-Billings, 1996; Hamilton and Pinnegar, 2000) during the preactive phase of curriculum planning and development. These areas of consideration can prove helpful to improving the curriculum planning and development processes in teacher education as well. The discussion moves now from planning that occurs prior to teaching to consideration of the importance and complexities of planning that happens during teaching, what Jackson (1968) termed interactive planning.

Interactive curriculum planning and development

Curriculum planning and development principle 2: Teacher educators enact the preactive plan by deliberately responding to the nuanced needs of the students during the lesson.

The preactive phase, the planning and development prior to teaching, is essential, but the interactive phase of planning and curriculum development is perhaps even more important. The interactive phase has to do with the planning – the thinking and reflection of teacher educators – while teaching. Beck and Kosnik (2001) wrote: "reflection while teaching is feasible and can result in more – rather than less – attentive teaching" (p. 223). Based on student questions, answers, informal assessments through writing, or even facial expressions or body language, the instructor is able to "read" the class in order to gauge understanding. Interactive planning is the decisions the teacher or teacher educators makes *in the moment*, the "teacher moves" that have the potential to reshape conceptual confusion, misconception of information shared, and to clarify points about teaching practices. For example, during the interactive phase of curriculum planning and development, some of Milner's teacher education students struggled with Claude Steele's (1997) construct of stereotype threat. According to the theory, stereotype threat can occur when members of a group worry that they can confirm a negative stereotype about their group. For instance, the pervasive stereotype in the United States that women are not as smart in mathematics as men is one that Steele would argue could impact the achievement of women on standardised test exams because the women may worry that they will confirm the stereotype.

Some students struggled to understand how pervasive stereotypes could influence people's self-conceptions, work ethic and ability to function in an organisation. Milner was able to gauge the students' lack of understanding and clarity related to the topic and attempted to illustrate the idea, relative to stereotype threat, during the interactive phase of planning. Preactively, the lesson plan was to cover the Steele reading, to discuss it, to think about how stereotype threat might be applicable to students' own work, and to think about ways the teacher education students (as teachers) could circumvent it in their P-12 work. However, interactively, because some of the students were not able to understand the construct in order to apply it, Milner had to rework his preactive plan in order to be responsive to the students; he had to plan interactively.

To redirect the plans interactively and to help explain the notion of stereotype threat, Milner used examples of his own concerns about earning tenure; he shared the tenure rate for other African Americans in his department, college, and university and attempted to convey how stereotype threat applied to his situation. He also shared that he always saw himself as an African American male and assumed that others perceived him as an African American male as well. It seemed that, through the sharing of a personal narrative and making overt connections to stereotype threat, the teacher education students were able to better grasp the construct. Again, it was through the assessment of the students' understanding (based on evidence provided such as their responses to questions) that he came to understand that they did not understand Steele's construct and could not move on to the next phase of the lesson, which was to apply stereotype threat to P-12 classrooms and to ultimately think about ways to work through and around it.

Unlike the curriculum planning and development of P-12 school teachers, teacher educators have to interactively gauge not only where teacher education students are in terms of the content being covered, but also in terms of the P-12 school students whom the teacher education students will someday teach. The decision to include lessons and readings on stereotype threat is an example of planning with both teacher education students and their future pupils in mind. It was included because stereotype threat is among the challenges P-12 students face in schools. Teacher educators need to get a sense of the knowledge-base and understanding of their teacher education students and also more deeply understand if these students are making connections to the material that will benefit their P-12 school students. This phase of planning requires teacher educators to pose several important questions:

- What evidence suggests that teacher education students are actually learning the curriculum covered during teaching practices?

- What contradictions and challenges between teacher education students and P-12 school students seem persistently evident in the lesson?

- In what ways does the preactively planned lesson attend to and meet the needs of the teacher education students as well as the needs of P-12 students with whom they will work?

- What lessons do teacher educators omit during the interactive phase (*i.e.* the null curriculum) and why?

- How are teacher educators responding to the needs of both teacher education students and their future students during the enactment of the curriculum?

In essence, the above questions can help teacher educators think through their planning while teaching. Responsiveness to a range of issues is necessary for teacher educators as they plan interactively. The idea of responsive planning means that teacher educators scaffold learning by building on teacher education students' prior knowledge, conceptions, understandings, worldviews, and belief systems. When teacher educators take teacher education students' interests, needs, and ideas into consideration while teaching, students are able to exhibit greater enthusiasm about the content and to connect their learning to their future teaching. What makes responsive planning in teacher education even more complex, though, is that not only should teacher educators account for their students' interests and needs, but they should also always keep in mind the diverse needs of P-12 students.

The interactive phase of curriculum planning and development concerns the rational, responsive decisions of teacher educators to emergent issues that they encounter with teacher education students and also cues about P-12 school students. The responsive nature of the interactive phase of curriculum planning and development means much more than teacher educators' merely adjusting their practice based on their interactions with teacher education students. Consistent with Freire's (1998) banking theory, which is a metaphor for teaching that involves teachers making "deposits" of knowledge into students by imparting information to them, Elbaz (1993) stressed that responsive teaching is a "vision of teaching" (p. 190) that requires teacher educators to understand a wide range of issues and phenomena. Elbaz wrote that responsive teaching negates the notion that "teaching consists essentially in the passing on of knowledge from one container (teacher) to another (student)" (p. 191). Rather, knowledge construction is garnered with and through all those in the learning environment, including teacher education students, and should be done with P-12 learners in mind.

The interactive phase of curriculum planning and development challenges teacher educators to respect the reality that teacher education students bring a diverse range of experiences and expertise into the learning environment – some that can be an asset to their work with P-12 school students and some that can be detrimental. Regardless of its benefit, the knowledge base of teacher education students as it emerges in teaching during the interactive phase of curriculum planning and development needs to be targeted and centrally considered. While teacher educators should work to respond interactively to the emerging knowledge and conceptions teacher education students have, they should also carefully and thoughtfully reflect on themselves and their students during the postactive phase of curriculum planning and development. This phase of planning represents an important opportunity for teacher educators to be responsive to their and P-12 students' needs. Some guidelines for postactive planning are introduced in Principle 3 below.

Postactive planning

> **Curriculum planning and development principle 3:** Teacher educators reflect upon the extent to which their preactively planned lessons are effectively enacted, the extent to which they have been responsive to the learning needs of their students during the interactive phase, and they consider future directions for curriculum planning and development.

Teacher educators plan before they teach (preactively), while teaching (interactively), and also after they have taught a lesson or a course. The postactive phase of curriculum planning and development is akin to the preactive phase because the reflective thinking that guides postactive planning helps teacher educators preactively construct future lessons and courses. Reflection is a key component to the postactive phase of planning and development. The literature makes clear the importance of teachers' self-, curricular- and pedagogical-examination and awareness in meeting the needs of their students (Howard, 2001; Medina, Morrone and Anderson, 2005; Zeichner and Liston, 1996). Woolfolk (2004, p. 8) wrote that "reflective teachers think back over situations to analyse what they did and why and to consider how they might improve learning for [all] their students". Valli (1997, p 67) explained that "reflective teaching emphasises the importance of teacher inquiry and counteracts a more limited interest in teachers' behaviour without considering what is going on in their minds and hearts". In this phase of postactive planning, it is important for teacher educators to write down (not necessarily in a formal or specific format) the features of the lesson and interactive planning that seemed to work well and also those areas that seemed to be less effective. Keeping a record of these areas of strength and weakness right after the lesson can prevent teacher educators from forgetting the most important experiences from the teaching episode or course. Such emphasis on the importance of writing down plans is consistent with the literature that suggests that writing down lessons is useful (see for instance, McCutcheon, 2002). Reflective questions that can guide teacher educators in the postactive phase of curriculum planning and development include, but are not limited to:

- What features of the lesson seemed most effective? Why?

- What features of the lesson seemed most ineffective? Why?

- How was the teacher educator able to respond to unexpected dilemmas during earlier phases of curriculum planning and development, especially during the interactive phase?

- Was the teacher educator able to respond to teacher education students' needs and to provide space where teacher education students were able to make meaningful connections with P-12 school students and their needs?

- Did the enactment of the lesson take into consideration the needs of P-12 students?

- What phases of curriculum planning and development appeared most effective (preactive, interactive, or postactive)? Why?

- What did the teacher educator choose to avoid and omit in the lesson? Why?

The postactive phase of curriculum planning and development allows teacher educators the opportunity to think back over all phases of the planning and development process and work through tensions inherent in the process and outcomes.

One area of concern has been teacher education students' inability to take some of the ideas, ideology and theories discussed and to transfer them into their teaching and analysis of teaching practices. For example, one of the ideas Tenore addressed in his work with teacher education students is the importance of considering contextual factors in teaching and planning. In postactive reflection following course meetings, he recognised that when teacher education students discussed teachers and students whom they had observed, their talk focused on evaluating or passing judgment on teachers or students as "good" or "bad" based on a single classroom interaction. During the postactive phase Tenore came to understand that the teacher education students were not considering the "big picture" of classroom life, which includes the context in which the class occurred, the shared history among teachers and students, the particular knowledge that teachers had of the students' idiosyncrasies, and so on. In subsequent course meetings, he used what he learned during postactive planning to preactively design lessons to help students apply what they had learned about the influences of contextual and social factors and power relations to the observations they were making in classrooms. Here, not only was he thinking of the learning of teacher education students, but also he was considering the P-12 students' need to have teachers who were able to draw on multiple sources of information concerning their contexts, histories and learning needs.

Postactively, teacher educators should think through ways to explicitly help teacher education students connect theory with practice. Teacher educators have to be explicit both in terms of what they model, share and expect with teacher education students and also with what they ask them to do. Teacher educators, in this phase of planning, write down, as soon as they leave class if possible, struggles and successes they face in their classes.

Conclusions and implications

In Box 7.1, an attempt is made to capture and summarise the three principles covered throughout this chapter. These principles focus on what teacher educators should consider during the preactive, interactive and postactive phases of curriculum planning and development. This chapter is written for the benefit of teacher education graduate students (and others) who will one day find themselves challenged by the complexity and tensions of preparing teachers to work with diverse learners. While teacher education graduate students are often prepared in how to conduct research, it is also very important that they have a window into how to plan and develop a meaningful, relevant and responsive curriculum. Moreover, these teacher education graduate students need to understand how complex and challenging planning and developing a curriculum can be when they are not only working to meet the needs of their teacher education students but also their responsibility to consider P-12 school students needs as well.

Box 7.1. **Curriculum planning and development principals**

Preactive Phase

Principle 1: Teacher educators think not only about who their teacher education students are, but also about the identities of P-12 school students the teacher education students will teach.

Interactive Phase

Principle 2: Teacher educators enact the preactive plan by deliberately responding to the nuanced needs of the students during the lesson.

Postactive Phase

Principle 3: Teacher educators reflect upon the extent to which their preactively planned lessons are effectively enacted, the extent to which they have been responsive to the learning needs of their students during the interactive phase, and they consider future directions for curriculum planning and development.

Clearly, teacher education graduate students sometimes have experiences where they are the lead teacher or are a teaching assistant in a teacher education course. Still, the curriculum planning and development of these courses are too often not transparent enough for teacher education graduate students. These students find themselves struggling to understand how to respond to both the teacher education students and also provide contextual insight into the needs of P-12 school students. This chapter presented three sets of questions that are important for all teacher educators to thoughtfully consider when planning and developing curriculum. These questions might serve as the basis for a series of professional development courses for teacher educators. However, for graduate students or new teacher educators working to negotiate the complex challenges and tensions of preparing teachers for diverse learners, they are vital starting points that can guide careful, reflective, responsive curriculum planning and development and instruction.

Teaching in any context for any purpose is challenging, complex work. We have argued, though, that curriculum planning and development in teacher education for diverse learners presents particular challenges and tensions that should be addressed specifically. Indeed, more attention should be placed on these matters because ultimately P-12 students either benefit or are hurt by what teacher education students have the opportunity to learn (or not).

References

Banks, J.A. (2001), "Citizenship Education and Diversity: Implications for Teacher Education", *Journal of Teacher Education*, Vol. 52, No. 1, pp. 5–16.

Baszile, D.T. (2003), "Who Does She Think She is? Growing Up Nationalist and Ending Up Teaching Race in White Space", *Journal of Curriculum Theorising*, Vol. 19, No. 3, pp. 25-37.

Beck, C. and C. Kosnik (2001), "Reflection-in-action: In Defense of Thoughtful Teaching", *Curriculum Inquiry*, Vol. 31, No. 2, pp. 217-227.

Clark, C.M. and P.L. Peterson (1986), "Teachers' Thought Processes", in M.C. Wittrock (ed.), *Handbook of Research on Teaching*, Macmillan, New York, pp. 255-296.

Cochran-Smith, M. (1995), "Uncertain Allies: Understanding the Boundaries of Race and Teaching", *Harvard Educational Review*, Vol. 65, No. 4, pp. 541-570.

Cochran-Smith, M. (2000), "Blind Vision: Unlearning Racism in Teacher Education", *Harvard Educational Review*, Vol. 70, No. 2, pp. 157-191.

Cochran-Smith, M. and K.M. Zeichner (2005), "Executive Summary", in M.C. Smith and K.M. Zeichner (eds.), *Studying Teacher Education: The Report of the AERA Panel on Research and Teacher Education*, Lawrence Erlbaum Associates, Incorporated, New Jersey, pp. 1-36.

Dinkelman, T. (2003), "Self-study in Teacher Education: A Means and Ends Tool for Promoting Reflective Teaching", *Journal of Teacher Education*, Vol. 54, No. 1, pp. 6-18.

Dinkelman, T. (2000), "An Inquiry into the Development of Critical Reflection in Secondary Student Teachers", *Teaching and Teacher Education*, Vol. 16, pp. 195-222.

Eisner, E.W. (1994), *The educational imagination: On the design and evaluation of school programs*, MacMillan College Publishing Company, New York.

Elbaz, F. (1993), "Responsive Teaching: A Response from a Teacher's Perspective", *Journal of Curriculum Studies*, Vol. 25, pp. 189-199.

Epstein, J. (1995, May), "School/Family/Community Partnership: Caring for the Children we Share", *Phi Delta Kappan, pp.* 701-712.

Freire, P. (1998), *Pedagogy of the Oppressed*, Continuum, New York.

Gay, G. and T. Howard (2000), "Multicultural Teacher Education for the 21st century", *The Teacher Educator*, Vol. 36, No. 1, pp. 1–16.

Hamilton, M.L. and S. Pinnegar (2000), "On the Threshold of a New Century: Trustworthiness, Integrity, and Self-study in Teacher Education", *Journal of Teacher Education*, Vol. 51, No. 3, pp. 234-240.

Hatton, N. and D. Smith (1995), "Reflection in Teacher Education: Towards Definition and Implementation", *Teaching and Teacher Education*, Vol. 11, No. 1, pp. 33-49.

Hopper, T. and K. Sanford (2004), "Representing Multiple Perspectives of Self-as-teacher: School Integrated Teacher Education and Self-study", *Teacher Education Quarterly*, Vol. 31, No. 2, pp. 57-74.

Howard, T.C. (2001), "Telling their Side of the Story: African American Students' Perceptions of Culturally Relevant Teaching", *Urban Review*, Vol. 33, No. 2, pp. 131–149.

Jackson, P. (1968), *Life in Classrooms,* Holt, Rinehart and Winston, New York.

Ladson-Billings, G. (1996), "Silences as Weapons: Challenges of a Black Professor Teaching White Students", *Theory into Practice*, Vol. 35, pp. 79-85.

Ladson-Billings, G. (2001), *Crossing Over to Canaan: The Journey of New Teachers in Diverse Classrooms,* Jossey-Bass Publishers, San Francisco.

Lewis, A.E. (2001), "There is No 'Race' in the Schoolyard: Color-blind Ideology in an (Almost) All White School", *American Educational Research Journal*, Vol. 38, No. 4, pp. 781-811.

Lieberg, C. (2005), *Teaching your First College Class: A Practical Guide for New Faculty and Graduate Student Instructors*, Stylus Publishing, Sterling, VA.

McCutcheon, G. (1980), "How do Elementary School Teachers Plan? The Nature of Planning and Influences on it", *Elementary School Journal*, Vol. 8, pp. 14-23.

McCutcheon, G. (2002), *Developing the Curriculum*, Educators' Press International, Troy, NY.

Medina, M.A., A.S. Morrone and J.A. Anderson (2005), "Promoting Social Justice in an Urban Secondary Teacher Education Program", *Clearing House* Vol. 78, No. 5, pp. 207-212.

Merryfield, M.M. (2000), "Why Aren't Teachers Being Prepared to Teach for Diversity, Equity, and Global Interconnectedness? A Study of Lived Experiences in the Making of Multicultural and Global Educators", *Teaching and Teacher Education* Vol. 16, pp. 429-443.

Milner, H.R. (2006), "But Good Intentions are not Enough: Theoretical and Philosophical Relevance in Teaching Students of Color", in J. Landsman and C.W. Lewis (eds.), *White Teachers/Diverse Classrooms: A Guide to Building Inclusive Schools, Promoting High Expectations and Eliminating Racism*, Stylus Publishers, Sterling, VA, pp. 79-90.

Milner, H.R. (2010), "What does Teacher Education Have to do with Teaching? Implications for Diversity Studies", *Journal of Teacher Education*.

Milner, H.R., J.C. Laughter, J.C. and F.B. Tenore (2008), "Multicultural Education in Teacher Education", in C.A. Lassonde, R. Michael, and J. Rivera Wilson (eds.), *Issues in Teacher Education*. Charles C. Thomas Publishers, Springfield Illinois.

Milner, H.R. and M. Smithey (2003), "How Teacher Educators Created a Course Curriculum to Challenge and Enhance Preservice Teachers' Thinking and Experience with Diversity", *Teaching Education*, Vol. 14, No. 3, pp. 293-305.

Moore, D.S. (2005), "Preparing Graduate Students to Teach Statistics: Introduction", *American Statistical Association*, Vol. 59, No. 1, pp. 1-3.

NCES (2003), *School and Staffing Survey, 1999-2000,* National Center for Education Statistics, United States Department of Education, Washington, DC, accessed 3 October 2003, *www.nces.ed.gov/surveys/sass.*

Polacco, P. (1994), *Pink and Say*, Penguin Putnam, New York.

Pike, M. (2000), "Keen Readers: Adolescents and Pre-Twentieth Century Poetry", *Education Review*, Vol. 52, No. 1, pp. 35-40.

Rearick, M. L. and A. Feldman (1999), "Orientations, Purposes and Reflection: A Framework for Understanding Action Research", *Teaching and Teacher Education*, Vol. 15, pp. 333-349.

Rubin, H.J. and I.S. Rubin (2005), *Qualitative interviewing: The Art of Hearing Data (2nd Edition).* Thousand Oaks, Sage.

Sardo-Brown, D. (1988), "Twelve Middle-School Teachers' Planning", *Elementary School Journal*, Vol. 89, No. 1, pp. 69-87.

Shulman, L.S. (1987), "Knowledge and Teaching: Foundations of the New Reform", *Harvard Educational Review,* Vol. 19, No. 2, pp. 4-14.

Steele, C.M. (1997), "A Threat in the Air: How Stereotypes Shape Intellectual Identity and Performance", *American Psychologist*, Vol. 52, pp. 613-629.

Valli, L. (1997), "Listening to Other Voices: A Description of Teacher Reflection in the United States", *Peabody Journal of Education*, Vol. 72, No. 1, pp. 67-88.

Wink, J. (2000), *Critical Pedagogy: Notes from the Real World* (*2nd edition*), Longman, New York.

Woolfolk, A.E. (2004), *Educational Psychology (9th edition)*, Allyn and Bacon, Boston.

Zeichner, K. (2005), "A Research Agenda for Teacher Education", in M. Cochran-Smith and K. Zeichner (eds.), *Studying Teacher Education,* Lawrence Erlbaum Associates, Incorporated, New Jersey, pp. 737-760.

Zeichner, K. (2008), "Introduction: Settings for Teacher Education", in M.Cochran-Smith, S. Feiman-Nemser, D.J. McIntyre, and K.E. Demers (eds.), *Handbook of Research on Teacher Education: Enduring Questions in Changing Contexts,* Routledge, Taylor, and Francis Group and the Association of Teacher Educators, New York, pp. 263-268.

Zeichner, K. and H.G. Conklin (2008), "Teacher Education Programs as Sites for Teacher Preparation", in M.Cochran-Smith, S. Feiman-Nemser, D.J. McIntyre, and K.E. Demers (eds.) *Handbook of Research on Teacher Education: Enduring Questions in Changing Contexts,* Routledge, Taylor, and Francis Group and the Association of Teacher Educators, New York, pp. 269-28.

Zeichner, K.M. and D.P. Liston (1996), *Reflective Teaching: An Introduction,* Lawrence Erlbaum Associates, Incorporated, New Jersey.

Zumwalt, K and E. Craig (2005), "Teachers' Characteristics: Research on the Demographic Profile", in M.C. Smith and K.M. Zeichner (eds.), *Studying Teacher Education: The Report of the AERA Panel on Research and Teacher Education,* Lawrence Erlbaum Associates, Incorporated, New Jersey, pp. 111-156.

Chapter 8

Intercultural competence teacher-training models: the Italian experience

Milena Santerini
Università Cattolica del Sacro Cuore, Italy

In order to address the challenges of cultural diversity Italian schools are facing, new initiatives are required in teacher education. This chapter surveys a number of theoretical models to identify the level of intercultural skills of practitioners and proposes a new training programme designed to increase the intercultural skills of teachers and social workers working in multicultural contexts. The experiences of teacher education initiatives at the Catholic University of Milan confirm the programme's initial assumptions: sensitivity, understanding, a critical reprocessing of personal experience and self-reflection (introspection) are all essential to improving the quality of intercultural skills training. The author argues that these assumptions are especially important in light of the increasing conflict and racism present in Italian schools today.

From the OECD online consultation : preparing the teachers

The majority of teacher respondents reported that they did not feel well prepared for diversity in their classrooms, neither by their initial teacher education nor by their professional development. How can education systems give teachers the tools they need to respond to their changing classrooms?

Introduction

In today's societies, where increasingly serious cultural conflict is becoming more and more common, the principles and methods of intercultural education in schools have undergone extensive revision. Paradigms based on *assimilation* have proven ineffectual and have done little to resolve social contradictions and conflict while those based on *absolute relativism* have affirmed the importance of cultural differences but run the risk of exempting such differences from critique and judgement, and impeding dialogue (Camilleri and Cohen Emerique, 1989; Banks, 2006). In the latter case, the undisputed need to respect and promote diversity (the aim of *openness*) has not gone hand in hand with building social cohesion and a sense of citizenship (the aim of *equality*). In fact, the glorification of diversity has had some adverse effects (Ouellet, 1991). For example, in schools the didactic activities which have highlighted ethnic differences have sometimes resulted in increasing the separation between students.

This seeming impasse in interpretations of intercultural education has been resolved by a new conceptual approach to culture. This approach is based on anthropological and philosophical contributions and has made a thorough revision of educational assumptions and methodologies possible (Geertz, 2000; Cuche, 2003). In this perspective, culture cannot be reduced to an essence because it is plural, an amalgam of many different voices. Even in individuals, culture cannot be regarded as an *unum* because individuals are themselves multicultural. Since culture is neither innate nor biologically transmitted but rather an accumulation of habits acquired from birth, it is learned through acculturation, education and – especially in adults – daily social intercourse. It is interactive, in that it is shared and transmitted within and through the group. Cultures are not static, they are dynamic and permeable; and apart from special instances of "closure", they tend to change over time.

This conception of cultural interaction is particularly important in a country like Italy, where the issue of the integration of diverse cultures has become urgent due to the rapid increase of immigrant students. In the period following the Second World War, Italian schools have chosen an *inclusive* type of orientation. The term *inclusive* refers to the tendency over the past 50 years to promote schooling of all types of students, absorbing internal immigrants (from the south to the north) and integrating disabled students into mainstream classrooms. Italian law also allows students to attend school even if they are undocumented immigrants. This situation could change if the laws regarding immigrants become more restrictive. To avoid this, a 2007 document of the Ministry of Public Education (*La via italiana alla scuola interculturale*) specifically states that the organisation of Italian schools is founded on the Convention of Children's Rights according to the principles adopted by the European Union. This openness to diversity, however, has not always been accompanied by the appropriate teacher education to deal with diversity on all levels.

Beginning in the late 1980s, Italy began receiving immigrant students, mostly from Eastern Europe, the Maghreb region, Latin America and Asia. The heterogeneity of the immigrant population in Italy put the principles and practices of integration to the test, and the variety of languages and countries of origin presented a new challenge for teachers. There are 191 nationalities present in Italian schools, with at least 60 different languages spoken. The largest groups of immigrant students come from Romania, followed by Albania, China, Ecuador and Morocco, with most of these students concentrated in certain cities in northern Italy. In addition, the Roma population, which includes nearly 12 000 students, represents a particularly complex case for teachers and teaching due to their history.

In the 2007/2008 school year, students with non-Italian citizenship numbered 574 133, representing 6.4% of the student population. This can be compared with the figures from 1998/1999 in which they made up only 1.1% of the student population. However, it is important to note that about 200 000 of these children were born in Italy and are thus second generation students. While they have grown up speaking Italian and many of their cultural habits are the same as their Italian schoolmates, under Italian law they remain foreigners. Citizenship laws in Italy, unrealistically modelled on a country of emigrants rather than immigrants, have favoured the *jus sanguinis,* the transmission of citizenship from an Italian father or mother to the children rather than the *jus soli,* or birthright citizenship, used in many other European countries as well as in North America. Although there is no distinction made in statistical data between non-citizens born in Italy and those who immigrate, there is a significant difference for the teacher. For those who immigrate, the date of arrival in Italy is equally important. Students who arrived in Italy as recently as 2007/2008 make up only 10% of the non-citizen student population.

The phases of integration of these varied groups have been similar to many other European countries. Initially, there was a phase of *assimilation*, or insertion of the minority culture with little or no attention paid to the culture of origin, followed by a phase of *multiculturalism*, understood as the "discovery" of pluralism but also the romanticising of other cultures. Today, there is the feeling that it is necessary to reach an intercultural model to accomplish integration without giving up social cohesion.

To create the conditions for communal life in a pluralistic context, intercultural education needs to convey an idea of culture that steers clear of essentialism ("all Muslims", the "African mentality", "Asian culture") and encourages a non-simplified understanding of minority groups. Intercultural education operates in the space between the *cultural zero* and the *cultural all* (Abdallah Pretceille, 2006 and 1990). A dynamic concept of culture such as this relies on a kind of moderate relativism if it is to strike the difficult balance between respect for specificity and universal principles. In this sense, it encourages a worldview based on mutual transformation, respecting other cultures while also promoting cohesion by emphasising common goals and values (Santerini, 2003).

This theoretical and conceptual framework ought to bring about far-reaching change in all teaching methods and curricula in both formal education (schools, universities, courses) and informal education (fostering communal life and intercultural dialogue in the social sphere, conflict resolution, etc.). The reality, however, is that this dynamic vision of culture and education is frequently ignored. Unsurprisingly, the explanation for this resistance lies in the fact that education based on a static concept of culture makes curricula "easier" to teach – but not more effective (Allemann-Ghionda, Perregaux and Goumoens, 1999). In a certain sense, the "mono" approach to teaching is simpler than the "inter" approach. Italian teachers are generally accustomed to a "mono" approach, which consists of the presentation of only one point of view (for example, in subjects such as sciences, geography and history). The intercultural approach, on the other hand, requires the consideration of other points of view, the exercise of critical capacity, the analysis of sources, the distinction between differences in cultural perspectives, etc.

A prime example of this is teacher and social-worker training in Italy, the primary concern of this paper. In addition to reformulating didactic principles, methods and practices into an intercultural approach, teachers today must also deal with the consequences of a political orientation that is becoming more and more restrictive towards immigration (new laws that render it a crime to be in the country without the proper authorisation, restrictions on the possibility of residency, etc.). This situation of conflict, fed by the mass media, has created the phenomenon of segregation of immigrant students into schools separate from those attended by native students. For example, the newspapers portray immigrant students as an "emergency" and "invasion" who will lower the quality of education for Italian citizens. Finally, especially in some cities in northern Italy, various groups of immigrants are beginning to demand cultural recognition, asking that their native language be taught in the schools or for concessions regarding special food requirements and religious holidays.

For all these reasons, it is necessary to rethink teacher training in light of new challenges. Intercultural teacher training is a fundamental means of constructing a school which is open to diversity rather than one oriented toward "segregated" education. It is important for Italian teachers to be trained to manage heterogeneity, which is to say to become sensitive to differences and to organise support and co-operation activities between students. In Italy, in-service teacher education takes place in the schools and is based on guidelines from the Ministry of Education. Initial teacher education, on the other hand, happens at university, which provides only a general training although some attention is given to intercultural and special education. Most intercultural training initiatives are organised by local government organisations or NGOs that focus primarily on the knowledge of immigrant cultures. The approach to training in Italy is generally a specialist or *segregated approach* (which promotes competence in specific fields, such as teaching the L2). The *infusion approach*, on the other hand, would update the teachers' general skills in managing heterogeneity, but it is less used.

In addition to the above, another limit is the "culturalist" conception of education, which inevitably tends to teach the culture of *"the other"* by simplifying it, thereby running the risk of reinforcing stereotypes, biases and prejudices rather than countering them. On the other hand, it seems more effective to provide experiential training based on personal encounters and competence in relating to immigrant students in order to bring about more profound changes in trainees' personalities and worldviews. The expectations of this training, as well as trainees' reluctance to question their own roles and view intercultural relations critically, have been described in teacher-oriented studies on this issue (Santerini, 2002, 2008).

Although the need for multidimensional training programmes has already been voiced in several studies (*e.g.* Milhouse, 1996), most teacher and social-worker training, in Italy at least, tends even now to be intellectual rather than experiential. For example, a research project based on focus groups and in-depth interviews with 30 teachers (from 14 elementary and middle schools in Milan with high percentages of immigrants) revealed that the teachers involved all had a theoretical form of cultural training rather than an experiential one. The teachers expressed the need for training that would help them to manage a heterogeneous classroom (Santerini and Reggio, 2004).

A transversal, multidimensional approach to competence

The interpretative, inclusive approach to culture discussed in the previous section is also essential if the aim is to create real competence and not merely "knowledge" of or familiarity with cultural differences. The concept of competence is a dynamic mix of knowledge and ability indicating that mastery has been achieved in given professional or business environments. Another word for this concept is "proficiency" – high-level internalised knowledge linked to the ability to read, analyse and interpret specific, complex situations.

These process features – interactions of motivation, lived experience and uniqueness of context – make the concept of competence particularly appropriate to intercultural relations, especially where teachers are concerned. Fantini (2007) affirms that intercultural competence means the skills set needed to act effectively and appropriately in relation to linguistically and culturally diverse immigrants. The field of definition is so vast that 19 alternative terms have been coined to describe the concept (intercultural, cross-cultural or trans-cultural competence, global competence, multiculturalism, etc.).

In Italy, the concept refers mostly to the knowledge and ability of educational, social and healthcare professionals who interact with immigrants although intercultural competence increasingly seems not so much a quality or entity *per se* as an essential set of training resources for people who are aware of living in a complex world where encountering cultural difference is becoming the norm.

It should be stressed that intercultural competence training (whether delivered by or received from teachers and professionals) is, in the broadest sense, a *political* task because it is integral to our awareness of living in an interdependent world, and because it is connected to migration policy and the way states and their institutions are programmed and run. Teachers and social workers need to enhance their skills in dealing with such complexity and, in particular, their intercultural competence not only as educational professionals, but also as social actors on the cutting edge of their country's democratic development, endeavouring to promote equal rights for all citizens.

Models for the definition and evaluation of intercultural competence

In a recent survey, Sinicrope, Norris and Watanabe (2007) examined the various conceptual frameworks that have been used to define intercultural competence and the rating scales created to measure these in individuals. Some of these frameworks are discussed below in a pedagogical perspective to determine which of their aspects may be useful in developing appropriate training programmes for diversity and intercultural competence.

Ruben's model (1976), for example, lists seven dimensions of intercultural communication effectiveness. Byram (1997) affirms that intercultural competence involves five elements. The resulting model, which is appropriate both for school students and for adults, applies especially to linguistic communication.

One of the best known is the *Developmental Model of Intercultural Sensitivity* (DMIS) (Hammer, Bennett, and Wiseman, 2003), in which Bennett conceptualises the dimensions of an individual's intercultural awareness, *i.e.* experience in the broad sense – of cultural difference. The model's underlying assumption is that when an individual's experience of cultural difference becomes more complex and sophisticated, his or her potential competence in intercultural relations increases. In this constructivist perspective, cultural difference is a key event in our experience of reality. The model was developed to identify the attitudes and viewpoints (ranging from mono-cultural to more complex mindsets) in a person's development.

A different approach, this time from an education expert rather than a psychologist, comes from Banks (2006). The aim of his six-step model is to outline ideal-types that can help educators to identify how people experience their ethnic identities and to help develop them. The six steps are:

- captivity (internalisation of negative racial/ethnic stereotypes and beliefs)

- encapsulation (characterised by separatism)

- clarification (development of a healthy sense of one's own identity)

- bi-ethnicity (participation in cultures other than one's own)

- multiculturalism (interaction and involvement with several cultures)

- globalism (positive identification with the global dimension)

Deardorff's multidimensional model (2004) reappears in *Intercultural Competence – The Key Competence in the 21st Century (*2007), which is based on the American researcher's intercultural competence models. In her original Delphi study, Deardorff interviewed 23 American intercultural experts regarding key elements and appropriate methods of intercultural evaluation so as to draw up a checklist of definitions of *intercultural competence*. Deardorff then reduced the components of intercultural competence (as indicated by the experts) to four dimensions:

- *attitude* (openness, respect, curiosity, tolerance of ambiguity)

- *knowledge and skills* (cultural awareness, knowledge of one's own and other cultures, observation, ability to evaluate)

- *internal outcomes* (adaptability, flexibility, empathy, the ability to see things from another's point of view

- *external outcomes* (situation-appropriate behaviours and communication)

In the models we have examined, the most useful analyses of intercultural competence for the purposes of this study – *i.e.* models that actually *increase* competence, rather than merely define and describe it – are those that adopt a dynamic, multidimensional approach (Deardorff, 2007). This is because they enable us to consider not only the development of competence over time, but also the extent to which its elements influence each other.

Models of this type are concerned with how an individual attains the highest possible level of self-awareness (Bennett, 1986). Most importantly, they invite reflection on how intercultural competence is *constructed* (*e.g.* through encountering and relating to the "other") rather than merely how it is described. To the extent that competence is a question not only of *knowing* but also of *being* and *doing*, the ability to increase competence depends not so much on describing its content as on being able to experience and reflect on the interaction with people from other cultures that activates the necessary comprehension skills and abilities.

Box 8.1. Enhancing intercultural awareness: training model

1. INTERCULTURAL KNOWLEDGE

    a. Acquisition of a theoretical framework encompassing major intercultural issues and concepts (universal *vs.* relative, etc).

        i. Discussion of major ethical issues.

        ii. The ability to understand and describe the evolutionary, subjective, historical and dynamic aspects of cultures.

        iii. Interpreting cultural difference in ways that take into account individual subjectivity, rather than in terms of static, unyielding worldviews.

        iv. The ability to make informed ethical choices (*e.g.* universalistic *vs.* relativistic) when comparing cultures.

    b. Increased knowledge.

        i. Of the life sciences (anthropological, psychosocial and pedagogical aspects of integration, assimilation, inter-group relations, theories of prejudice, concepts of ethnic difference, race/racism).

        ii. Of geo-historical and socio-political issues (globalisation, geo-political information, migration and ethnic difference, migrants' countries of origin, the composition of multicultural societies).

        iii. Of language and linguistics (differences of idiom, verbal and non-verbal communication, sociolinguistic issues).

Box 8.1. **Enhancing intercultural awareness: training model** *(continued)*

2. INTERCULTURAL UNDERSTANDING

   a. Development of cultural sensitivity.

      i. The ability to acknowledge (accept) people who are different.

      ii. The acquisition of interpretative ability (relating to others as unique individuals, perceiving differences as variants of a shared humanity).

      iii. Encouraging de-centring/other-centredness (overcoming self-centredness so as to be able to adopt the other's point of view).

      iv. Empathy (an intentional process through which a profound relationship with the other is achieved by accepting his/her uniqueness while maintaining a sense of one's own personal autonomy and identity).

      v. Trust (a moral resource that makes sharing and co-operation possible).

      vi. Flexibility and emotional resilience (the ability to tolerate ambiguity and react to it in a constructive and appropriate way).

   b. Encouragement of self-reflection.

      i. Modifying and reconstructing one's previous attitudes and views.

      ii. Understanding how one's own thinking may be biased.

      iii. Questioning stereotypes and prejudices.

      iv. Developing a critical and dialectic approach.

3. INTERCULTURAL SKILLS

   a. Enhancement of relational skills.

      i. Developing the ability to communicate.

      ii. Developing the ability to handle emotional conflict and moral divergence, and to mediate and negotiate democratically.

      iii. Developing awareness of communication signals.

      iv. Developing the ability to handle stress and culture shock.

      v. Developing willingness to engage in new activities and experiences, and to interact with people in new situations.

Box 8.1. **Enhancing intercultural awareness: training model** *(continued)*

b. Construction of methodological tools that can add an intercultural perspective to working and professional activities.

   i. Developing the competences needed to gather ethnographic data on pupils, their families and their socio-cultural environment, and then to interpret and apply it in strategy building.

   ii. Developing the competences needed to review school subjects and informal system content in an intercultural perspective.

   iii. Acquiring the knowledge and skills needed to handle direct contact with people from other cultures.

Structuring the training

Having surveyed academic models of competence and the components of intercultural training, the following section outlines a training programme designed to enhance the intercultural awareness of social workers and teachers professionally involved in ethnic diversity. This training model incorporates the dynamic, multidimensional features appropriate to training in a complex field, and is based on the three classic dimensions of intercultural training – *knowing*, *being* and *doing*.

The training model above has a number of specific features:

- The concept of culture is dynamic and subjective (it is people who enter into contact with each other, not cultures). This means that competence rests on an anthropological interpretation of reality rather than on knowledge of preordained notions.

- Personality and self-reflection are crucial because they make affectivity the basis of cultural relations. In this sense, training must act on the personalities of teachers and social workers, who in turn must "mediate" or facilitate understanding between people from different cultures. For example, various studies have shown the tendency of some teachers to have stereotypes regarding immigrants. A critical analysis of his or her own stereotypes may help him or her to mediate problems between Italian families and immigrant families.

- The various elements are mutually influential. For example, interest in and respect for the other determine the ability to communicate which, once learned, can create empathy. Revisiting one's stereotypes and prejudices creates openness, and openness is, in turn, a necessary condition for self-reflection.

- Training is not limited to promoting the ability for tolerance and mere acceptance, which would mean leaving people in separate spaces that never intersect. To achieve training objectives and overcome prejudice and cultural misunderstandings, it is not enough to know about the other culture: a third space of trust and mutual transformation needs to be constructed, in which people are prepared to adapt to each other (Marandon, 2001, 2003).

- Intercultural competence has an ethical-political dimension because it fosters a global, non-nationalistic concept of citizenship based on interdependence and peaceful understanding between peoples.

These elements constitute a working basis that can be adapted to the varying needs of teachers and the contexts in which they find themselves. The self-reflective nature of the approach suggests a personalised form of training, as trainees can decide how they want to communicate their experiences and theoretical insights. This individual work can be the basis upon which the trainer develops additional skills in the trainees. To be effective, programmes of this type need active methodologies – discussion, case study, simulation, role-playing, problem-solving, exploration of cultural dilemmas and culture shock – that can personalise learning, and tools that encourage self-reflection (*e.g.* logs, self-assessment, narrative writing, literary criticism, portfolios). These activities should be done in a group setting with other teachers.

The connection between theoretical knowledge and practice is fundamental to this training curriculum, and takes the form of frequent or less frequent (depending on need) alternations of work experience, traineeship/teaching practice, extramural activities, and periods spent abroad or living in minority communities. It is also essential that trainees are expected to report on the competence they have acquired by producing a teaching or educational project.

Trainees' thoughts on intercultural competence

The training programme outlined above was tested as a component of the M.A. in Intercultural Training in the Faculty of Education (Facoltà di Scienze della Formazione) at the Catholic University of Milan in the academic year 2007/2008. To test some of the programme's hypotheses, the 28 participants were asked to fill in a short questionnaire of six open questions. The participants, who came from varying backgrounds (teachers, social workers, university students, professionals), had already completed Module I of the M.A., consisting of courses and workshops on intercultural education and anthropological and communication models of particular relevance to migration issues. The aim of our questionnaire was to explore some of the *autobiographical aspects* of the participants' experience, *i.e.* their knowledge and beliefs concerning the intercultural sphere when they filled in the questionnaire, and the experiences (professional, cultural, daily life, etc.) that had helped shape their opinions. The *training aspects* of the questionnaire were designed to elicit the definitions and aims of intercultural competence resulting from the participants' experience of the course. The perceptions of students intending to become teachers in intercultural contexts are especially useful because they suggest practical ways of improving competence (Mushi, 2004).

In their descriptions of the knowledge and beliefs they thought they possessed (as a result of training or otherwise), all the participants discovered, in their various ways, that the dynamic process of intercultural relations was fundamental to any kind of meaningful intercultural relationship. Half of them (14) stressed the social dimension because they saw intercultural relations as a pervasive feature of both daily life and society as a whole. In their view, the social dimension is an aspect not only of ethnic relations in the narrow sense, but also of the ability to relate to other people in general through dialogue and mutual respect. Intercultural activity is, then, a *way* of encountering and coping with the range of thought-processes typical of complex societies.

Five students laid even more emphasis on the idea of inter-relationship and the notion that mutual transformation and influence leads people not only to compare themselves with others, but also to question who they are in their search for shared values.

Finally, nine students related their heightened awareness of the social dimension to the conceptual content of the course itself (essentialism, the subjectivity of culture, universalism *versus* relativism, etc).

The participants also had to indicate, in the "training" section of the questionnaire, their definition of intercultural competence. In terms of the three dimensions of the training model (*knowing, being, doing*), there was a marked preference for intercultural sensitivity and understanding (being). Twenty of the 28 students stressed that self-reflection was a fundamental part of competence: the ability to risk, to be self-critical, to re-examine their beliefs, to be able to see things from another's point of view and so on. Of these 20 students, five expressed this idea in an explicitly "relativistic" way (with non-judgemental openness, unconditional acceptance, etc.), while another seven stressed the *transformative* power of intercultural competence (achieving competence entails changing all one's partners, creating mutual understanding, searching for shared values and the things that bring people together).

By contrast, only four participants chose knowing (knowledge) as their main definition of competence (*"understanding of theoretical intercultural concepts", "knowledge of socio-political and life sciences"*). Another four opted for the third dimension (doing), the ability to communicate, relate and negotiate (*"the ability to listen and communicate effectively"*).

Conclusions and next steps

This chapter has reviewed a number of theoretical models to identify the salient dimensions of intercultural competence. A brief survey of participants in an M.A. course in Intercultural Training confirmed the programme's initial assumptions, in particular the dynamic, transformative nature of intercultural competence training in which sensitivity, understanding, critical reprocessing of personal experience and self-reflection (introspection) are of key importance.

The conclusions suggest a new training programme designed to increase the intercultural competence of teachers and social workers involved in intercultural contexts, especially in situations of conflict and racism that appear to be present in Italian society today. It is necessary to continue the research in order to understand the impact of this training on participants, and in particular, teachers' intercultural competences should be evaluated according to the three aforementioned levels (intercultural knowledge, understanding and skills). Future steps of this research will include evaluating intercultural competences of a group of teachers before and after the training through the use of a questionnaire and other methodology.

The research will be accompanied by a specific assessment, consisting of the collection of continuous monitoring data of teachers' training to identify the impact of intercultural training. The evaluation will be designed to reveal the evolution and critical aspects of the various dimensions of intercultural competence – intercultural knowledge, understanding and skills. These elements will be gathered from a group of teachers who attend a post-graduate intercultural training course who are simultaneously actively teaching in schools. The characteristics of the participants will be observed throughout the training course to shed light on the learning process and weak points relative to skills mastered or acquired. A final round of data collection will be performed at the end of the training regarding the skills developed.

We will employ methodological tools that encourage the ability of teachers to reflect on their training and professional experience. The data on skills developed will be analysed by the participants along with intercultural training experts, through a dialogue that develops awareness and critical capacity. The tools to be utilised are suitable for research and individual evaluation (personal themes, diaries, case analyses, interviews) as well as for group evaluation: brainstorming and the "scale of required priorities" (Bezzi, Palumbo, 1997), focus groups, and case analyses carried out within the group. The data gathered will be used to form evaluation judgments to be discussed and shared with teachers. These judgments will be formulated using specific criteria and relevant indicators which will be identified with the teachers in the establishment phase of the intercultural training assessment.

References

Abdallah Pretceille, M. (1990), *Vers une Pédagogie Interculturelle*, Publications de la Sorbonne, Paris.

Abdallah Pretceille, M. (2006), "Interculturalism as a Paradigm for Thinking about Diversity", *Intercultural Education*, Vol. 5, pp. 475-483.

Allemann-Ghionda, C., Perregaux, C., de Goumoens, C. (1999), *Curriculum pour une Formation des Enseignant(e)s à la Pluralité Culturelle et Linguistique*, Programme national de recherche 33 (Centre suisse de coordination pour la recherche en éducation – CSRE), Genève.

Banks, J.A. (2006), *Cultural Diversity and Education. Foundations, Curriculum, and Teaching* (5th edition), Allyn and Bacon, Boston.

Bennett, M.J. (1986), "A Developmental Approach to Training to Intercultural Sensitivity", *International Journal of Intercultural Relations*, Vol. 2, pp. 179-186.

Bennett, M.J. (1993), "Toward Ethno-relativism: A Developmental Model of Intercultural Sensitivity", in R.M. Paige (ed.), *Education for Intercultural Experience*, Intercultural Press, Yarmouth, pp. 21-71.

Bennett, M.J. (2002), *Principi di Comunicazione Interculturale*, Franco Angeli, Milano.

Bezzi, C., and Palumbo, M. (1997) (eds.), *Valutazione: Materiali di Lavoro*, Arnaud – Gramma, Perugia.

Bhawuk, D.P.S., and Brislin, R. (1992), "The Measurement of Intercultural Sensitivity Using the Concept of Individualism and Collectivism", *International Journal of Intercultural Relations,* Vol. 16, pp. 413-436.

Byram, M. (1997), *Teaching and Assessing Intercultural Communicative Competence*, Multilingual Matters, Clevedon.

Camilleri, C., Cohen Emerique. M. (eds.) (1989), *Choc de Cultures. Concepts et Enjeux Pratiques de l'Interculturel*, L'Harmattan, Paris.

Clanet, C. (2000/1), "L'Interculturel et la Formation des Maitres: Institution et Subjectivation", in Dasen, P.R. and C. Perregaux (eds.), *Pourquoi des approches interculturelles en sciences de l'éducation? Raisons Educatives*, Vol. 2, No. 3, pp. 223-242.

Cuche, D. (2003), *La Notion de Culture dans les Sciences Sociales,* La Découverte, Paris.

Cui, Geng., and S. A. van den Berg (1991), "Testing the Construct Validity of Intercultural Effectiveness", *International Journal of Intercultural Relations*, Vol. 15, pp. 227-241.

Deardoff, D.K. (2004), "The Identification and Assessment of Intercultural Competence as a Student Outcome of Internalization at Institutions of Higher Education in the United States", Ph.D Thesis, North Carolina State University.

Deardoff, D.K. (2006), Identification and Assessment of Intercultural Competence as a Student Outcome of Internationalization, *Journal of Studies in International Education* Vol. 10, pp. 241-266.

Fantini, A.E. (2007), *Exploring and Assessing Intercultural Competence,* Center for Social Development Research Report, Washington, DC., *www.sit.edu/ publications/docs/feil_research_report.pdf 2006.*

Geertz, C. (2000), *Available Light: Anthropological Reflections on Philosophical Topics,* Princeton University Press, Princeton, NY.

Glaser, E., M. Guilherme, M. Méndez Garcia and T. Mughan (2007), *ICOPROMO – Compétence Interculturelle pour le Développement de la Mobilité Professionnelle*, Editions du Conseil de l'Europe, Strasbourg.

Hammer, M.R., M.J. Bennett and R. Wiseman (2003), "Measuring Intercultural Sensitivity; the Intercultural Development Inventory", *International Journal of Intercultural Relations* Vol. 27, pp. 421-443.

Hannerz, U. (2001), *La Diversità Culturale,* Il mulino, Bologna.

Hofstede, G. (1980), *Culture's Consequence: International Differences in Work Related Values*, Sage Publications, Beverly Hills.

Kelley, C. and J. Meyers (1992), *The Cross-Cultural Adaptability Inventory*, National Computer Systems, Minneapolis.

Lázár, I., M. Huber-Kriegler, D. Lussier, G.S. Matei and C. Peck (eds.) (2007), *Developing and Assessing Intercultural Communicative Competence – A Guide for Language Teachers and Teacher Educators*, Conseil de l'Europe / Centre européen pour les langues vivantes, Strasbourg / Graz.

Olson, C.L. and K.R. Kroeger (2001), "Global Competency and Intercultural Sensitivity", *Journal of Studies in International Education*, Vol. 5, No. 2, pp. 116-137.

Marandon, G. (2001), *L'Empathie et la Rencontre Interculturelle*, L'Harmattan, Paris.

Marandon, G (2003), "Au-delà de l'Empathie, Cultiver la Confiance: Clés pour la Rencontre Interculturelle", *Revista CIDOB d'Afers Internacionals*, Vol. 61, No. 6, pp. 259-282.

Milhouse, V.H. (1996), "Intercultural Communication Education and Training Goals, Content, and Methods", *Intercultural Journal of Intercultural Relations*, Vol. 20, pp. 69-95.

Mushi, S. (2004), "Multicultural Competencies in Teaching : A Typology of Classroom Activities", *Intercultural Education,* Vol. 15, 179-194.

Ouellet, F. (1991), *L'Education Interculturelle. Essai sur le Contenu de la Formation des Maitres*, L'Harmattan, Paris.

Ouellet, F. (2002), *Les Défis du Pluralisme en Education. Essais sur la Formation Interculturelle*. Les Presses de l'Université Laval – L'Harmattan, St. Nicolas (Quebec), Paris.

Ruben, B.D. (1976), "Assessing Communication Competence for Intercultural Communication Adaptation", *Group and Organization Studies*, Vol. 1, No. 3, pp. 334-354.

Santerini, M. (2002), "La Formation des Enseignants à l'Interculturel : Modèles et Pratiques", *Carrefour de l'éducation,* Vol. 14, pp. 97-104.

Santerini, M. (2003), *Intercultura*, La Scuola, Brescia.

Santerini, M. and P. Reggio (2004), "La Scuola dell'altro. Intercultura e Formazione degli Insegnanti", in V.Cesareo (ed.), *L'altro. Identità, Dialogo e Conflitto nella Società Plurale,* Vita e Pensiero, Milano, pp. 261-302.

Santerini, M. (2008), "School Mix e Distribuzione degli Alunni Immigrati nelle Scuole Italiane", *Mondi Migranti*, Vol. 3, pp. 235-249.

Sercu, L. (2004), "Assessing Intercultural Competence: A Framework for Systematic Test Development in Foreign Language Education and Beyond", *Intercultural Education*, Vol.15, No. 1, pp. 73-89.

Sinicrope, C., J. Norris and Y. Watanabe (2007), *Understanding and Assessing Intercultural Competence: A Summary of Theory, Research, and Practice*, Technical Report for the Foreign Language Program Evaluation Project 2007, *http://nflrc.hawaii.edu/evaluation/publications.htm.*

Sleeter, C.E. (2001), "Preparing Teachers for Culturally Diverse Schools. Research and the Overwhelming Presence of Whiteness", *Journal of Teacher Education*, Vol. 52, 94-106.

Vinsonneau, G. (2002), *L'identité culturelle*, Armand Colin, Paris.

Part III

Moving into practice

Chapter 9

From homogeneity to diversity in German education

Anne Sliwka

Heidelberg University of Education, Germany

Germany is currently changing its self-perception as it shifts from a culturally homogenous nation to a more pluralistic society shaped by immigration. Education is thus evolving to be more inclusive although heterogeneity is still considered a challenge with which to cope rather than a potential strength. This approach can be compared with countries that have longer histories of immigration, such as Canada, having moved from merely "dealing with heterogeneity" to embracing diversity as a resource for education. Teacher education plays a key role in this transition, and there are many approaches it can use to facilitate this shift. These approaches range from increasing the intake of teacher trainees with diverse backgrounds, to applying didactic approaches that will encourage communication about their different identities, to exploring basic philosophical concepts such as diversity, identity and controversy.

From the OECD online consultation : resistance to change

The perceived importance of diversity issues varied across countries and contexts. Although many practitioners acknowledged its significance, in some countries there was still resistance to addressing diversity in education systems.

Introduction: changing perceptions of German reality

Understanding diversity in the German educational system calls for first taking a broader look at diversity and how it is regarded in German society. As is the case in most OECD member countries, Germany's perception of itself has been changing rapidly in recent years. Even if ethnic, linguistic and religious plurality have been a reality in Germany since the 1960s, the country has not come to terms with this fundamental change from its longstanding image of itself as a homogeneous society until a decade ago.

The "economic miracle" of the 1960s triggered an influx of foreign workers from Greece, Italy, Spain and Turkey. Immigrants into Germany were called "Gastarbeiter", guest workers, because of the assumption that they would eventually be returning to their home countries. In reality, most not only remained but brought their families from their home country to Germany. This influx of immigrant families has changed the demography of German classrooms. In the past 30 years, most classrooms in the urban areas of Germany (particularly in former West Germany) have become multicultural.

Germany: an immigrant society?

The perception of "foreigners" living "temporarily" in Germany began to change when German politicians of all parties realised that the absence of an official policy to accommodate immigrants had created a parallel world of immigrant communities outside mainstream German society (with ensuing social problems),. This delayed awareness is not without repercussions. With the beginning of the new millennium, the need to develop an understanding of Germany as a nation of "immigration" has found an increasingly stronger voice.

The successful integration of individuals with an immigrant background has become the declared aim of successive governments (Bommes and Krüger-Potratz, 2008). The current political discourse considers an immigrant to be successfully integrated if he or she speaks and writes German fluently and is able to participate fully in the education system and the labour market to earn a living. Whereas well-integrated immigrants were also expected to adopt German customs and cultural traits, the concept of diversity as an asset is slowly becoming tangible in the country's fabric. In recent years, several of the large private foundations have started programmes to support gifted migrant students on their way into higher education and positions of leadership. The Green Party is the first political party to have elected a chairman with an immigrant background, the son of Turkish workers born in Germany. The other political parties are opening their ranks to individuals with immigrant backgrounds, increasingly making them common-place rather than merely token figures. At the same time, Germany is still reluctant to ensure that minority groups are equally represented in the government and to grant immigrants without European citizenship full political rights at the local level.

Other diversity issues: gender equality and inclusion of individuals with special needs

Seen from the outside, media reports of xenophobia in some parts of the country make it seem as if Germany has a problem with linguistic, cultural and religious diversity. But to grasp Germany's persistent discomfort with perceiving diversity as an asset rather than a problem, one must look beyond the cultural dimension of diversity. This discomfort also becomes apparent when examining gender and special needs.

For example, in spite of Angela Merkel being one of the few female heads of state in OECD member countries, women are significantly underrepresented in the higher ranks of German companies and universities. The majority of leadership positions in business and academia are held by white men of German origin. A highly emotional public debate on the compatibility of raising children and having a professional career is indicative of the lingering uncertainty regarding gender roles. It has taken Germany longer than many other OECD countries to ensure public infrastructure for high-quality early childcare that enables both women and men to pursue careers and have children without remorse. It is only in the past four years that a coalition government, formed by the two big left-of-centre and right-of-centre parties, decided to make the necessary infrastructure investments while providing pecuniary incentives.

Another challenging learning process with regard to diversity has been the debate about inclusive education for disabled students and students with learning disabilities or behavioural problems (Wansing, 2005). After the persecution of disabled individuals under the Nazi regime, post-war Germany felt a special obligation towards the disabled, which resulted in the creation of an intricate system of special schools for the various forms of special educational needs. Special schools were created for the deaf, the blind and for individuals with other forms of physical disability as well as for children and youth with learning disabilities or behavioural problems. The underlying assumption was that those with special needs would get the best possible developmental support if they were taken out of mainstream schooling and were taught and cared for by teachers with specialist training. The argument was that special needs required special investments in highly specialised institutions. Special schools were well-equipped and special needs teachers well-paid, highly qualified professionals, working outside the main school system.

In spite of recurrent debates about being more inclusive, the overall system of separating students with various special needs from students in mainstream education remained fundamentally unchanged for 50 years. Finally, parents – most of them with an academic background – of disabled children began to challenge the idea that their children had to be separated from mainstream education in order to get optimal support. They felt that special education in separate institutions failed to deliver the educational outcomes their children needed for graduating. For many years, a vocal but comparatively small group of parents legally challenged the system. Some of them were successful, achieving for their child (but not for disabled children in general) the right to be educated in a mainstream school.

In recent years, some of the German Länder* have responded by creating more integrated schools, predominantly in primary education. Yet it was not until Germany ratified the United Nations Convention for the Rights of the Disabled on 1 January 2009 that legal certainty for individuals with special needs was finally achieved. They can now demand to be fully integrated into mainstream schools and receive the individual support needed to succeed. This is an important milestone towards diversity in education.

Early selection and educational stratification as a barrier to diversity

Mainstream education at the secondary level is highly stratified in several ways. As educational policy is the responsibility of the 16 individual German states, it is difficult to make universally valid statements about the

---

* *i.e.* "states".

German school system. Compared with most other school systems across the OECD, the German system shows several specificities:

1. After four (in some states, six) years of elementary schooling for all, children's schooling continues in different types of schools based on an assessment of their competence level at ages nine to eleven.

2. Despite the common perception that Germany has a tripartite school system, the reality is more complex. In addition to different types of mainstream secondary schools, most German Länder still maintain a large number of special schools for children with physical and learning disabilities or behavioural challenges. Furthermore, several of the German Länder have created new highly selective special schools for gifted students. It would thus be more correct to speak of a four or five-partite school system.

For individuals socialised in comprehensive school systems, it is often difficult to understand the logic behind a system that sustains so many separate institutional tracks of schooling for students at such a young age. It is one of the core issues and should be more closely examined as Germany begins to move towards a culture of diversity.

The fundamental paradigm that has underlaid and shaped German education is the assumption that the homogeneity of learners in a group best facilitates their individual learning. Thinking along the lines of a "norm", and deviations from it, has a long history in German educational thought (Tillmann, 2006). When asked about the most challenging task for teachers in classrooms, early German educational thinker Johann Friedrich Herbart (1776-1841) responded, "The difference in heads". The first German professor of education, Ernst Christian Trapp (1745-1818) at Halle University wrote, "As it is impossible to take into account everyone's individual, special and momentary disposition in a heap of children who are educated and trained together, teachers should base their work on the approximate average" (Trapp, 1780). Trapp's advice to teachers was to cater to the needs of the *Mittelköpfe*, the "middle heads" or average students in a given class. This approach developed a long-standing consensus on certain norms that provided guidance for selecting and sorting children into the "right" type of school for them. This resulted in allegedly homogenous groupings in the various institutional tracks of the German system:

- *Förderschule*, a special-needs school for students with behavioural or developmental challenges;

- *Hauptschule*, a lower-track school traditionally geared towards educating future blue-collar workers;

- *Realschule*, traditionally geared towards future white-collar workers without a university education;

- *Gymnasium*, a cognitively more demanding type of school with an upper secondary level leading to higher education; and

- special schools for the gifted – a small number of schools with an enriched and accelerated curriculum.

This excessive tracking enabled the idea of homogeneity in German education to continue for so long.

The didactic focus on "the average" within these different types of schools has been paralysing the German education system. Calculating resources on the basis of the "average" legitimises uniform teaching for large groups: equal aims, equal content, equal learning steps, equal amount of time assigned for learning, and equal criteria for success. It is not surprising that in a culture of alleged homogeneity, assessment has predominately been norm-referenced, *i.e.* focusing on a given peer group. The paradigm of homogeneity required that learners were seen as similar in many ways and that differences were deliberately not acknowledged. Those in the same school and in the same classroom were treated the same, regardless of their interests and abilities.

Studies on teachers and the teaching profession have shown that an orientation along the lines of the "average students" in class has become almost impossible, given the cultural, socio-economic and linguistic differences in almost all of today's classrooms (Gomolla, 2005; Gomolla and Radtke, 2009). Reliable data on the makeup of German classrooms along these lines is scant, however (Stanat and Segeritz, 2009). The lack of awareness of diversity issues meant that these data were not collected, and as a result, educational accountability with regard to diversity is still in its infancy. It was only in 2006 that the German government began to publish diversity-related data in its biannual report on the state of education in Germany, but compared to data available in North America, for example, they lack disaggregation (Autorengruppe Bildungsberichterstattung, 2009).

Psychological and neuroscience research published at the end of the 20th century has finally encouraged German educators to start seeing every child as a unique human being with great individual potential to learn and develop. Ideas of reformist pedagogy are now making their way into mainstream schooling. Many primary schools are now applying didactic approaches developed by Maria Montessori, Celestin Freinet and other reformist pedagogies of a century ago. Mixed-age groupings as developed in the Jena-Plan pedagogy can now be found in more or less conventional state schools.

Primary school teachers have long known for a long time that homogeneity does not exist in education. But even for the secondary level, the OECD's

PISA study, analysing the educational outcomes of students from the different types of schools in Germany, showed that there are learners at the *Realschule* who perform better than students at the *Gymnasium*, and some students at the *Hauptschule* sometimes surpass the results of those at the *Realschule*-level. No matter how much effort is invested in selecting wisely, the result is never a truly homogenous grouping of learners. The data collected in the context of the PISA study also revealed profound equity issues in the German education system (Baumert, Stanat and Watermann, 2006; Stanat and Christensen, 2006). Immigrant students and students with an immigrant background, *i.e.* those whose parents and even grandparents migrated to Germany, are severely over-represented in the lower tracks of the German secondary school system, even when allowing for differences in cognitive ability and grade average at primary school level. Children of parents with little formal education are also significantly disadvantaged. While this applies to German and immigrant children alike, immigrant children are especially affected since parents from certain immigrant communities often have little formal education. In other words, schools are currently unable to remediate differences in educational background.

From homogeneity to heterogeneity in German education

While the school system has not yet changed significantly, several changes at the micro-level indicate a shift in thinking among those responsible for the education system. Individualised support, *Individuelle Förderung*; differentiation within the classroom, *Binnendifferenzierung*; and heterogeneity, *Heterogenität*; are the buzz words of the current educational debate. Not only do they shape the educational research agenda (chairs in education are now being redesignated to encompass these new concepts); regional and national policy programmes also aim to strengthen the system's capacity to deal productively with the heterogeneity of students and their needs.

One example of the change in what is perceived to be "best practice" is the German School Award, first offered in 2006 by a group of influential German foundations. It was established to single out and make widely known mainstream schools that have successfully responded to the educational and equity challenges that PISA and other studies have exposed. It is quite revealing that although diversity is one of the six criteria for the nomination of award-winning schools, this aspect is referred to as "Dealing with Diversity", which sounds equally reserved in German (*Umgang mit Vielfalt*). The award is given to schools "that have found ways and means to deal productively with the different educational backgrounds, interests and abilities of their students, with their cultural and national origin, their family's educational history, and their gender; to schools that effectively compensate disadvantages and continuously and strategically support individualised learning." In other words, diversity is not celebrated but something with which to cope.

The award-winning schools:

- Take in learners with different abilities and disabilities.

- Apply diagnostic assessment to find out what kind of support each child needs to be able to learn and develop successfully, taking into account prior learning and aiming to organise learning in each student's "zone of proximal development".

- Personalise learning, apply peer learning and provide individualised support for learning.

- Have changed their culture of assessment to move away from norm-referenced towards self-referenced and criterion-referenced formative feedback. Rather than comparing individual children with other children in the classroom, every child's development is considered separately. Children and parents receive feedback on the child's learning progress in relation to the child's previous development and in relation to a rubric of overall learning goals.

However, it is important to bear in mind that these schools are not yet representative of the German school system. More and more teachers are adopting these practices, but their work is not always part of a whole-school approach. Wherever there is a whole-school approach, it tends to stem from strong school leadership and local support for change.

From homogeneity to heterogeneity: the difficult process of changing deep-seated mental models

As a teacher educator, I have often noticed that German teacher trainees' mental concept of schooling is deeply influenced by the school system in which they have been socialised. Many students in teacher education have understood the need to diversify pedagogical and didactic strategies applied in the classroom, yet at the same time they perceive the differences among learners as one of the most challenging tasks they will face. In a way, they are right. Given the fact that early selection of students into the various types of schooling has been the norm in German education, the equally separate institutional tracks for teacher education did not recognise the need to develop pedagogies and teaching strategies to productively deal with diverse student abilities, interests and needs. Teacher education is now beginning to focus on the different developmental stages (childhood, early adolescence, late adolescence), rather than on the different tracks.

This change is taking place alongside other shifts in the system. After PISA, the old way of early selection and alleged homogeneity has lost much of its credibility (Auernheim, 2006; Gogolin, 2008; Neumann 2008).

Empirical educational research is receiving massive funding. Many young researchers are examining the equity issues at stake. Additional issues are coming to the fore. Education for heterogeneity is not only about doing justice to each individual's learning needs, it is also about the development of the social and democratic skills that a pluralistic society needs to flourish, and it is about understanding the mutual benefits society as a whole (and smaller communities and groups within it) can gain from a wide range of abilities, perspectives, interests and skills.

This learning process in German education has allowed for a paradigm shift from homogeneity to heterogeneity, but can go even further.

Futures thinking: from heterogeneity to diversity

Societies with longer histories of ongoing immigration seem to have responded with more thorough and sustainable school change to address the kind of challenges facing Germany today. I first noticed this during a research stay in Ontario/Canada in the late 1990s. I remember being very impressed at the time by the fact that teacher trainees in practice teaching not only had to have a curricular and didactic understanding of how they were going to teach but also needed to show an elaborate and well-developed plan about how they were going to work with a specific diverse class to enhance social cohesion in the classroom and to teach pro-social values and social skills.

As a prerequisite, these trainees needed to have substantial knowledge about the students with whom they were working: their ethnic, cultural, religious and socio-economic background, their level of language acquisition and their educational history. That requirement in itself significantly broadened the knowledge base of teacher training. I hardly ever heard the term "heterogeneity" in Canadian schools and universities. It seemed to me that the system had moved one step further. Whereas the paradigm of heterogeneity perceives difference as a challenge to be dealt with actively, diversity as a systemic paradigm perceives difference as an asset. The pedagogy that I came to know there was based on the idea that difference between individuals is one of the most important resources for mutual learning. A world without difference of interests, abilities and perspectives, on the one hand, and differences in cultural, religious and ethnic identities, on the other hand, would have been considered a barren learning environment. This educational philosophy was very different from what I had learned during my own education in Germany and proved to be a real eye-opener. As I will show later, there is much to be learned from this different mindset for teachers and teacher educators in Germany.

Figure 9.1. **Paradigm shifts: from homogeneity to heterogeneity to diversity**

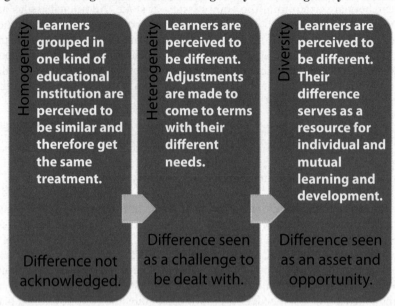

I would like to argue that German education has taken some important steps in the right direction in recent years but would have to make more significant changes to reap the fruits of diversity in education. "Schools of diversity" would move beyond the schools of heterogeneity that we currently see emerging (see Figure 9.1). In addition to diagnostic and formative assessment as well as personalised learning and individual support for learning, the German education system would have to make full use of diversity, perceiving and communicating it as a core value and a key resource of education that needs to be cherished, safeguarded and fully explored. To do that, individuals would have to be perceived as having multiple, hybrid and changing identities. Their cultural knowledge and the individual perspective would be valued and used as a resource for learning, not just in socio-emotional but also in cognitive terms.

All of this would require not only changes in the structure of the German education system but also in the organisation of learning. This would require strengthening norms of mutual support and peer learning, a culture of formative assessment based on self-referencing and criterion-referencing, elements of choice and self-determination in learning, and finally a culture of public deliberation and citizenship. There is a long road ahead to make this vision come true, but Germans have already made strides in this direction, and they should go further.

The potential role of teacher education as a change agent

As a teacher educator, I ask myself about the role of teacher education in the development of a culture of diversity. These are the steps that we ought to be taking in the coming years:

- Teacher education institutions need to increase the intake of students with diverse backgrounds, for example, by actively recruiting students from immigrant families and students with disabilities.

- Teaching and learning in initial teacher education need to make use of diversity to enhance student awareness of diversity as a resource for learning. This implies deliberately taking the perspectives of different students into account and applying didactic approaches that will draw students into communicating about their different identities and perspectives in a respectful manner.

- In teacher education courses, students should have opportunities to explore basic philosophical concepts such as diversity, identity, democracy, pluralism, controversy and deliberation. This will allow students to make connections and understand the bigger picture.

- Teacher education needs to significantly broaden its knowledge base to incorporate cultural and psychological knowledge on cultural, religious, ethnic and gender identities as well as intercultural communication. Any manager sent abroad is now required to undergo training in intercultural communication – why not do the same for teacher trainees?

- Training in foreign languages, internships and study abroad should become a requirement for teacher trainees as it will enable them to extend their frames of reference. Having experienced another culture firsthand, they will be more understanding of other cultures at home or even develop an understanding of culture itself as hybrid and changing.

- Students in teacher education programmes should take advantage of the learning opportunities that exemplary schools offer so that they may observe and apply "best practice" in diversity education. Internships in local schools with highly diverse populations would provide teacher trainees with essential classroom practice.

These are steps that German teacher education will have to make in the coming years. Many teacher trainees and teachers are eagerly looking for tools that will help them succeed in their diverse classrooms. On the other hand, there are others who simply feel that addressing diversity means extra work. Thus, changing the way the German educational systems views and embraces diversity also entails cultural change in the society at large, and that, as we all know, takes time.

References

Auernheimer, Georg (2006), *Schieflagen im Bildungssystem. Die Benachteiligung der Migrantenkinder, Wiesbaden*, VS Verlag für Sozialwissenschaften 2006.

Autorengruppe Bildungsberichterstattung (2008), *Bildung in Deutschland 2008. Ein indikatorengestützter Bericht mit einer Analyse zu Übergängen im Anschluss an den Sekundarbereich I, www.bildungs-bericht.de* [18.9.2008].

Baumert, Jürgen, Petra Stanat and Rainer Watermann (eds.) (2006), *Herkunftsbedingte Disparitäten im Bildungswesen, Differenzielle Bildungsprozesse und Probleme der Verteilungsgerechtigkeit: Vertiefende Analysen im Rahmen von PISA 2000,* VS Verlag, Wiesbaden.

Bommes, Michael and Marianne Krüger-Potratz (eds.) (2008), *Migrationsreport 2008: Fakten – Analysen – Perspektiven*, Campus, Frankfurt am Main.

Gogolin, Ingrid (2008), "Migration und Bildungsgerechtigkeit", in Liebau, Eckart and Jörg Zirfas (eds.), *Ungerechtigkeit der Bildung – Bildung der Ungerechtigkeit*. Opladen (Barbara Budrich), S. 55-68

Gomolla, Mechthild (2005), *Schulentwicklung in der Einwanderungsgesellschaft. Strategien gegen institutionelle Diskriminierung in Deutschland, England und in der Schweiz*, Waxmann, Münster.

Gomolla, Mechthild and Frank-Olaf Radtke (2009), *Institutionelle Diskriminierung: Die Herstellung ethnischer Differenz in der Schule*, VS Verlag, Wiesbaden.

Neumann, Ursula (2008), "Integration and Education in Germany", in, Becker, Frans, Karl Duffek and Tobias Mörschel (eds.), *Social Democracy and Education*, Mets & Schilt, Amsterdam, pp. 198-220.

Stanat, Petra and Michael Segeritz (2009), "Migrationsbezogene Indikatoren für eine Bildungsberichterstattung", in R. Tippelt (ed.), *Steuerung durch Indikatoren? Methodologische und theoretische Reflexionen zur deut-*

schen und internationalen Bildungsberichterstattung, Barbara Budrich, Opladen, pp. 141-156.

Stanat, Petra and Gayle Christensen (2006), *Where Immigrant Students Succeed – A Comparative Review of Performance and Engagement in PISA 2003,* OECD, Paris.

Tillmann, Klaus-Jürgen (2006), *Lehren und Lernen in heterogenen Schülergruppen: Forschungsstand und Perspektiven, http://www. reformzeit.de/fileadmin/reformzeit/dokumente/pdf/heterogenitaet_tillmann.pdf* [18.10.2009].

Wansing, Gudrun (2005), *Teilhabe an der Gesellschaft: Menschen mit Behinderung zwischen Inklusion und Exklusion,* VS Verlag, Wiesbaden.

Chapter 10

Teacher education for diversity in Spain: moving from theory to practice

Miquel Angel Essomba
Autonomous University of Barcelona, Spain

The school and teacher education systems in Spain have traditionally considered students who were "different" as a problem to be addressed rather than as an opportunity to learn. Recent educational reforms have required not only that diversity be accepted as a reality but have also emphasised it as an asset. These reforms have also stated that teacher education must be redesigned for this to be formally reflected. However, moving from theory to practice is not always easy and changing minds and culture takes time and resources. For a first impression of this process, this chapter looks at the status and role of diversity issues in the curricula of four Spanish universities offering new degrees in teacher education (academic year 2009-10). Initial observations indicate that the system has not yet been reformed successfully and that it could be a result of simply changing discourse instead of practices.

> *From the OECD online consultation :*
> *diversity as an asset – moving from*
> *theory to practice*
>
> **One strategy often suggested by teachers was that diversity be considered a "resource" and not a "problem". This is easier said than done as changing behaviours and attitudes require ongoing support and guidance.**

Introduction

For diversity to be valued and not treated as a difficult reality with which school systems must cope, proper teacher education is crucial. While it is crucial to implement strategies to transform this into reality, this is an extremely complex endeavour. The underlying difficulties may be identified around two issues: teacher education in general and the role of diversity in education. This chapter first analyses the challenges surrounding teacher education and diversity in Spain in order to provide an understanding of the past and shed light on the current situation. It then provides a number of ideas that emerge from the Spanish case, opening new paths for further research and innovative action.

Teacher education in Spain: background

The Spanish teacher education system comes from a strongly inspired rationalistic paradigm (Perez Gomez, 2007), in which, for the last three or four decades, teacher education has been developed according to particular principles, including:

- The mission of schools is to provide academic knowledge to young students in order to prepare them for further education.

- Teacher education is based on the perception of teachers' roles as pure "academic content translators" to the younger generations.

- Teacher education activities must therefore be focused on transmitting the academic knowledge and pedagogical tools required.

- The key factors driving educational success are mainly set up around the interaction between the teacher and the pupil inside the classroom.

- Finally, teacher education is a pre-service activity which consists of modelling teacher behaviour by mentoring, encouraging the use of good practices, benchmarking and observation. Continuing teacher education follows the same path.

The process of turning these principles into reality was and remains intensive. With the role of school perceived as the scientific preparation of youth, childcare and pre-primary education became less relevant. Teacher education for the lowest level (ISCED 0) was structured within the framework of vocational education (upper-secondary education, ISCED *(3)* and segregated from the rest of teacher education usually included in the first stage of tertiary education (ISCED 5). Reasons for this include the low social status assigned to childcare and pre-primary education. It was not until the 1990s and the implementation of LOGSE (the Education Act of 1990[1]) that childcare and pre-primary education were officially recognised, and teacher education for these levels was integrated into the tertiary education framework.

Historically, there has also been a clear distinction between primary and secondary teacher education. For primary education teachers, teacher education became compulsory in the 1970s thanks to the LGE (Education Act of 1970[2]), and was structured as a short-cycle degree (three-year bachelor's degree), focused primarily on specific subject knowledge. In contrast, teacher education was practically absent as a basic requirement for becoming a secondary school teacher, as candidates merely had to complete a long-cycle degree (four or five-year bachelor's degree) in a concrete scientific discipline and take a 120-hour course (less than half of a semester), which included educational content (pedagogy, psychology, sociology, teaching methodology) to obtain the CAP (a certificate of pedagogical aptitude). The LOGSE tried to solve this lack of training with the introduction of an additional one-year course called the CCP (a certificate of pedagogical qualification), but it was never implemented due to insufficient resources as well as the low status of teacher training among secondary teachers.

Another important element of previous versions of teacher education was the absence of a strong and significant relationship between teacher education and the educational system as a whole, including schools and colleges. There were some opportunities for classroom teaching practice for teachers taking courses in initial teacher education, but these internships were too short, and the lack of co-ordination between trainers and schoolteachers made them traditionally poor from a learning perspective. Little essential classroom experience during training was the norm in the 1970s and 1980s.

Diversity and education in Spain: background

The predominant educational paradigm in Spain has traditionally been rationalistic, and the Spanish educational system has not historically acknowledged diversity. This has been the case both from an ideological and operational point of view. In general, Spanish teachers strongly defend principles like equality, equity and respect for differences. However, dealing with children or young people who are "different" does not work well with an approach that requires teaching a "normalised" population to achieve standardised outputs. It could be argued that this attitude is the result of a lack of professional competence to face the new challenges of education, a situation which is similar to that of many other countries (OECD, 2005).

In general, diversity in the classroom is perceived more as a problem than as an opportunity, with some of the following attitudes commonly expressed by teachers:

- Schools are for "normalised" students. Those who are different from the majority for some reason (*e.g.* special needs, mentally ill or foreign students) must be placed in special schools.

- Differences should be eliminated as they are considered anomalies.

- The Spanish educational system must be selective instead of comprehensive (young students were segregated based on academic performance at the age of 14 until the late 1990s).

- Methodologies must be universal, and groups must be homogeneous. Schools aim to minimalise differences by building standardised patterns of citizenship.

- More recently, "diversity" has become synonymous with "cultural diversity" due to the arrival of a significant number of immigrants in the last ten years throughout Spain. Prevailing public opinion suggests that gender, age, socio-economic and other forms of diversity are currently considered as secondary after cultural diversity.

This shift in the way diversity is viewed has meant that most policies and resources pay great attention to the inclusion of migrant families' children, including special classrooms for advanced language learning within schools, specific programmes for the provision of materials and grants for migrant pupils and others.

There are, of course, many Spanish teachers who adopt an attitude that involves the "acceptance of differences". These teachers realise that their students are not all the same and some of them belong to ethnic minority groups. Others may have a disability, but this does not mean that they cannot be taught in the same classroom. Their role consists of helping all students achieve the same goals by various means and strategies. For these teachers, integration is the preferred approach to dealing with differences. However, there is a distinction between integration, which involves accepting "difference", and inclusion,[3] which would entail embracing "diversity". At the moment, no process has been proposed for progressively moving away from the integration approach and towards inclusion as the convenient teaching framework for managing and enhancing diversity.

Despite the 1990 Education Act's stipulation that teacher education must prepare teachers to face differences in the classroom, only a minority of teachers take this approach. However, these goals were not immediately reflected in initial teacher education due to the aforementioned separation between the school system and the teacher education system. Teacher educators' incapacity to update teacher training content to take into account this new aspect of the Act posed another significant problem.

This gap between the "integration" and "inclusion" approaches has been reflected in many aspects of the educational system. This situation has been reproduced in several areas, from educational literature to school practice. Teachers' opinions on the issue provide much insight. An analysis of their discourse provides evidence that diversity is not seen from a global perspective but rather is viewed with a restrictive, simplified and fragmented eye. The following table provides a summary of research on the discourse of teachers and other educational agents in Catalonia (northeastern Spain).

However, the situation is evolving. There are an increasing number of teachers taking a global approach to diversity, with the Special Needs UNESCO Conference in 1994 in Salamanca (northwestern Spain) and new juridical frameworks (LOE – 2006 Education Act) contributing to this change of perspective. A decentralised system which transferred the management of the school system to the *comunidades autónomas* (autonomous communities) during the 1980s-1990s also contributed to a better understanding of, and practices for coping with, diversity at school. All these changes are still in progress and may have more of an effect on discourse than on the practice of teaching. This nonetheless represents an important first step.

The current context of teacher education and diversity: adapting the discourse to new realities

As explained above, teacher education in Spain has not been explicitly training teachers to manage diversity in education (in some cases, for example, secondary education did not prepare them to manage education). There has thus been relatively little progress made on these issues.

However, imperatives coming from recent political and social changes (European integration, the European Space for Higher Education,[5] the huge number of new migrants coming from overseas, and the development of Spanish democracy after the death of General Franco in 1975) have all put diversity on the agenda. The increasingly central role of diversity within the educational system means that teachers must be trained in order to build their capacity and professional competencies in this area. Current teacher education in Spain must thus be adapted to reflect the changing roles of teachers, including the teaching of foreign languages and national language(s) as a second language to immigrant students, the use of ICT as new learning tools, and the importance of planning both specific learning activities and general lessons in ordinary classrooms for immigrant students.

In short, teachers must transform traditional practices into more intercultural[6] practices to acknowledge cultural diversity in daily school life. After the approval of the 2004 Gender Equality Act, gender issues must also be present in the curricula. Inclusive education for all is the new approach, and all students (including those with disabilities and "gifted" students) count.

Table 10.1. **Perspectives of diversity regarding a global or a simplified, fragmented and restrictive approach**

	Global approach to diversity: ideal situation	Restrictive approach to diversity: current situation in Spain
WHO are the students who must be assisted from a diversity perspective?	All students	Only those students with special needs[4]
HOW can teachers assist students from a diversity perspective?	Using a combination of individual, peer, small group and larger group learning strategies	Using individual strategies
WHICH dimension(s) of diversity must be considered?	All dimensions: intellectual, social, cultural, linguistic, gender, religious, age etc.	The cultural dimension
WHAT is the aim of a diversity perspective?	The development of the full potential of all students	The solution of educational problems
WHEN is the diversity perspective relevant?	At all educational stages	Mainly during lower secondary education (ISCED 2)
WHERE must a diversity perspective be implemented?	In all significant student contexts (classroom, school, community, media and society)	In the classroom

Source: Essomba, 2005.

Diversity within the educational system in Spain

The current situation in Spain is defined by the 2006 Education Act[7] (LOE). In this Act, diversity is clearly introduced in the article concerning the principles and aims of the educational system as well as those articles concerning the role of teachers and their training needs. Diversity must not only be respected but integrated from a cross-curricular perspective as it is part of the essential structure of the system, as the following articles suggest:

- Quality of education for all students, independent of their conditions and circumstances (LOE, article 1a).

- Equity, guaranteeing equal opportunity, educational inclusion and non-discrimination, plays a role in compensating for personal, cultural, economical and social inequalities, being especially attentive to those related to disabilities (LOE, article 1b).

- The transmission and practice of values for personal freedom, responsibility, democratic citizenship, solidarity, tolerance, equality, respect and justice, and all those that contribute to eliminating any sort of discrimination (LOE, article 1c).

- The flexibility to adapt education to the diversity of aptitudes, interests, expectations and needs of students as well as to social changes (LOE, article 1e).

- The development of equal rights and opportunities as well as the promotion of an effective equality between men and women – not only formally but also in social practices (LOE, article 11).

The approach to diversity is global and not restrictive, taking into account all its dimensions (intellectual, social, cultural, linguistic and others). These dimensions can be further identified through some of the aims reflected in articles of this Act:

- The full development of the student's personality and his/her abilities (LOE, article 2a): *intellectual diversity.*

- Education respecting fundamental rights and freedom, equal rights and opportunities for both men and women, and equality of awareness and non-discrimination of disabled people (LOE, article 2b): *gender diversity and special needs.*

- Peace education, respect for human rights, living together, social cohesion, solidarity and co-operation amongst peoples … (LOE, article 2e): *socio-economic diversity.*

- Education respecting and acknowledging the linguistic and cultural plurality of Spain and considering interculturality as an enriching element of society (LOE, article 2g): *linguistic and cultural diversity.*

Legal context of teacher education for diversity in Spain

It has taken a long time for all Spanish governmental bodies, teacher unions and teacher associations to agree that teachers should modify their role with respect to diversity (LOE, 2006; *Associació de Mestres Rosa Sensat*, 2005). The current Education Act (*op. cit.*) makes it clear that students are not a homogeneous group, and every child or young person has the right to be considered unique. Thus, teaching goes beyond dealing with academic contents and tests. All teachers, apart from giving lessons and assessing their students' achievement, have to provide personal guidance, counselling and support for the full intellectual, emotional, physical, social and moral development of students (LOE, article 91).

Teacher education has moved into a new era marked by new recommendations outlined by the European Common Principles for Teacher Competences and Qualifications (European Commission, 2005 – reflected in LOE, articles 100 and 102):

- Teacher education must be adapted to the challenges of the educational system, including increasing diversity. This implies prioritising teaching methods and strategies (how to teach) over contents to be taught (what to teach).

- All teachers must obtain at least a four-year bachelor's degree. This is an important departure from the past, when teachers needed a three-year bachelor's degree, or in some cases, only some vocational education courses (*e.g.* for childcare and pre-primary education). Teacher education for secondary school teachers is also significantly extended (four-year bachelor's degree in a specific area plus a one-year master's degree focusing on teaching methods and strategies).

- There must be close collaboration between educational authorities and universities when defining and assessing teacher education needs in order to ensure that teacher education responds to the reality of the school.

- Teacher education must follow the guidelines and the structure of the European Space for Higher Education.[8]

- Continuing teacher education must focus on diversity among other topics.

All these principles must promote the acquisition of core competences which embrace diversity and are common to all member states of the European Union (European Commission, 2007). These competences are:

- to identify the special needs of every pupil and respond to them by using a wide variety of teaching strategies;

- to help young people learn autonomously within the context of a life-long learning perspective;

- to help young people learn the basic competences described in the European Reference Framework of Key Competences (European Parliament, 2006);

- to work within multicultural settings (understanding the value of diversity and respecting differences); and

- to work closely with teachers, parents and community.

Universities have been progressively adapting their planning to meet the requirements of the curriculum reform regarding teacher training in Spain since 2004 although it is too early to state whether the process has been successful as a whole.

The "natural" gap between policy and implementation

Despite the fact that teacher education for diversity should cover both initial and continuing levels, most resources and expectations are focused on initial teacher education. It is still considered that, in teacher education, this initial experience is crucial for further professional development (Imbernon, 1998), and that these early stages help teachers to become competent in the methods and strategies that must be put into practice at schools.

Now we turn to the challenging current situation of teacher education regarding diversity, especially focusing on teacher education for those professionals who want to work at ISCED 0 and ISCED 1 levels.[9]

The state educational authorities context

As with other tertiary degrees at Spanish universities, teacher education has traditionally been centralised, with the Spanish Ministry of Education and Science determining 70% to 80% of the curriculum content and each university responsible for 20% to 30% of content selection.

However, this rule was modified recently because of the adaptation to the European Space for Higher Education, which requires a high level of autonomy for every university. This procedure has been established in the LOU (2007 Universities

Act), a legal framework that aims to respond to the recommendations and instructions of international bodies related to this matter. This means that each institution can design its own curriculum with no initial prescriptions from the state. However, due to the importance of teacher education, the Spanish Ministry of Education and Science has determined some core competences that each student should achieve by the end of his/her teacher education. There are two categories of core competences: *(1)* childcare and pre-primary education; and *(2)* primary education.

Of the core competences for those professionals who work with children from ages 0 to 6, two out of 23 are clearly related to diversity. At this level, teacher education must provide learning opportunities to become competent in:

- Designing and implementing learning opportunities in diversity contexts, while being attentive to the special needs of students, gender equality and respect for human rights.

- Leading situations of language learning within multicultural and multilingual contexts.[10]

For those professionals who wish to work with children from ages 6 to 12, two out of 18 core competences that must be acquired during the training process are directly related to diversity (basically the same as those required for their colleagues in childcare and pre-primary teacher education):

- Designing and implementing learning opportunities in diversity contexts, while being attentive to the special needs of students, gender equality and respect for human rights according to the values of citizenship education.

- Leading situations of language learning under efficacy criteria within multicultural and multilingual contexts.[10]

This means that the State educational authorities believe that teachers must be competent in dealing with diversity and that teacher education must play a preparatory role. It is relevant to see that the focus is on the learning process and not on diversity; diversity is the context, not the content. With this approach, diversity is identified as a value and a principle for which schools strive. What is promising is that the scope of diversity is broad: intellectual, gender, social, cultural and linguistic. All teacher education curricula in Spain are required to include diversity and such inclusion is well-received.

The university context

As the legal and structural frameworks for teacher education and diversity have changed, it is important to determine whether these changes have taken effect within the universities which are responsible for this kind of training.

This may not be the best moment because, as previously mentioned, teacher education is currently undergoing extensive reform. According to the fundamental norm which guides this process (*Real Decreto 1393/2007 por el que se establece la ordenación de las enseñanzas universitarias oficiales*), the eight teacher education degrees available[11] must be progressively phased out from the academic year 2010-11 on, so that all education faculties and departments can plan and programme new teacher education curricula. A state co-ordination of the Conference of Deans of Education has met regularly since 2002 in order to share criteria as well as to plan the challenges and processes that this innovation involves.

At the moment, a few universities have already launched the new teacher education curricula in the academic year 2009/2010. Four (Universitat Autònoma de Barcelona [UAB]; Universidad Autónoma de Madrid [UAM]; Universitat de València [UV]; Universitat de les Illes Balears [UIB]) were selected with the purpose of obtaining some initial data on the focus on diversity in the new teacher education curricula. Given that this is a process of initial implementation, it is not possible to obtain definitive conclusions on how this will play out, but this early analysis can serve to identify tendencies and provide a rough idea of the possibilities and limitations that teacher education for diversity might have in Spain in the coming years.

The list of the coursework for teacher education for diversity is presented in the following table, which includes those descriptors written in the curriculum directly related to one or more dimensions of diversity (intellectual, linguistic, cultural, social, special needs), their quantitative importance within the overall curriculum (measured by the number of credits, or ECTS) and their qualitative importance (measured by the scope of the content: the basic curriculum for all students; other compulsory courses; and optional courses for some students).

From this first glance, the following observations emerge:

- The percentage of courses on diversity available to all students is low (the average is between 6 ECTS and 12 ECTS – between 2.5% and 5% of a curriculum comprised of 240 ECTS).

- Teacher education for childcare and pre-primary education (ISCED 0) provides fewer courses on diversity issues than teacher education for primary education (ISCED 1) .

- All initial teacher education curricula for primary teachers provide some expertise in diversity issues. However, because diversity training is not the only expertise available (other expertise includes, for instance, music education, physical education or arts and crafts education); it is always optional and covers about 30 ECTS (12.5% of a 240 ECTS curriculum).

- The diversity perspective still remains within a rationalistic paradigm. It is seen as a problematic deficit for which to be compensated instead of an opportunity for the enrichment of all.

In this early analysis it appears that these reforms tend to involve structural adaptation rather than a transformation of content. Further analysis as the reforms progress will be able to refute or corroborate these initial impressions, but it should be highlighted that the teacher trainers, as well as universities, are the same as before, and they have had to face this challenge with no extra resources and without specific training. In addition, the percentage of compulsory education on diversity for students still remains more or less the same compared to the previous curricula (for another study on this topic see Essomba, 2006). Despite the changes in legal and institutional frameworks, it appears that diversity is still sometimes seen as an "abnormal" context, to be controlled in order to achieve a standardised educational environment that allows for the acquisition of scientific knowledge.

The approach used in teacher education is closer to the previous "integration" model than the currently stated goal of "inclusion" (despite the titles of the courses in Table 10.2). This means that the teacher's role is seen as an expert on those learning processes that allow "different pupils" (mainly special needs and immigrant pupils) to share in some activities with the "ordinary and normal pupils", an approach that is far from conceiving the teacher's role as that of a supporter of diversity within the same classroom. Diversity management is thus viewed as a matter to be carried out by specialists rather than all staff, with the mastery of teaching for diversity considered an optional specialisation. Despite the common vision of state authorities and universities when defining teacher competences in diversity to be learnt, at the moment it seems that diversity is the context but not the content. Changing discourse thus does not necessarily translate automatically into changing practices.

Table 10.2. **Diversity contents in new teacher education curricula at four Spanish Universities (UAB, UAM, UV, UIB)**

University	Teacher education for childcare and pre-primary education (0-6 years)	Teacher education for primary education (6-12 years)
UAB	Language learning for newcomers (Optional, 6 ECTS)	Linguistic school project and multilingualism (Compulsory, 5 ECTS)
Learning difficulties and developmental handicap: inclusive education. (Basic, 6 ECTS)	Differences and inclusion (Compulsory, 5 ECTS)	Expertise in Inclusive Education (Optional, 30 ECTS): special needs and learning processes; special needs and cognitive development; special needs and behavioural problems; special needs and sensory disabilities; mediation/language learning for newcomers.

Table 10.2. **Diversity contents in new teacher education curricula at four Spanish Universities (UAB, UAM, UV, UIB)** *(continued)*

University	Teacher education for childcare and pre-primary education (0-6 years)	Teacher education for primary education (6-12 years)
UAM	Expertise in Early Care (Optional, 27 ECTS): early care, disabilities and its evaluation; special programmes for disabled or at-risk pupils.	Expertise in Support for Inclusive Education (Optional, 27 ECTS): needs for educational support; counselling and team work for inclusive education; programmes for pupils with different abilities; socio-emotional skills for pupils with social relation problems.
Psychological and educational basics for the inclusion of pupils with special needs (Basic, 9 ECTS)	Psychological and educational basics for inclusive education (Basic, 6 ECTS)	
UV	Difficulties with written and oral language development (Basic, 6 ECTS)	Development of communication skills in multilingual contexts (Compulsory, 6 ECTS)
Special needs (Basic, 6 ECTS)	Special needs (Basic, 6 ECTS)	Expertise in Diversity and Individual Differences Care (Optional, 30 ECTS): school management and counselling for diversity; self-regulation and behavioural problems; compensatory education; curriculum development for learning disabilities; curriculum development for special abilities, family situations and school disaffection.
UIB	Language learning in multicultural contexts (Optional, 3 ECTS)	Expertise in Counselling and Academic Guidance (Optional, 30 ECTS): social exclusion at school; intercultural education.
Inclusive education (Basic, 6 ECTS)	Inclusive education (Basic, 6 ECTS)	Expertise in Counselling and Academic Guidance (Optional, 30 ECTS): social exclusion at school; intercultural education.
Delayed development (Basic, 6 ECTS)	Specific learning difficulties (Basic, 6 ECTS)	Expertise in Counselling and Academic Guidance (Optional, 30 ECTS): social exclusion at school; intercultural education.
		Expertise in Language Development (Optional 30 ECTS): language difficulties; educational intervention for language development problems; prevention of language development problems.

Source: Essomba, 2009.

Further steps towards understanding and learning: the case of Spain

We would like to conclude with some additional remarks that could be interesting for an international audience. First, if diversity is becoming a challenging issue at schools, simply changing teacher education in itself is not enough. An innovation process like this requires the involvement of teacher education institutions, of course, but in close interaction with other agents: educational authorities, schools and teacher associations. It is not clear that teacher education curricula strongly consider this a relevant topic, especially as diversity education is not given its due importance in teacher training.

Second, continuing teacher education is as important as initial teacher education. The profile and treatment of diversity issues in initial teacher education curricula is poor and in continuing teacher education it is no better. Logically, it is of no use to train new education professionals for diversity if they will be in schools in which their colleagues have fewer tools to manage diversity than they do, although, it must start somewhere.

Third, it is important that teacher education explicitly include diversity content in the curricula. The diversity perspective should be cross-curricular instead of another topic to be learned separately. However, when attempting to make this sort of change, it is necessary to provide some explicit courses in order to facilitate the increasing importance of the issue in the whole curriculum (even considering the evident risk of a permanent specialisation instead of a transversal approach).

Finally, although it is outside of the scope of this chapter, it is important to address the training of trainers. If teacher education is to be redesigned and this work is to be done in close collaboration with educational agents with diversity being a basic element rooted in the ethos and curricula of teacher education institutions, then the training of trainers is crucial. It is worth looking into international co-operation in this area, including how the role of institutions like the OECD can be helpful in the organisation and implementation of teacher training.

Notes

1. This is the third Education Act of the Spanish democracy. It aimed to set new educational stages, new curricula and to increase the age of compulsory education from 14 to 16.

2. This was the previous Education Act of the Spanish dictatorship, which tried to update and modernise the Spanish education system according to emerging needs based on the new economic development framework of the 1960s and 1970s.

3. Inclusive education is "an ongoing process aimed at offering quality education for all while respecting diversity and the different needs and abilities, characteristics and learning expectations of the students and communities, eliminating all forms of discrimination" (UNESCO, 2008).

4. Traditionally, the Spanish school system considered "special needs" as those related to physical, mental or sensorial disability. However, nowadays the term "special needs" involves a broader scope, including linguistic needs of immigrant students, behavioural issues and even talented students. For further information see the last educational reform in the 2006 Education Act.

5. The purpose of the European Space of Higher Education is to enhance the employability and mobility of citizens and to increase the international competitiveness of European higher education. More information can be found at: *http://ec.europa.eu/education/policies/educ/bologna/bologna.pdf*.

6. A note on terminology: in Spanish literature, the term "multicultural" refers to social reality while the term "intercultural" pertains to the social agenda of inclusion and cohesion that is to be promoted in relation to this social reality.

7. Ley Orgánica de Educación

8. Teacher education in Spain is centred on the learning process of the student. The curriculum is based on a competence approach and is flexible, with mobility considered a fundamental practice during initial training.

9. Information on teacher education for teaching at lower secondary education (ISCED (2) and upper-secondary education (ISCED (3) is not included in this discussion as this curriculum is still in the process of legal definition as a one-year course (Master's level), and only some experimental universities have developed non-compulsory courses to test training methods. Nevertheless, there

are concerns regarding the feasibility of this proposal for two reasons: the lack of time (only two semesters) and the commonly held opinion among secondary school teachers and trainers that for ISCED 2 and ISCED 3 tackling diversity is not as important as teaching content.

10.   This means that all teachers must be competent to make use of multilingualism as an ordinary situation for learning activities (to teach a lesson in Spanish but look up information in English to solve an exercise and/or translate the output into another language and exchange it with some students abroad within the framework of a mobility programme).

11.   Childcare and pre-primary education, primary education, musical education, physical education, language education, special needs education and CAP.

References

Associació de Mestres Rosa Sensat (2005), *Per una nova educació pública*, AMRS, Barcelona.

European Commission (2005), *European Common Principles for Teacher Competences and Qualifications, http://ec.europa.eu/education/policies/2010/ testingconf_en.html.*

Essomba, M.A. (2005), *L'atenció a la diversitat a Catalunya*, EUMO, Vic.

Essomba, M.A. (2006), "Quand le présent dépasse l'avenir. Dix ans de formation d'enseignants en diversité culturelle en Espagne", *Revue des Hautes Études Pédagogiques*, Vol. 1, pp. 149-169.

Imbernon, F. (1998), *La formación y el desarrollo profesional del profesorado. Hacia una nueva cultura profesional*, Graó Barcelona.

OECD (2005), *Teachers Matter,* OECD, Paris.

Pérez Gómez, A. (2007), "Aprender a enseñar. La construcción del conocimiento en la formación del profesorado", in Pérez Gómez, A., M. Martínez, A. Tey, M. A. Essomba and M. T. González (eds.), *Profesorado y otros profesionales de la educación*, Octaedro Barcelona.

Legal documents

Ley General de Educación de 1970 (LGE).

Ley Orgánica de Ordenación General del Sistema Educativo de 1990 (LOGSE).

Ley Orgánica de medidas de protección integral contra la violencia de género de 2004 (LOMPIVG).

Ley Orgánica de Educación de 2006 (LOE).

Ley Orgánica de Universidades de 2007 (LOU).

Orden ECI/3854/2007 sobre las competencias específicas o profesionales de la titulación de Maestro en Educación Infantil referida al Real Decreto 1393/2007.

Orden ECI/3857/2007 sobre las competencias específicas o profesionales de la titulación de Maestro en Educación Primaria referida al Real Decreto 1393/2007.

Real Decreto 1393/2007 por el que se establece la ordenación de las enseñanzas universitarias oficiales.

Recommendation 2006/962/CE of the European Parliament and the Council.

Chapter 11

School leader approaches to multicultural education: a Northern Ireland case study

Claire McGlynn
Queen's University, Northern Ireland

This chapter critically examines a variety of approaches to diversity in integrated schools (i.e. mixed Catholic and Protestant) in Northern Ireland and considers their implications in the context of the wider debate around multiculturalism. It presents a study of integrated school principals and their responses to diversity in their schools. It furthermore provides a summary of the characteristics of different approaches to integration and how they can be viewed with respect to teacher education. Given the range of possible educational responses to cultural diversity, it is important to determine which are the most contextually relevant in order to encourage their adoption throughout initial and ongoing teacher education. This chapter argues that multiculturalism and multicultural education can provide a valuable frame for analysis of integrated education policy and practice.

From the OECD online consultation :
role of school administration

Less than half of teacher respondents felt well-supported by their school administration in their attempts to address diversity in the classroom. How can school administrators effectively support teachers working in diverse classrooms?

Introduction: challenges to multiculturalism[*]

All modern states need to reconcile the claims of minority groups of people who are perceived as having identities that differ from those of the majority (Kymlicka, 2007; Kelly, 2002). In many countries, the response has been to employ models of pluralistic citizenship in which common societal goals provide cohesion whilst respecting the diverse cultural, ethnic, linguistic, and religious backgrounds of the population. However, multiculturalism has been significantly challenged by liberal egalitarians, such as Barry, who assert that such policies reinforce cultural difference and can inhibit the development of common values such as liberty and equality (2001). Multiculturalists retort that cultural neutrality neglects, for example, the role of culture and group identity in defining harms and causes of injustice and they continue to contend a social thesis that culture matters. Indeed, Jenkins suggests that we are powerless to resist the "socialising tyranny of categorisation" (2004, p. 183). He also argues that identity is made up of both individual and collective aspects that interact. For Taylor (1994), the politics of recognition leads him to favour collective over personal identification but he maintains that people should not be compelled to organise their lives around their group identity. However, in societies such as Northern Ireland that have suffered from protracted conflict, such organisation is a common characteristic.

Kymlicka (1995) attempts to reconcile the social thesis with the primary liberal value of autonomy. He proposes that collective identity and culture provide

* A version of this paper was first published in the journal *Multicultural Perspectives*. This study was made possible by a grant from the International Fund for Ireland, with grateful thanks to the Northern Ireland Council for Integrated Education and all participants.

the resources from which an autonomous and valuable life can be constructed. In practice, however, the reconciliation of individual freedom and collective cultural expression is problematic (Benhabib, 2002). We must be very careful here to be critical in our use of the concept of culture. Gjerde (2004) contends that we must challenge any representation of culture as an objective referent, when it is in fact a human creation, shaped by hegemonic interests. It may be that cultural difference is not as great as sometimes claimed and also that it does not always map neatly onto communities (Phillips, 2007). More recent conceptualisations of multiculturalism challenge reified notions of culture and homogenised views of cultural groups (Phillips, 2007; Parekh, 2006). Some continue to hold to "culture" as the unit of analysis (Banks, 2008; Parekh, 2006) whilst others prefer to use "identity" (see Modood, 2007). Modood (2007) argues that in post-immigration societies, such as Britain, identity is a more useful construct as identities may persist even when cultural practices decline or adapt. That is not however to essentialise identity, which is increasingly viewed as "multiple, changing, overlapping and contextual, rather than fixed and static" (Banks, 2008, p. 133; Parekh, 2006). Whilst we may consider then either culture or identity or both to be a vital source from which to construct our life, we must also acknowledge that both are constantly evolving and are not finite.

Multicultural education in conflicted societies

In societies that have suffered from conflict, issues of cultural recognition come into sharp relief. How can/should educators respond to issues of cultural diversity when group rights are often central to the conflict? What approaches can be taken, both in formal education and teacher education, when structural inequalities such as segregated education systems mediate against a reconciliatory role for education? We must always be aware that the education system can be a powerful force for maintaining the social *status quo*.

Proponents of critical multicultural education theory (Mahalingham and McCarthy, 2000; Nieto, 2000; Kincheloe and Steinberg, 1997 and Sleeter and McLaren, 1995) argue that acknowledging diversity without seriously challenging inequality is not only fraudulent but potentially harmful. Indeed, adopting a critical multicultural perspective brings into question the role of teachers and schooling in perpetuating dominant values and common culture. Critical theorists denounce liberal forms of multiculturalism that support belief in a natural equality and a common humanity (Kincheloe and Steinberg, 1997). They argue that if commonalities are stressed rather than difference, the promotion of cultural invisibility fails to address bias. Liberal multiculturalists counter this by claiming that positive ideals such as liberty and equality must be endorsed, rather than emphasising cultural difference. They contend that this liberal standpoint gives hope for the stable coexistence of people with diverse values (Duarte and Smith, 2000).

Once again we must be careful in our use of the concept of "culture". Sen (2006) argues that the inaccurate presumption that people can be uniquely categorised based on their culture constitutes a major source of conflict in the contemporary world. He rejects a plural monocultural approach that essentialises identity in favour of multicultural practice endowing the freedom to cultivate a reasoned choice of identity priorities. Phillips (2007) also argues that people need to be treated as agents, rather than as captives, of their cultures. Sen (2006) critically distinguishes between two approaches to multiculturalism – one that promotes diversity as a value in itself (see Parekh, 2006) and one that focuses on the freedom of reasoning and decision-making, and celebrates cultural diversity to the extent that it is as freely chosen as possible by the persons involved. I would argue that we more usually see the former, rather than the latter, approach to diversity reflected in formal education. We should question the value of each approach carefully.

Davies (2004) warns us that attempts to preserve distinct cultures can present communities as homogenous and fixed, rather than dynamic and emerging. In conflicted societies, we must be acutely aware that to prevent essentialist identities being mobilised for conflict we need to acknowledge complexity and hybridity and to avoid stereotyped portrayals of the "other" (Davies, 2004). All multicultural societies must also "navigate between the '*pluribus*' whilst also promoting a '*unum*'" (Reich, 2002, p. 116). Reich (2002) proposes an adapted liberal theory of multicultural education that tries not to script students for a predetermined cultural identity but rather to treat them as evolving, self-governing persons. Whilst autonomy is clearly the goal, Reich (2002) readily concedes that education about alternative cultures is also needed to address the narrow ethnocentric educational practices of the past. As such, the emphasis is not on the promotion of commonality, but rather on the development of self-reflective individuals. The caveat here is that such a model must then maintain sufficient attention on cultural difference in order to sufficiently challenge cultural bias and inequality.

Integrated education in Northern Ireland

As elsewhere in the United Kingdom, community tensions in Northern Ireland have risen due to the impact of the events of 11 September 2001 in New York, 7 July 2005 in London and the Iraq war. In a thinly veiled attack on separatist multicultural policy (from a somewhat unlikely quarter) the Chair of the Commission for Racial Equality warned of the dangers of sleepwalking to social segregation (Phillips, 2005). Government policy of increasing the number of funded faith-based schools in Britain has also been questioned with regards to the possible impact on community cohesion and also with regards to the use of public funds to sustain religious schools (Parker-Jenkins, Hartas and Irving, 2004; McGlynn, 2005). Indeed Brighouse

(2006) goes as far as to contend that faith-based schools undermine the opportunity for autonomy of those who do not attend them, as they limit the opportunity for inter-cultural contact in non-faith based schools.

This raises important questions regarding the role of contact and curriculum in promoting social cohesion. An American Educational Research Association research brief (2006) presents a body of evidence for maintaining formally desegregated schools in the United States. Further to this, Reich claims that "the efficacy of multicultural education likely increases to the degree that the school in which the children learn is integrated, not segregated, by cultures" (2002, p. 131). The current trend, however, is educational resegregation (Orfield and Lee, 2006) both in the United States and elsewhere, driven largely by the ability of better-off parents to move to nicer neighbourhoods and subsequently enrol their children in socio-economically and racially separate schools, with those who cannot afford to move becoming increasingly ghettoised.

Northern Ireland is a particularly interesting case study of educational response to diversity. Progress towards a more peaceful and democratic society in Northern Ireland has been painstaking. Indeed, some commentators have observed that the Good Friday Agreement of 1998, the settlement that heralded the end of the recent thirty year conflict, has actually served to institutionalise sectarianism, resulting in greater political and social segregation due to its very careful attention to acknowledging the differences and demands of the conflicting groups. Gallagher (2005) argues that the overprivileging of difference by the peace process has left little space for a discourse of the common good. There remain many challenges to break down the boundaries between members of the Catholic and Protestant communities who continue for the main part to live, work and play separately. Education remains largely segregated, with children either attending Catholic maintained schools or *de facto* Protestant-controlled schools. In addition the arrival of new minority group members, particularly from newly acceded eastern European countries, brings a new national, cultural and linguistic diversity to many of our classrooms. It is only in the last few years that children with first languages other than English have arrived in Northern Irish schools. As the most recent population census was conducted in 2001,[*] these new arrivals do not feature in the statistics but they have certainly made an impression in schools which previously only had English speaking pupils. In most schools, English language learners represent approximately 2-3% of the school population, although in some areas the number may be higher due to greater availability of jobs for migrant workers. According to the 2001 census, 40.26% of the Northern Ireland population was Catholic; 45.57% was Protestant, 0.3% other religions and 13.88% of no religion. By contrast

---

[*] See *www.nicensus2001.gov.uk/nica/public/index.html.*

minority ethnic groups constitute only 0.85% of Northern Ireland's 2001 population, one of the smallest ethnic minority populations in the European Union. One third of all ethnic minorities live in Belfast and the largest group is Chinese, with significant number recorded in the 2001 census as Irish Travellers, Black Caribbeans, Black Africans and Other Blacks. However, we will not get more accurate census data of new arrivals from Eastern Europe until 2011.

Whilst many see this diversity as enriching, others feel threatened and there has been a proportionate growth in societal race hate crime. The total number of "racial incidents", for example, increased from 226 in 2002/3 to 990 in 2008/9 (Police Services of Northern Ireland Archives, 2009). After a series of race hate attacks in June 2009, more than 100 members of the Romanian Roma community left Belfast (BBC News, 2009). This then is the Northern Ireland context, a society still divided by religion, sectarianism and needing to respond to the legacy of conflict, but also a society facing the challenges of incoming populations and new forms of racism. One hopeful development is the emergence of integrated education.

Integrated education was established in Northern Ireland with the opening of the first planned integrated post-primary school by parents in 1981. A further 59 primary and post-primary schools have since been established either by parent groups or by parental ballot. Integrated education is defined as the education together, in equal numbers, of Catholic and Protestant children, who are more usually educated separately, providing an opportunity for them to develop respect and understanding for alternative cultures and perspectives. Under the 1989 Education Reform (Northern Ireland) Order the government has a duty to meet the needs of parents requesting integrated education but only 18 000 children (6% of all pupils) attend integrated schools (either planned integrated or Protestant schools that have transformed to integrated status). The phenomenon has thus been described as voluntary integration by parental consent rather than by compulsory desegregation as in the United States (Gallagher and Smith, 2002).

Research evidence to date suggests that integrated education may impact positively on identity, outgroup attitudes and forgiveness, with potential to heal division (McGlynn, Niens, Cairns and Hewstone, 2004; Montgomery, Fraser, McGlynn and Smith, 2003; McGlynn, 2001) and promote a less sectarian outlook (Hayes, McAllister and Dowds, 2006). However, it would appear issues of religion and politics are avoided in some integrated schools (Donnelly, 2004; Hughes and Donnelly, 2007). Research also suggests that integration often relies on the interpersonal contact that arises from sharing classrooms, rather than intergroup contact (Niens and Cairns 2008). This passive approach was observed in a review of integrated education practice (Montgomery, Fraser, McGlynn and Smith, 2003), although reactive and pro-active models of integration were also noted. The difference here is between reactive approaches, responding to events only when and if they occur (such as sectarian bullying), and pro-active approaches that include planned curriculum activities to address issues of religion, politics and identity in a bid to increase understanding. In a previous study of leadership in several integrated schools, McGlynn (2008) reports that some principals adopt liberal approaches to multicultural education.

This paper is concerned with exploring approaches to integrating diversity in the integrated schools in Northern Ireland and thus with investigating approaches to multicultural education in a segregated society. The theoretical perspectives on multiculturalism and identity outlined above will be brought to bear on qualitative data collected in a study of the leadership approaches of integrated school principals.

Methods

In Northern Ireland, a still divided society moving out of conflict and challenged by the presence of new minority group members, how do the formally integrated schools respond to diversity? How do they manage cultural difference? A study of integrated school principals, funded by the International Fund for Ireland, was carried out to explore these issues. Semi-structured interviews were conducted with principals of planned and transformed integrated schools. 52 of the 58 integrated principals agreed to be interviewed, of whom 33 were principals of planned and 19 were principals of transformed schools. Interviews lasted approximately one hour and aimed to determine what the principals understand by integration and to explore their leadership visions. Data were analysed using qualitative methods, whereby units of relevant meanings were clustered and common themes determined before themes general and unique to all interviews were identified (Freebody, 2003; Mason, 1996; Punch, 1998).

Findings

Before considering the findings there are two provisos that should be considered. Firstly, it should be noted that the breadth and depth of response to questions regarding vision and practice of integration varied greatly between principals, indicating a variation in the degree of importance allocated to the "integrating" function of the school. It was also apparent that some principals were not satisfied with their current approach to integration and wished to develop it further.

However, distinctive categories of approach to integration, identified by the emphasis placed on cultural difference or similarity and/or willingness to tackle inequalities, emerged from the data. Principals' approaches to integration constituted five main categories, namely liberal, plural, critical, liberal/plural and liberal/critical, of which two categories were further self-divided (see Table 11.1). Each approach will be considered in turn.

Table 11.1. **Approaches to integration shown by integrated school principals, where P = planned and T = transformed integrated school**

Type of principal	Liberal pro-active	Liberal passive	Plural inclusive	Plural limited	Critical	Liberal/ plural	Liberal/ critical	Total
P primary principals 1-21	2	1	3	1	3	5	6	21
T primary principals 22-36	2	6	4	2	0	1	0	15
P post-primary principals 37-48	3	2	5	0	0	0	2	12
T post-primary principals 49-52	2	0	1	0	1	0	0	4
Total	9	9	13	3	4	6	8	52

Liberal integration

Eighteen principals described approaches to integration that can be categorised as liberal; that is, where the emphasis is placed on cultural commonality rather than difference, reflecting the liberal position that individuals from diverse groups share a natural equality and common humanity and endorsing the joint ideals of liberty and equality. However, the approaches reported can be further divided into *liberal pro-active* where the emphasis on commonality is deliberate (nine principals) and *liberal passive* where it is coincidental (nine principals).

The *liberal pro-active* approach is typified by the following comments:

Integration is everyone working together, all classes and all creeds. It should be all one family under the one sky. Respect is the core value. It is important how you treat people and children should experience how to deal with conflict (Principal 2).

In this principal's school there is active work on developing conflict resolution skills, including a peer mediation programme. This was reflected by other pro-active liberal principals, for example:

Integration here is not too much in your face. It is about more than the things that divide us. A balanced celebration of events is difficult ... Conflict resolution is a central plank at the micro and macro level. Integration features through all levels in the school (Principal 37).

Such comments reflect a conscious effort to find common ground ("we are all human first and foremost" – School 49) but also indicate a deliberate reluctance to focus on difference. Instead there is a desire to build a united school community:

> *We see integration as being welcoming, friendly and serving the wider community. It is about breaking down suspicions ... we are seeking to encourage the sense of community within the school (Principal 38).*

By contrast the *liberal passive* approach is characterised by a belief that integration can happen "naturally" (Principal 25).Whilst integration is perceived as a child-centred and welcoming concept, there is some evidence of the avoidance of divisive issues ("Do we look at symbols and emblems? No!" – Principal 27) and also evidence of an acknowledgement that it is a challenge to keep integration to the fore. A typical comment illustrates the reluctance to prioritise integration:

> *Our core business is the education of children. We would love to have more time on the integrated ethos but it is a bit of a luxury being able to do that (Principal 39).*

For this principal integration is about the day to day contact with Catholics and Protestants that happens naturally in the school. No particular further leadership or curricular emphasis is required.

Plural integration

A pluralist approach to integration that embraces the celebration of diversity, history and cultural heritage is exhibited by 16 principals. However, these principals do not stress any critical multicultural perspective. The plural approach noted can be further sub-divided into *plural inclusive*, where the focus is on celebrating all aspects of difference (13 principals) and *plural limited*, where although world religions and ethnic minority groups are recognised, references to Catholic/Protestant differences are actively avoided (three principals).

Principals reflecting a *plural inclusive* approach articulate a clear focus on all forms of cultural and religious difference:

> *We recognise differences and encourage children to celebrate these differences. Everything should be out in the open – for discussion. We celebrate all religions (Principal 31).*

This approach to integration is clearly an intrinsic part of school development planning and is reflected in the formal and informal curricula. The celebration of cultural tradition and the expression of cultural identity is a priority:

We celebrate cultural diversity ... you should be proud of who you are and what you believe in but have respect for others' cultures (Principal 45).

By contrast three principals describe an approach to integration that is *plural limited* in that overt references to Catholic/Protestant differences are avoided although recognition is given to other diverse groups. These principals report a range of curricular and other activities that celebrate "world religions and culture, for example, Ramadan" (Principal 7). Whilst attempts are made to celebrate some traditions, these principals do not focus on denominational, cultural or political differences between Catholic and Protestant pupils. Thus the "exotic" is worthy of celebration but that which is at the root of the conflict is ignored.

Critical integration

A small number (4) of principals exhibit a *critical* approach to integration. This is characterised not only by a policy of recognising and celebrating all differences, both denominational and other, but also by a desire to tackle social injustice:

While we recognise and celebrate difference, we appreciate that school in not a neutral haven. Issues of prejudice must be addressed. We are inclusive in all respects ... we address the needs of all faiths and we are challenged by supporting the needs of our ethnic minority pupils (Principal 9).

These principals describe a range of initiatives that promote the celebration of difference, including the existence of integration committees and integration development plans; whole school celebration of the Catholic sacraments of confession, communion and confirmation; the teaching of world faiths; visits to Christian and non-Christian places of worship and displays of cultural symbols and emblems. What distinguishes this approach from the *plural inclusive* one, however, is an accompanying emphasis on challenging inequality:

School should be different. We are tackling controversial issues and conflict resolution. You need to be comfortable with difference. This is the challenge of an increasingly multicultural society. We have to confront racist attacks (Principal 8).

Principals also report human rights and anti-bullying initiatives as central to their *critical* practice of integrated education. This approach recognises that diversity must be considered alongside issues of social justice.

Liberal/plural integration

An approach that incorporates aspects of both *liberal* and *plural* models of integration is reported by six principals. Whilst cultural difference is acknowledged, commonality and equality are also stressed:

> *Integration is primarily about equal opportunity, all are welcome. School is safe and child-centred. All children are special and unique – we value and celebrate difference and promote tolerance and respect (Principal 14).*

While offering pupils "the freedom to be different" (Principal 34) the *liberal/plural* approach attempts to construct an inclusive school community where "children and staff feel valued" (Principal 34). The inclusion of diverse groups pivots on the liberal principle of equality:

> *Children come first. Everyone is welcome and all are treated with respect ... all children are educated together. Children are treated equally. Our school tries to instill an attitude of respect (Principal 15).*

As such the *liberal/plural* approach promotes a model of integration that reconciles cultural difference within the concept of a common school community, a "unity through diversity" model.

Liberal/critical integration

The *liberal/critical* approach to integration reported by eight principals also seeks common ground between diverse groups. Whilst overtly acknowledging commonality, this approach also commits to challenging injustice such as sectarianism and racism head on:

> *Integration is about a shared community open to everyone. An all inclusive school should be at the heart of a shared community. Integration should drive all areas and the teaching should reflect this. Children will be looking at contentious issues ... we have a constant awareness of anti-bias, anti-bullying and conflict resolution (Principal 16).*

A further principal, whilst clearly in favour of seeking commonality, views initiatives on difference and injustice as a route to promoting equality;

> *The ideal is no awareness of Protestant or Catholic. We have a firm discipline policy on sectarianism ... we tackle sectarian abuse. Integration is promoted through assemblies – we take a compassionate view of those in need, for example, tsunami victims and children in need (Principal 47).*

The data indicates that this group of principals actively reflect on how they might draw together an eclectic school community comprising Catholics, Protestants, those of other faiths and no faith, boys, girls, all abilities, social classes and ethnic backgrounds. Pro-active anti-bias and anti-prejudice work is seen as vital. In addition two principals report on the importance to their model of integration of an emphasis on developing pupil actualisation. This is exemplified by the comment:

> *Each child is special and should be given opportunities to develop good self-esteem and achieve success. There is a place in the sun for everyone (Principal 17).*

Discussion

Previous research indicates positive outcomes for integrated education in Northern Ireland (Hayes, McAllister and Dowds, 2006; McGlynn, Niens, Cairns and Hewstone, 2004; Montgomery *et al.*, 2003; McGlynn, 2001), but also suggests that opportunities for pro-active practice are missed in some schools (Montgomery *et al.*, 2003; Donnelly, 2004; Donnelly and Hughes, 2007). This study reports a much wider range of approaches to integrated education, including liberal, plural, critical, liberal/plural and liberal/critical (see Table 11.2 for summary of approaches noted in this study).

Thus within even a small education sector, deliberately established to educate Catholic and Protestant children together, there are a number of quite different approaches to dealing with cultural diversity. Whilst such a typology may provide us with a useful tool for categorising approaches to

Table 11.2. **Summary of approaches to integration**

Approach	Characterised by
Liberal pro-active	Deliberate emphasis on commonality
Liberal passive	Coincidental emphasis on commonality i.e. avoidance of difference
Plural inclusive	Recognition and celebration of all aspects of cultural difference
Plural limited	Recognition of world religions and ethnic minority groups but Catholic/ Protestant difference avoided
Critical	Recognition and celebration of all cultural difference plus commitment to tackle prejudice and injustice
Liberal/plural	Deliberate emphasis on commonality balanced with recognition of cultural difference
Liberal/critical	Deliberate emphasis on commonality plus commitment to tackle prejudice and injustice

multicultural educational efforts, we must go further with our analysis and consider the potential implications of this variation, not least for teacher education. Ongoing research projects by the author are now investigating the characteristics of good practice in response to cultural diversity in two case study integrated schools, one with a *critical* approach and one with a more *liberal* approach. It is hoped that eliciting detailed, multi-perspectival insights and observations into the practices of response to cultural diversity will increase our understanding of how these approaches are experienced by culturally diverse children and of how teachers translate them into practice.

Central here is surely the necessity to strike a balance between respecting group and individual rights, Reich's navigation between the *"pluribus"* and *"unum"* (2002, p. 116). Kincheloe and Steinberg (1997) warn that *liberal* approaches may promote cultural invisibility and fail to challenge prejudice and injustice towards minority groups. However, *liberal pro-active* endorsement of commonality, liberty and equality might also help to construct the common ground that is sorely needed between conflicting communities. The weaker *liberal passive* model, also reported in this study may, at best, leave the building of such common ground to chance. More *plural* approaches that purely advocate the celebration of diversity also have their limitations. It is difficult to defend a *plural limited* model that, whilst willing to recognise "exotic" minorities, appears to deny recognition to the two majority groups, Catholics and Protestants. Although the *plural inclusive* approach may be more easily supported, due to its willingness to acknowledge and celebrate all forms of diversity, without a critical edge it appears to promise equality it cannot deliver. *Plural* approaches also risk the reification of difference by presenting group identities as homogeneous and fixed. This is also a difficulty for *critical* approaches, which whilst challenging hegemonic culture, may also unintentionally reinforce group boundaries.

Sen (2006) resists over-simplistic categorisation of people purely on the basis of their religion or culture. He argues for the autonomy of the individual in celebrating whichever aspects of their culture that they choose. Only 2 of the 52 principals interviewed reported that the development of pupil autonomy was a central aspect of their approach to integration. This does not imply that the other 50 principals believe that education cannot contribute to this, but rather that they tend to prioritise the bringing together of groups of children. Niens and Cairns (2008) suggest that the contact hypothesis, that states that contact between members of opposing groups will promote positive intergroup attitudes in individuals and improve relationships between groups (Allport, 1954; Pettigrew and Tropp, 2000), has been an unspoken guiding principle behind integrated education. However, developments of the contact hypothesis (Hewstone, 1996) indicate the importance of group salience in the process of prejudice reduction. This risks reifying difference. Whereas contact theory foregrounds difference, Sen's approach challenges our tendency to reduce difference to the lowest common denominator. Indeed to promote a culture of peace he advocates the development of understanding of the pluralities of human identity (Sen, 2006). Davies suggests:

> *Efforts to "preserve" or "celebrate" distinct cultures ... may be counterproductive: it would be better to acknowledge hybridity as a positive identity (Davies, 2004, p. 87).*

As suggested earlier identity may be a more helpful construct to us than the much contested "culture", not least because in Northern Ireland identity as a "Catholic" or "Protestant" can be understood as a complex amalgam of religious, political, social and ethnic aspects. We must also recognise that identities are complex and continually in flux. It is difficult, however, to imagine how recognition of identity hybridity might be reflected in classroom practice whilst also effectively tackling bias, when the latter requires a recognition of group distinctiveness. Reich (2002) outlines a theory of liberal multicultural education that promotes the development of self-reflective individuals who are empowered to make autonomous decisions about shaping their own lives, but his model lacks the critical edge needed to counteract sectarianism and racism. The *liberal/critical* approach reported here represents an attempt to unify, whilst also proactively challenging prejudice and injustice. An extension of this *liberal/critical* model that acknowledges hybridity as a positive identity and that promotes the development of more autonomous individuals may be a useful policy direction for multicultural societies. In conflicted societies like Northern Ireland the multicultural project must affirm and protect minority group members, but also be fit to tackle the legacy of conflict by challenging stereotypes, engaging with the "other" perspective and reducing prejudice.

We have seen here that multiculturalism and multicultural education can provide a valuable frame for analysis of integrated education policy and practice. One thing must be remembered: the socialising role of schools is limited and it remains to be seen whether educational initiatives such as integrated education can overcome the "socialising tyranny of categorisation" (Jenkins, 2004, p. 183). This study reports a range of approaches to managing cultural difference. The motto *"Ut sint unum"* (together we are one) of the first integrated school in Northern Ireland is a powerful rallying call to integration and cultural interaction: its translation into practice is an ongoing challenge when the needs of individuals and groups must be negotiated and prejudice must also be tackled.

What are the consequences then for preparing our teachers for diversity in initial and ongoing teacher education? In a study of students at the two institutions responsible for the initial education of the majority of primary school teachers in Northern Ireland, Montgomery and McGlynn (2009) report that much more needs to be done to embed diversity and community relations in teacher education. However, this is constrained by the absence of an explicit community relations role for teachers in both the statements of teacher competency and in the revised national curriculum. The present chapter would suggest that central to the preparation of teachers for diverse classrooms is engagement in critical debates surrounding the social purposes of education; explorations of identity as a social construction and the impact of education on identity construction; the development of classroom tools such as critical multicultural pedagogy that enable teachers to increase the participation and achievement of culturally diverse children; and the ongoing development of critically reflexive teachers who are constantly working towards inclusion by evaluating their practice.

References

American Educational Research Association (2006), *Brief of the American Educational Research Association as Amicus Curiae for the respondents, www.aera.net/uploadedFiles/News_Media/AERA_Amicus_Brief.pdf.*

Allport, G.W. (1954), *The Nature of Prejudice,* Addison-Wesley, London.

Banks, J.A. (2008), "Diversity, Group Identity and Citizenship Education in a Global Age", *Educational Researcher,* Vol. 37 No. 3, pp. 129-139.

Barry, B. (2001), *Culture and Equality: An Egalitarian Critique of Multiculturalism,* Polity Press, Cambridge.

BBC News (2009). Romanians Leave NI after Attacks, 23 June 2009, *news. bbc.co.uk/1/hi/northern_ireland/8114234.stm.*

Benhabib, S. (2002), *The Claims of Culture: Equality and Diversity in the Global Era,* Princeton University Press, Princeton.

Brighouse, H. (2006), *On Education,* Routledge, Oxon.

Davies, L. (2004), *Education and Conflict: Complexity and Chaos,* Routledge Falmer, London.

Donnelly, C. (2004), "What Price Harmony? Teachers' Methods of Delivering an Ethos of Tolerance and Respect for Diversity in an Integrated School in Northern Ireland", *Educational Research,* Vol. 46, No. 1, pp. 3-16.

Duarte, E.M. and S. Smith (2000), *Foundational Perspectives in Multicultural Education,* Longman, New York.

Education Reform (Northern Ireland) Order (1989), S.I 1989, No. 2406 (NI20). Belfast: Her Majesty's Stationery Office.

Freebody, P. (2003), *Qualitative Research in Education: Interaction and Practice,* Sage Publications, London.

Gallagher, T. (2005), "Balancing Difference and the Common Good: Lessons from a Post Conflict Society", *Compare,* Vol. 35, No. 4, pp. 429-442.

Gallagher, T. and A. Smith (2002), "Selection, Integration and Diversity in Northern Ireland", in A.M. Gray, K. Lloyd, P. Devine, G. Robinson and D. Heenan (eds.), *Social Attitudes in Northern Ireland: the Eighth Report*, Pluto, London.

Gjerde, P.F. (2004), "Culture, Power and Experience: Toward a Person-Centred Cultural Psychology", *Human Development*, Vol. 47, pp. 138-157.

Government of the United Kingdom of Great Britain and Northern Ireland, the Government of Ireland (1998), *The Agreement: Agreement Reached in the Multi-party Negotiations*, Northern Ireland Office, Belfast.

Hayes, B.C., I. McAllisterand and L. Dowds (2006), "In Search of the Middle Ground: Integrated Education and Northern Ireland Politics", *Research Update,* No 42, ARK (Northern Ireland Social and Political Archive), *www.ark.ac.uk/publications/updates/update42.pdf.*

Hewstone, M. (1996), "Contact and Categorisation: Social Psychological Interventions to Change Intergroup Relations", in C.N. Macrae and C. Stangor and M. Hewstone (eds.), *Foundations of Stereotypes and Stereotyping*, Guilford, New York, pp. 323-368.

Hughes, J. and C. Donnelly (2007), "Is the Policy Sufficient? An Exploration of Integrated Education in Northern Ireland and Bi-lingual/Bi-national Education in Israel", in Z. Bekerman and C. McGlynn (eds.), *Addressing Ethnic Conflict through Peace Education,* Palgrave Macmillan, New York.

Jenkins, R. (2004), *Social Identity,* Routledge, London.

Kelly, P. (2002), *Multiculturalism Reconsidered,* Polity Press, Cambridge.

Kincheloe, J.L. and S.R. Steinberg (1997), *Changing Multiculturalism,* Open University Press, Buckingham.

Kymlicka, W. (2007), *Multicultural Odysseys,* Oxford University Press, Oxford.

Mahalingham, R. and C. McCarthy (2000), *Multicultural Curriculum: New Directions for Social Theory, Practice and Policy,* Routledge, New York.

Mason, J. (1996), *Qualitative Researching,* Sage Publications, London.

McGlynn, C. (2005), "Integrated Schooling and Faith-Based Schooling in Northern Ireland", *Irish Journal of Education*, Vol. 36, pp. 49-62.

McGlynn, C. (2008), "Leading Integrated Schools: A Study of the Multicultural Perspectives of Northern Irish Principals", *Journal of Peace Education*, Vol. 5, No. 1, pp. 3-16.

McGlynn, C.W. (2001), "The Impact of Post Primary Integrated Education in Northern Ireland on Past Pupils: A Study", Ed.D Thesis, University of Ulster at Jordanstown, Belfast.

McGlynn, C., U. Niens, E. Cairns, and M. Hewstone (2004), "Moving Out of Conflict: The Contribution of Integrated Schools in Northern Ireland to Identity, Attitudes, Forgiveness and Reconciliation", *Journal of Peace Education,* Vol. 1, No. 2, pp. 147-163.

Modood, T. (2007), *Multiculturalism,* Polity Press, Cambridge.

Montgomery, A. and C. McGlynn (2009), "New Peace, New Teachers: Student Teachers' Perspectives on Diversity and Community Relations in Northern Ireland", *Teaching and Teacher Education,* Vol. 25, No. 3, pp. 391-399.

Montgomery, A., G. Fraser, C. McGlynn, A. Smith and T. Gallagher (2003), *Integrated Education in Northern Ireland: Integration in Practice,* UNESCO Centre, University of Ulster, Coleraine.

Nieto, S. (2000), *Affirming Diversity: The Sociopolitical Context of Multicultural Education,* Longman, New York.

Niens, U. and E. Cairns (2008), "Integrated Education in Northern Ireland: A Review", in D. Berliner and H. Kupermintz (eds.), *Fostering Change in Institutions, Environments, and People: A Festschrift in Honor of Gavriel Salomon,* Lawrence Erlbaum, Mahwah, NJ, pp. 193-210.

Orfield, G. and C. Lee (2006), Racial Transformation and the Changing Nature of Segregation. *www.civilrightsproject.harvard.edu/research/ deseg/Racial_Transformation.pdf.*

Parker-Jenkins, M., D. Hartas and B. Irving (2004), *In Good Faith: Schools, Religion and Public Funding,* Ashgate Press, Abingdon.

Phillips, A. (2007), *Multiculturalism Without Culture,* Princeton University Press, Princeton.

Pettigrew T.F. and L.R. Tropp (2000), "Does Intergroup Contact Reduce Prejudice? Recent Metanalytic Findings", in S. Oskamp (ed.) *Reducing Prejudice and Discrimination,* Lawrence Erlbaum, Mahwah New Jersey, pp. 93-114.

Phillips, T. (2005), "After 7/7: Sleepwalking to Segregation," Speech given by Chair of the Commission for Racial Equality at the Manchester Council for Community Relations, 22 September 2005, *www.cre.gov.uk/Default. aspx.LocID-0hgnew07s.RefLocID-0hg00900c002.Lang-EN.htm.*

Police Services of Northern Ireland Archives (2009), Domestic and Hate Motivation Archive, *www.psni.police.uk/index/updates/updates_statistics/updates_domestic_and_hate_motivation_statistics/updates_domestic_and_hate_motivation_statistics_archive.htm.*

Punch, K.F. (1998), *Introduction to Social Research: Quantitative and Qualitative Approaches,* Sage Publications, London.

Reich, R. (2002), *Bridging Liberalism and Multiculturalism in American Education,* University of Chicago Press, Chicago.

Sen, A. (2006), *Identity and Violence,* Norton, New York.

Sleeter, C. and P. McLaren (eds.) (1995), *Multicultural Education, Critical Pedagogy and the Politics of Difference,* State University of New York Press, New York.

Taylor, C. (1994), "The Politics of Recognition", in A. Gutmann (ed.), *Multiculturalism: Examining the Politics of Recognition,* Princeton University Press, Princeton, pp 25-73.

Chapter 12

Classroom practices for teaching diversity: an example from Washington State (United States)

Geneva Gay
University of Washington, United States

It is difficult to identify classroom practices for teaching cultural diversity that could be applicable across national and cultural contexts. So much weight in research on ethnic and cultural diversity is given to the environmental, sociological and historical influences which mitigate learning that "universal" strategies are almost unthinkable. The author proposes that teacher education programmes focus on principles to guide classroom practices rather than specific practices themselves. Prospective teachers can be taught how to translate these principles into effective strategies for their particular classroom settings. Four principles are discussed: (i) *how beliefs about diversity shape instructional behaviours;* (ii) *using multiple perspectives in learning about diversity;* (iii) *multiple techniques to achieve common learning outcomes; and* (iv) *developing skills to cross borders between different cultural systems. Specific examples are provided to illustrate what these principles look like in actual instructional practice, but the emphasis is on encouraging teachers to develop their own.*

From the OECD online consultation : addressing diversity in practice

Teachers provided examples of practices they adapt for their changing classrooms. As student populations become more diverse, it is clear that there is no "one-size fits all" method that will work for everyone. How can teachers be supported to choose practices that have the most potential for their particular context?

Introduction

In discussions on instructional strategies for teaching diversity, it is important to take into account the importance of *contextual specificity* in determining techniques for meeting the needs of different students (see Verma, Bagley, and Jha, 2007; Paik and Walberg, 2007; Arzubiaga, Noguerón, and Sullivan, 2009). This is more valid than looking for "universal best practices" for two reasons. First, teaching and learning are cultural processes that take place in social and political contexts. Without knowing the specifics of who is teaching what to whom, when, where and why, suggested techniques are unavoidably general and broad. Second, while it is acceptable for *principles* of teaching diversity to transcend context, *strategies* for their implementation should be targeted to particular audiences, purposes and locations if they are to be most effective.

The idea of contextual specificity in the learning experiences designed for different individuals and groups of students based on more than intellectual abilities is a significant departure from long-held beliefs and practices in education. Ideological claims have been made repeatedly by many educators about the need to respond to the individual identities and needs of students, while actually using the same or similar practices for large groups. However, the idea of educational programmes and practices tailored to specific communities and student populations has theoretical precedents that date back many years as well. In the United States context, these include the thoughts of John Dewey, Lev Vygotsky, and African American educators such as W. E. B. Du Bois, Mary McLeod Bethune, and Carter G. Woodson in the early years of the 20th century. It also has been a constant theme in multicultural education theory since its beginnings in the late 1960s.

Invitations and challenges

Not all categories of diversity are synonymous and, therefore, cannot be treated identically in teaching and learning. However, they cannot be handled entirely discretely either. Racial, gender, ethnic and social class inequities are not the same even though there are points of intersection among them. Nor do any or all of them function in identical ways for members of different ethnic groups or even for all members within the same ethnic group (Verma, Bagley, and Jha, 2007; Paik and Walberg, 2007; Banks, 2009). Time and location are other factors that cause diversity challenges and need to be nuanced.

One example of this "variance within diversity" that must be considered when designing instructional strategies is the ethnic student enrolment patterns in different countries. As can be seen in Figure 12.1, in the latest statistics available from the National Center for Educational Statistics (NCES), the number of students from different ethnic and racial groups in public schools in the United States is growing significantly. The percentage of increase between 1972 and 2007 varies by region of the country and ethnic group, but students of Latino ancestry account for the largest amount of growth in all regions. African American student enrolments have remained relatively stable across regions of the United States over the last 35 years; however, regional patterns do exist as can be seen when, in 2007, African American student enrolments comprised a quarter of student enrolments in the South and only a small minority in the West.

Figure 12.1. **Percentage distribution of the race/ethnicity of public school students enrolled in kindergarten through 12th grade: selected years, October 1972-October 2007**

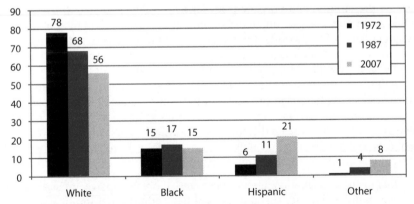

Notes: "Other" includes all students who identified themselves as being Asian, Hawaiian, Native American Indian, or two or more races.

Estimates include all public school students enrolled in kindergarten through 12th grade.

Other groups of colour (Asian, Pacific Islander, Native American, Alaskan Native, and bi/multiracial) are also increasing in public school enrolment, but the numbers remain very small, while students of European ancestry are declining, with by far the highest decline in the Western region of the country.[1]

Oppression and discrimination are an illustration of how time and location influence the teachings of diversity. The features and effects of racism directed at African Americans differ from those toward Asian, Native and Latino Americans, and racial discrimination is manifested differently today than it was 50 years ago. This is also true for different regions of the country – that is, the North, East, South and West. While they are not immune to oppression and racial profiling, educated and middle class individuals of colour receive somewhat better treatment than those who are poor and uneducated. In most instances, females in different ethnic groups in the United States are not treated as harshly as their male counterparts. However, across time African American females have been perceived and treated more negatively than other women of colour by mainstream society in the United States. They have been profiled as aggressive, angry, unattractive, hostile and domineering. Ethnic and gender stereotypes such as these have negative effects on the social, psychological, educational and identity achievement of both African American females and males (see Collins, 1990; Jewell 1993; West, 1995; Woodard and Mastin, 2005). For example, research by Steele (1997) shows that stereotypes attributed to African Americans can derail the academic achievement of students from this ethnic group even when they are normally high achievers and even if they do not believe that the stereotypes apply to them personally.

International variations in diversity need to be considered as well in teacher preparation and practice (see Verms, Bagley, and Jha, 2007; Banks, 2009; Arzubiaga, Noguerón, and Sullivan, 2009). The arrival of people from different parts of the world, at particular points in time and under particular conditions, creates different educational, political, social, economic and cultural challenges. The language that educators use to discuss diversity varies by country or regions of the world as do the particular issues of analysis. For instance, the language of choice in the United States for people relocating to the country includes terms such as immigrants and newcomers, with qualifiers added to indicate differences in political status, such as sojourners, refugees and undocumented newcomers. In many European nations these individuals are referred to as migrants, migrant minorities and resettlers.

Insightful information about these and more extensive cross-national nuances within diversity discourses, and their educational implications, are presented by contributors to a recently edited volume by Banks (2009) on international multicultural education. It is a helpful resource for prospective teachers and teacher educators on a variety of diversities in countries in the Americas, Europe, Africa and Asia.

This topic has already generated much discussion. According to Storti (2001), some tensions are inevitable when different cultures intersect, and this reality should not be avoided in cross-cultural teaching and learning. Instead, cultural differences should be confronted directly and skills taught to negotiate them. This is necessary because:

> *People from different cultures have ... deeply ingrained ideas about what is right, good, normal and natural ... These values and beliefs determine how those individuals behave and what they are supposed to say and do, as well as not say and do, in various situations. As children we learn and internalise the values and behaviours of our culture, what we might call the code of conduct in that society, until it becomes entirely natural and instinctive for us to behave in certain ways and to never behave in others. Needless to say, when people from different countries come in contact with each other ... they are bound to say and do things that will confuse, frustrate, and offend each other. And the more this happens ... the harder it will be for them to live and work together (Storti 2001, pp. 2-3).*

If these various complications and configurations are ignored in teaching, then the complexities of existing inequities and interventions required to resolve them are minimised. The resulting reform is likely to be overly simplified, focus too much on the presumed common denominators among diversities, and have limited value in teaching students important information and skills about diversity.

Therefore, designing classroom practices for teaching diversity cross-nationally should begin by specifying the particular type of diversity that is to be the primary focus of instructional attention, and its contextual characteristics and dynamics. In theory, all forms of diversity should be understood by teachers and students, but, in practice, all of them simply cannot be taught with the same degree of emphasis and depth at the same time. Priorities have to be established about which one will be the primary focus of the *instructional centre*,[2] how others will be woven into the analyses, and what these will be. Thus, ethnic diversity could be the primary unit of teaching and learning in one socio-political setting while incorporating gender, language, social class, and immigration/migration perspectives and experiences to gain greater insights into its complexities and dynamics. In another school or national setting, the crux of diversity studies could be immigration/migration, with gender, nationality and language as the intervening variables. In yet another, the focus of analysis could be race and racism. Professional preparation programmes should help prospective and practicing teachers learn how to make informed and valid choices about addressing, characterising and analysing diversities so that they and their students learn significant, accurate and authentic information.

The notion of *intersectionality* proposed by Gillborn and Youdell (2009) for studying interconnections and interrelationships among multiple diversities is a viable strategy for accomplishing these goals.[3] These relationships are configured differently for various groups of people in assorted socio-political, national and historical contexts and they have different implications for how specific educational programmes and practices are organised and implemented. For instance, educating immigrant students is affected by their pre-migration education status, as well as other social and political conditions in their countries of origin, and their reception in the receiving countries (Arzbugiaba *et al.,* 2009).

In the United States some developments in multicultural education theory and practice are occurring that recognise these complexities of diversity. Most scholars in this field routinely declare and name particular kinds of diversity as their areas of concentration. It is the rare exception that these major scholars make references to "diversity" without including a qualifier – hence, cultural diversity, racial diversity, ethnic diversity, gender diversity and linguistic diversity. Separate bodies of research, theory and practice have developed on these various diversity categories. For instance, many multicultural education specialists routinely include ethnic, racial and cultural diversity in their scholarly discourse and proposals for practice; educational disability specialists typically form the professional communities of Special Education, and Gifted and Talented Education (GATE); and immigrants students who are not native speakers of the dominant mainstream language of the United States (English) fall within the jurisdiction of Bilingual Education (BE), English as a second language (ESL), and/or English Language learning (ELL).

The number of "cross-over" scholars and school practitioners is growing. These individuals combine analyses of more than one area of diversity to serve the needs of the constituent students for whom they advocate. For instance, some special educators of colour are including race, ethnicity and culture into their analyses of the educational needs of and instructional programmes for students who need specialised ability-based instructional interventions. Some gender equity and women's studies scholars are examining how race, ethnicity and culture interact with gender. Also, some scholars who promote educational equity for African, Asian, Latino and/or Native American students are incorporating critical race theory into their analyses and reform proposals.

William Ayers' (2004, pp. 3, 43) statement that *teaching is an intellectual task of perpetual decision-making* symbolises another factor contributing to the challenge of identifying classroom practices for teaching diversity across multiple cultural and national contexts. He explains that in teaching,

"Nothing is settled once and for all. No view is all views and no perspective is every perspective ... Good teaching is not automatic; it is always a struggle. It is filled with initiative and risk, but also with satisfaction and joy. It is intricate, complex, deep and wide. It is never twice the same".

If teachers can never know with certainty how their practices will unfold and the effects they will generate in the interactive dynamics with students in classrooms, the chances are even less so in ethnically and culturally diverse classrooms or with practices proposed by outsiders. The best that people who are not an intimate part of the classroom communities of teachers can do is offer some general guidelines for practice, and help teachers learn to make these their own by personalising them to fit the particulars of their classrooms. This orientation offers ample space for prospective and practicing teachers to be active partners in the process of constructing instructional strategies for teaching diversity in their own classrooms. These strategies will be behaviourally unique but must be ideologically consistent with established parameters of educational equity, social justice and excellence for students diversified by a wide variety of factors.

Principles for practice in teaching diversity

Possible principles and practices for teaching diversity are too numerous to name them all. Four are included here to illustrate the idea of principles guiding practice, to suggest the range of possibilities, and to invite teacher educators and teachers to make their own additions. They are: (1) beliefs shape behaviour, (2) multiple perspectives, (3) multiple instructional means and (4) crossing cultural borders. In presenting these principles, this chapter provides an explanation of what these terms mean and provides a few examples (mostly from schooling in the United States) to demonstrate what they may look like in practice. The principles are at once discrete and interconnected, which implies that classroom practices should deal with various dimensions and types of diversities separately and in concert with each other. Hopefully, they will entice teacher educators, scholars as well as prospective and practicing teachers to add others gleaned from their personal backgrounds, academic knowledge and professional experiences with diversity. The larger challenge and invitation are for teachers in different cultures, communities and countries to not merely understand and accept these principles but to translate them into classroom teaching practices that are appropriate for their particular contexts and situations. Teacher education programmes can assist these processes by providing sample lessons, demonstrations and guided practice in converting general ideas about diversity into instructional actions appropriate for different learning situations. Video recordings and personal narratives can also serve as valuable tools for showing how these ideas are embodied as actions.

Beliefs shape instructional behaviours

The first principle for practice is that *personal and professional beliefs about diversity based on race, ethnicity, language, culture, social class and nationality shape instructional behaviours.* If diversity is perceived as a positive, enriching and valuable resource for teaching, learning and living, then it will be systematically and explicitly included in teaching practices, with an air of excitement, expectancy and adventure. Conversely, negative beliefs about diversity generate behaviours characterised by avoidance, denial, dismissal, anxiety and even fear. It is considered a pathology, or an obstacle to successful teaching and learning. Some teachers have ambivalent beliefs about diversity; they are positive about some related aspects, negative about others, and unsure about still others.

Regardless of their ideological positions, many teachers have not clarified their beliefs or critically analysed their behaviour with students. Correcting this is a good starting place for developing classroom practices for teaching diversity. Deep analyses will reveal that some long-standing beliefs about students from different ethnic groups are somewhat negative and become problematic for teaching them effectively. Among them are beliefs such as: some ethnic groups (such as African and Latino Americans in the United States) do not value education and are not motivated to learn; focusing on ethnic and cultural differences in schools is divisive and breeds hostilities; minority groups maintaining their first languages interferes with their learning the dominant language; students of Asian ancestry are "model minorities" (S. Lee, 2009; Pang and Cheng, 1998) because they are motivated to learn and are high achievers; children from all ethnic, cultural and social backgrounds should adapt to the existing norms of the mainstream cultures of the countries where they live; and racism is a thing of the past.

Teaching for and through diversity requires very different beliefs if the intended outcomes are equity, maximum achievement and genuine acceptance of the validity of and the right to existence for different cultures. Such positive beliefs attribute low school achievement of ethnic minorities and immigrants to factors other than inherent individual and cultural pathologies. These include: cultural incompatibilities between home and school; the failure of schools to include cultural diversity in the heart of their policies, programmes and practices; negotiating multiple cultural systems which command intellectual and emotional energy, thus drawing attention away from academic pursuits; high levels of stress, anxiety and distrust experienced by many ethnically and culturally diverse students; and the lack of familiarity faced by minority, migrant and immigrant students with the way teaching and learning are conducted in mainstream schools of their host countries. Therefore, achievement problems are often due more to the failure of educational systems to respond appropriately to the interactions among teaching, learning, and cultures, and diverse students not having the cultural and social capital to successfully negotiate unfamiliar school protocols, than they are to students' intellectual ability and motivation (Gay, 2000; Pang and Cheng, 1998).

Techniques well-grounded in theory, research and practice are available to help teachers articulate, analyse and revise their beliefs about various forms of diversity, and their role and function in the educational enterprise. One of these is cultural therapy: a series of self-study questions to help individuals become aware of their own cultural attitudes, values and behaviours, and how these affect teaching actions (Spindler and Spindler, 1994). It is especially helpful for White teachers in the United States because so many of them believe that they have no culture and ethnicity, and that these terms apply only to individuals and groups of colour. Another is the Developmental Model of Intercultural Sensitivity (DMIS) and related measurement tool, the Intercultural Development Inventory (IDI). The DMIS describes six stages of sensitivity and receptivity to cultural differences, and it suggests stage-appropriate interventions for building capacity for intercultural competence. The IDI, used to identify these developmental stages in individuals, groups and organisations, has been translated into 12 languages including Chinese, English, French, German, Italian, Japanese, Korean, Portuguese and Russian (see M. Bennett, 1986; Landis, Bennett, and Bennett, 2004; Van Hook, 2004). Other formal tools and techniques exist for diagnosing and developing receptivity to different kinds of diversity, including those described by Feng, Bryam and Fleming (2009).

Many instructors involved in diversity studies use a variety of more informal, self-constructed tools to help teachers become cognizant of their attitudes and beliefs about diversity. Among them are: cultural profiles; critical encounters with ethnic, racial and cultural diversity; personal narratives and storytelling; courageous conversations and dialogue analysis (Singleton, 2006; Storti, 2001); and procedures for observing, recording and reflecting on cultural diversity in everyday life. I have used three different techniques to serve similar purposes. I ask prospective teachers to: (1) create *multicultural codes of ethics* for their classrooms that state how they expect students to receive and respond to cultural diversity; (2) compose letters of *multicultural appreciation to parents* indicating excitement about having their children in class, and anticipation of how parents and children will contribute to the class' ventures into and adventures with diversity; and (3) write *multicultural pedagogical creeds* that combine general beliefs about ethnic, racial and cultural diversity with specifically related instructional behaviours. The structural format for these creed statements is, "I believe … ; therefore I will …." An example is "I believe content on *multicultural* diversity should be taught regularly within the context of other subjects and skills; therefore I will incorporate information from African, Asian, European, Latino and Native American cultures and experiences (at the same time and for all students) as

I teach word recognition, vocabulary, comprehension and interpretation in reading." An underlying premise of all these strategies is that teachers need to develop more positive beliefs about and behaviours toward diversity, but little if any progress can be made in doing so until those that already exist are revealed and subjected to critical analysis. Similar attitudes and actions can be used with students in primary and secondary schools.

Multiple perspectives

A second principle for developing classroom practices is *using multiple perspectives in teaching knowledge about different kinds of diversities and skills for engaging with these diversities.* Addressing diversity in classroom practices entails – at a minimum – paying special attention to curriculum, pedagogy and relationships. It is important for all students, subjects and school settings, regardless of whether they are minority or majority populations, immigrant or indigenous residents, high or low achievers, or enrolled in academic or vocational training programmes. How diversity education is actually delivered will vary by environmental settings and student populations. Thus, teachers' decisions regarding how to teach math, science or reading to students from different ethnic backgrounds should be informed by knowledge of their cultural heritages and living experiences. Both minority and majority students should learn about their own and each others' histories and heritages.

Another way to address multiple perspectives is to deal with both the general and the particulars of diversity, *i.e.* things that are common among groups as well as aspects that are unique to them. Both are necessary to avoid over-simplifying or over-generalising very complex and contextually-bound issues. This principle may be actualised by organising teaching and learning around major concepts, issues, events and experiences that are common among various groups, in different locations and times. Some of these *universals* are diaspora, identity, culture, oppression and survival. Virtually all groups throughout the world have experienced these in some form or another, and continue to do so, but not for the same reasons, in the similar ways, or with the identical consequences. Therefore, specific groups' experiences should be used as case studies to demonstrate how common concerns are manifested differently in actual behaviours. For example, in studying resistance to oppression, teachers should help students understand that some groups use political protest as their primary means while others use music, art, literature and drama. Students might analyse any one of these means of resistance (such as politics and protest) from the vantage point of different ethnic groups within and among different countries to determine similarities and differences in causes, techniques and effects.

Classroom practices for teaching ethnic and cultural diversity also can be directed toward and guided by commonly accepted goals and objectives as identified by scholars. These include increasing the academic achievement of students from marginalised groups; combating racism and other forms of oppression; providing equity and social justice in access to educational opportunities; teaching knowledge about the histories, heritages and contributions of different ethnic groups; developing competencies for cross-cultural personal interactions and relationships; acquiring skills for citizenship in multicultural communities, nations and the world; enhancing self-concepts and ethnic identities; and improving the socio-political empowerment, agency and activism of ethnically and culturally diverse students (see Gay, 1994; King, Hollins, and Hayman, 1997; C. Bennett, 2007; Grant and Sleeter, 2007). A number of analyses and recommendations presented by scholars from different ethnic identities, national locations and areas of specialisation[4] offer valuable insights into similarities and differences among the histories and experiences of ethnic groups, and provide some useful starting points for teachers and teacher educators to develop appropriate strategies for teaching to and through them.

In-depth understandings of diversity issues demand knowledge, insights and techniques from a wide-range of disciplines, viewpoints, individual and group experiences as well as from historical and contemporary explorations. This *multivocality* avoids falling into the trap of assuming that the "truth" of one group, individual, culture or nation is the only "correct" one that exists. Music, poetry, personal stories and literary texts (such as fiction, biographies, autobiographies and children's picture books) provide insights into diversity, and students respond to these materials differently than they do to information generated by empirical research in the social sciences, demographic analyses, political policies and legal regulations.

Multiple instructional strategies

A third principle for practice endorsed by scholars of cultural diversity, equity and social justice in education is *using multiple instructional means to achieve common learning outcomes for ethnically, racially and culturally diverse students*. Other educators refer to a variant of this idea that emphasises intellectual diversity as *differentiated instruction* (Forsten, Grant, and Hollas, 2002; Educational Leadership, 2008; The New England Reading Association Journal, 2009). This strategy is based on the fact that students learn in various ways and at different rates, and that these learning styles are strongly influenced by cultural socialisation and prior experiences (Shade, 1997; Park, 2002; Woodrow, 2007).

From his review of research on learning styles in Austria, India, the United Kingdom, and the United States, as well as his own studies of Chinese ancestry students in England and Hong Kong-China, Woodrow (2007; Woodrow and Sham, 2001) concluded that different societies develop different assumptions about the nature of knowledge and ways of learning. This "cultural capital" can be problematic when ethnically diverse students are learning in multicultural and multinational settings with teachers who do not understand, value or accommodate their students' cultural capital. As it is extremely difficult for both students and teachers to transcend or set aside their underlying beliefs and assumptions that drive the act of learning, it is important to acknowledge that these assumptions may be present despite the best intentions of the teacher or student. In designing strategies for teaching diversity, these different beliefs about learning and ways of learning need to be accommodated and complemented, not denied, ignored or eradicated.

Research evidence indicates that when teaching styles are compatible with students' learning styles, the achievement of ethnically and culturally diverse students is much higher in the areas of academic, personal, social, political, moral and ethical performance as well as on different measures, such as standardised tests and teacher-made assessments. In addition such outcomes as improved school attendance; fewer disciplinary referrals; feelings of efficacy and empowerment; and greater satisfaction with schooling for both students and teachers are noted as well (see Tharp and Gallimore, 1991; Gay, 2000; Banks and Banks, 2004; Au, 2006; O. Lee and Luykx, 2006; C. Lee, 2007; Palk and Walberg, 2007; Ladson-Billings, 2009).There are numerous strategies that can be used in classroom practices to accommodate the learning styles of ethnically and culturally diverse students, including the use of co-operative and collaborative groups; learning communities; teacher modelling; peer coaching; using theatre (or performance), poetry, music and drama as pedagogy; mentoring; cross-cultural exchange programmes among ethnic groups in local, national and international settings; student-produced narratives; oral histories; storytelling; learning partnerships with senior citizens and business people; and computer discourses among students from different backgrounds and living in different cultural environments (see Gay, 2000; Shorr, 2006; C. Lee, 2007; Banks, 2009; Tiedt and Tiedt, 2010).

Specific practices for teaching diversity should also be shaped by the many different aspects of teaching that regularly exist in classrooms. They include: curriculum content; teacher-student and student-student rapport and relationships; physical and psycho-emotional classroom climates; instructional materials and resources; beliefs about and expectations for performance; the many different delivery techniques used in the act of teaching; diagnosis of students' needs and assessment of their achievement; and social etiquette and behaviour management. The different subjects, knowledge and skills typically taught in schools and classrooms also demand different approaches to teaching diversity. Thus, teaching ethnic and cultural diversity within the context of reading will differ somewhat in math, science, literature and social studies. Various skills (acquiring factual information, problem-solving, critical thinking, values clarification, etc.) within different subjects require various techniques as well. For instance, a major part of social studies education is teaching students the symbols, signs and iconic representations of national identity (such as the national flag, motto and anthem) to evoke feelings of loyalty, affiliation and citizenship. In most countries there are new residents who are not yet citizens, and do not have any strong feelings of sentimentality toward these symbols, or even recognise them. Some may even feel conflicted because of continuing identity and strong affinity with their countries of origin. Yet, most social studies teachers do not ask students to critically examine what national symbols mean to different groups within a country, as they should in teaching diversity. All of these situations reinforce the need to use multiple means to teach the many aspects of diversity, and to ensure that these techniques are compatible with different arenas of classroom practices.

Another way to employ multiple instructional means to improve achievement is through using multicultural and multi-ethnic examples, scenarios and vignettes to illustrate academic concepts, ideas, and skills, and for students to practice and demonstrate mastery of knowledge. It is a powerful strategy for incorporating diversity into the heart of teaching because examples are fundamental to and consume much of the actual time devoted to teaching in all subjects and school settings. Relevant examples link school knowledge to the lived experience of diverse students and improved academic achievement. For instance, in schools in the United States a particular artistic, musical, rhetorical or dance technique might be illustrated with examples from European, African, Asian, Latino or Native American culture, as well as ethnic group traditions in other countries. Math skills such as ratios and graphing might be taught by using population distributions of different ethnic groups in the schools, cities, regions or countries where they are being taught. Or, students could be taught writing skills through conducting oral history interviews with significant individuals in their lives within their own families, cultural communities and countries of origin. It is impossible to provide an instructional example from every ethnic group within a given country, but surely more than those representing only the dominant culture can be easily identified and used routinely in teaching.

One of the teaching frameworks I use for ensuring that students receive varied engagement opportunities and participate in multiple kinds of learning is "*know, think, feel, do, and reflect*". This requires different kinds of student involvement, including comprehension, analysis, emotional responding, introspection and action. I do not consider a teaching exchange complete until I have had students engage in each of these processes. They are particularly powerful when used in concert with co-operative groups and project-based learning. Since some students are more skilful and amenable to some of the levels of engagement than others, they complement each other's strengths and compensate for weaknesses. I also frequently have students practice using different expressive modalities to acquire information and demonstrate their understanding of key concepts, ideas and theories. They may read scholarly texts; interpret statistical data sets; engage in observation exercises; compare accounts of culturally diverse events and experiences transmitted through personal memories, poetry, prose, song lyrics, novels, visual arts and films; and analyse insider and outsider perspectives. I also challenge prospective teachers in my classes to use a variety of expressive genres to convey what they know. These might include the conventional academic essay very familiar to college students; verbal presentations in small and large groups; photo essays; newspaper and various literary forms of writing; storytelling; role playing, simulation and dramatic performance; games; letter writing; creating DVDs; scrapbooking; constructing portfolios; and creating metaphorical imagery.

Tiedt and Tiedt (2010) use *esteem, empathy and equity* as the foundational anchors for their multicultural teaching. They suggest that building positive self-esteem is necessary to counteract feelings of inferiority that have been imposed upon many students from non-mainstream groups; empathy enables people to connect with others, accept differences, and work co-operatively; and equity recognises that diverse students do not come to school with equal learning backgrounds but must be given full access to resources that will help them achieve their maximum potential. These commitments shape the contours of all subsequent programmes and practices.

Teachers do not have to accept the models outlined above or any others found in educational theory and practice scholarship for structuring their teaching. They should, however, create some kind of explicit framework to give structure and order to their teaching diversity routines. It helps in organising, replicating and regularising one's teaching regime, and for acclimating students to established patterns in pedagogical processes. Experiencing multiple techniques in their own learning is an effective way for teachers to appreciate (based on actual experience instead of only theoretical ideas) the need for and benefits of using a wide range of teaching strategies to improve the engagement and achievement of ethnically, culturally and racially diverse students. In making these choices it is imperative that teachers are guided by knowledge of the cultural heritages and socialisation of their ethnically diverse students, which have strong influences on shaping their learning styles.

Crossing cultural borders

Crossing cultural borders is a fourth principle for practice. Cultural diversity educators view cultural and linguistic heritages as valuable personal and educational resources that should be preserved and used as teaching tools in diverse classrooms. They believe that cultures and languages practiced in homes and communities should be embraced by schools but not to the exclusion of diverse students learning the mainstream languages and cultures of the countries in which they reside – or what Lisa Delpit (2006; Delpit and Dowdy, 2002) calls the "culture of power and privilege". She argues, for example, that immigrants from North African countries to Italy and Spain should maintain their home languages and cultures while learning Italian and Spanish; first nation peoples in Canada and the United States should learn English along with preserving their indigenous languages; and dialect speakers in any country should maintain their cultural practices and social language facilities while learning the academic versions of the dominant languages and cultures of their respective countries. In doing so, they develop skills necessary to function effectively in multiple cultural systems and settings.

Cultural and experiential scaffolding is a consensual proposal among multicultural educators for building bridges across cultural borders. It is based on the general principle of learning that new knowledge is easier to master when it is connected to prior knowledge, and the socio-cultural idea that students from different ethnic and cultural backgrounds develop "funds of knowledge and skills" that are functional in their own daily lives, cultures and communities which can facilitate school success (Gonzáles, Moll, and Amanti, 2005; Moll and Gonzáles, 2004; C. Lee, 2007; McCarty, 2002; and Lipka, 1998). O. Lee and Luykx (2006, p. 150) capture the essence of these ideas in their comments that:

Students from all ethnic/racial, cultural, linguistic and socio-economic backgrounds come to school with already-constructed knowledge, including their home languages and cultural values, acquired in their home and community environments. Such knowledge serves as the framework for constructing new understandings.

Additionally, different ethnic groups have accumulated noteworthy bodies of knowledge and contributions in virtually all disciplines typically taught in schools. This social, cultural and intellectual capital can be used to improve academic achievement in schools for diverse students, and cultural competence for both members and non-members of various ethnic groups.

Carol Lee (2007; 2009) has used two approaches for teaching African American students communication skills that are effective both within their cultural community and mainstream schools. These are *cultural modelling* and *cultural data sets*. The first involves teaching students to critically analyse some of the knowledge and skills embedded in the routine speech practices of their cultural communities, discern parallels between them and features of different literary genres as well as transfer performance abilities from one domain of functioning (social) to another (academic). The teaching technique used is called *contrastive analysis*, and the learning outcome is *style or code-shifting*.

Lee and others scholars and practitioners also use *cultural data sets* to facilitate the academic learning of under-achieving African, Asian, Latino and Native Americans. These include "informal texts" such as the lyrics of contemporary popular songs and social speech, formal literary texts (fiction and non-fiction), the visual arts and indigenous knowledge and practices produced by ethnic authors, artists, customs and traditions. Students' cultural competencies become bridges to and resources for academic learning and these resources have been applied in teaching non-native speakers in a number of specific academic areas.[5] In all of these culturally responsive teaching efforts the results are impressive and are similar across grades, subjects and ethnic groups. Student achievement improves significantly on multiple levels, including higher grade point averages, higher standardised test scores, less disciplinary problems, better school attendance, greater interest in and satisfaction with school, and higher self-concept and academic efficacy.

Conclusion

Ochoa (2007) offers several recommendations for teaching Latino students in the United States that are relevant for other ethnic groups and national settings, and are useful for summarising the key ideas underlying the principles discussed above:

- integrate multicultural content into school curricula that combine analysis of ethnically diverse contributions, power, privilege and inequity with multiple histories, perspectives, experiences and voices;

- help students see themselves as active and empowered agents of change in social, political and economic situations beyond the classroom;

- value the cultural knowledge and experiences outside school as viable resources for and bridges to academic learning;

- know students culturally, socially, ethnically, experientially and intellectually; and genuinely care for them in the process of teaching;

- accommodate the different learning styles of diverse students to affirm their prior competencies and make new knowledge easier to master;

- create inclusive learning environments in which the experiences and perspectives of diverse students are always prominent in teaching and learning activities; and

- develop open lines of communication between schools and teachers, and diverse students, families, and communities based on cultural knowledge, human dignity, respect, and egalitarian reciprocity.

Translating general recommendations and principles for teaching diversity into specific classroom practices is a complex, compelling and exhilarating challenge. The difficulty increases when the learning sites are multi-ethnic and transnational. However, it is a necessity if the educational opportunities and outcomes for students from various ethnic, cultural, racial and linguistic backgrounds in different countries are to be improved substantially. These are important international needs but with significant local nuances. Both must be attended to in classroom practices. They also are comprehensive in that they affect all dimensions of teaching and learning as well as other aspects of the educational enterprise. The benefits are broad-based: theory, research and practice indicate that *all* students benefit from diversity education in multiple ways (although configured differently). These include improved academic, social, personal, moral, civic, interpersonal and cultural achievements. Even when teaching diversity is not as thorough or complete as it should be, the results are still positive. Therefore, everybody wins – students and teachers; mainstream and marginalised students; high and low achievers; immigrants and indigenous residents.

Given these effects, one wonders why there would be even a hint of reluctance among educators to embrace ethnic, racial, cultural, social and linguistic diversity? Yet it happens far too often. This failure must be driven by motivation other than pedagogical effectiveness or genuine moral and social justice commitments to doing what is right for all students. The unresolved question is not whether teaching for and about diversity is something that should be done. It is whether educators have the skill and will to do it and to proceed without equivocation – even when teaching diversity defies easily identifiable classroom practices that are transcendent across cultural, social and national boundaries. Although teaching diversity is challenging, children everywhere deserve the best efforts and investments imaginable as well as the instructional benefits of receiving high quality, relevant and empowering education. The difficulty and complexity involved should stimulate, not inhibit, this teaching commitment and the imagination, creativity, courage and perseverance that it requires.

Notes

1. *http://nces.ed.gov/programs/coe/2009/section1/indicator07.asp.*

2. The "instructional centre" is defined as "the primary emphasis or focus of attention." Among United States educators, conversations about diversity often address "the centre" and "the margins".

3. Intersectionality asks that educators "pay attention to more than one axis of subordination and inequality, more than one category of identity, and attend to the relationships between inequities, between identities, and between inequities and identities" (Gillborn and Youdell, 2009).

4. Cf. the anthologies edited by Banks and Banks (2004; 2007), Verma et al. (2007), Paik and Walberg (2007), and Banks (2009), and the book authored by Storti (2001).

5. These include academic English (Fogel and Ehri, 2000; Shorr, 2006; Palmer, Chen, Chang, and Leclere, 2006); math, science, reading and writing to Native Alaskans (Lipka, 1998), Navajos (McCarty, 2002), Mexican Americans (Civil, 2002; Moll and Gonzáles, 2004), African Americans (Moses and Cobb, 2001), and Native Hawaiians (Au, 1993; Boggs, Watson-Gegeo and McMillen, 1985; Tharp and Gallimore, 1988); and basic literacy skills to multi ethnic students in the same classrooms (Diamond and Moore, 1995; Krater, Zeni and Cason, 1994).

References

Arzubiaga, A. E., S.C. Noguerón and A. L. Sullivan (2009), "The Education of Children in Im/migrant Families", in V. L. Gadsden, J. E. Davis, and A. J. Artiles (eds.), *Review of Research in Education: Risk, Schooling, and Equity*, Vol. 33, pp. 246-271, American Educational Research Association, Washington, D.C.

Au, K. H. (1993), *Literacy Instruction in Multicultural Settings,* Harcourt Brace, New York.

Au. K. H. (2006), *Multicultural Issues and Literacy Achievement*, Lawrence Erlbaum, Mahwah, NJ.

Ayers, W. (2004), *Teaching the Personal and the Political: Essays on Hope and Justice*, Teachers College Press, New York.

Banks, J.A. (ed.) (2009), *The Routledge International Companion to Multicultural Education*, Routledge, New York.

Banks, J.A., and C.A.M. Banks (eds.) (2004), *Handbook of Research on Multicultural Education* (2nd edition), Jossey-Bass, San Francisco.

Banks, J.A., and C.A.M. Banks (eds.) (2007), *Multicultural Education: Issues and Perspectives* (6th edition), John Wiley, New York.

Bennett, C. I. (2007), *Comprehensive Multicultural Education: Theory and Practice* (6th edition), Pearson Allyn and Bacon, Boston.

Bennett, M.J. (1986), "A Developmental Approach to Training for Intercultural Sensitivity", *International Journal of Intercultural Relations*, Vol. 10, No. 2, pp. 179–196.

Boggs, S. T., K. Watson-Gegeo, and G. McMillen (1985), *Speaking, Relating, and Learning. A Study of Hawaiian Children at Home and at School,* Ablex, Norwood, NJ.

Carnoy, M. (2009), "Social Inequality as a Barrier to Multicultural Education in Latin America", in J. A. Banks (ed.), *The Routledge International Companion to Multicultural Education,* Routledge, New York, pp. 512-525.

Civil, M. (2002), "Culture and Mathematics: A Community Approach", *Journal of Intercultural Studies,* Vol. 23, No. 2, pp. 133-148.

Collins, P. (1990), *Black Feminist Thought: Knowledge, Consciousness, and the Politics of Empowerment,* Routledge, New York.

Delpit, L. (2006), *Other People's Children: Cultural Conflict in the Classroom* (2nd edition), New Press, New York.

Delpit, L., and J.K. Dowdy (eds.) (2002), *The Skin that We Speak: Thoughts on Language and Culture in the Classroom*, New Press, New York.

Diamond, B.J., and M.A. Moore (1995), *Multicultural Literacy: Mirroring the Reality of the Classroom*, Longman, New York.

Educational Leadership (2008), *Special Issue on Giving Students Ownership of Learning*, Vol. 66, No. 3.

Feng, A., M. Bryam and M. Fleming (2009), *Becoming Interculturally Competent through Education and Training,* Multilingual Matters, Buffalo, NY.

Fogel, H., and L.C. Ehri (2000), "Teaching Elementary School Students who Speak Black English Vernacular to Write in Standard English: Effects of Dialect Transformation Practice", *Contemporary Educational Psychology*, Vol. 25, No. 2, pp. 212-235.

Forsten, C., J. Grant and B. Hollas (2002), *Differentiated Instruction: Different Strategies for Different Learners*, Crystal Spring Books, Peterborough, NH.

Gay, G. (1994), *A Synthesis of Scholarship in Multicultural Education*, North Central Regional Educational Laboratory, Oak Park, IL.

Gay, G. (2000), *Culturally Responsive Teaching: Theory, Research, and Practice*, Teachers College Press, New York.

Gillborn, D., and D. Youdell (2009), "Critical Perspectives on Race and Schooling", in J. A. Banks (ed.), *The Routledge International Companion to Multicultural Education,* Routledge, New York, pp. 173-185.

Gonzáles, N., L.C. Moll and C. Amanti (eds.) (2005), *Funds of Knowledge: Theorizing Practices in Households, Communities, and Classrooms,* Lawrence Erlbaum, Mahwah, NJ.

Grant, C.A., and C.E. Sleeter (2007), *Doing Multicultural Education for Achievement and Equity*, Routledge, New York.

Jewell, K. S. (1993), *From Mammy to Miss America and Beyond: Cultural Images and the Shaping of U. S. Social Policy,* Routledge, New York.

King, J.E., E.R. Hollins and W.C. Hayman (eds.) (1997), *Preparing Teachers for Cultural Diversity*, Teachers College Press, New York.

Krater, J., J. Zeni and N.D. Cason (1994), *Mirror Images: Teaching Writing in Black and White,* Heinemann, Portsmouth, NH.

Ladson-Billings, G. (2009), *The Dreamkeepers: Successful Teachers of African American Children* (2nd edition), Jossey-Bass, San Francisco.

Landis, D., J.M. Bennett and M.J. Bennett (eds.) (2004), *Handbook of Intercultural Training,* Sage, Thousand Oaks, CA.

Lee, C.D. (2001), "Is October Brown Chinese? A Cultural Modelling Activity System for Underachieving Students", *American Educational Research Journal,* Vol. 38, No. 1, pp. 97-141.

Lee, C.D. (2007), *Culture, Literacy, and Learning: Taking Bloom in the Midst of the Whirlwind,* Teachers College Press, New York.

Lee, C.D. (2009), "Cultural Influences on Learning", in J.A. Banks (ed.), *The Routledge International Companion to Multicultural Education,* Routledge, New York, pp. 239-251.

Lee, O., and A. Luykx (2006), *Science Education and Student Diversity: Synthesis and Research Agenda*, Cambridge University Press, New York.

Lee, S. J. (2009), *Unraveling the "Model Minority" Stereotype: Listening to Asian American Youth* (2nd edition), Teachers College Press, New York.

Lipka, J. (1998), *Transforming the Culture of Schools: Yup'ik Eskimo Examples,* Lawrence Erlbaum, Mahwah, NJ.

McCarty, T.L. (2002), *A Place to be Navajo: Rough Rock and the Struggle for Self-Determination in Indigenous Schooling,* Lawrence Erlbaum, Mahwah, NJ.

Moll, L., and N. Gonzáles (2004), "Engaging Life: A Funds of Knowledge Approach to Multicultural Education", in J. A. Banks and C.A.M. Banks (eds.), *Handbook of Research on Multicultural Education* (2nd edition), Jossey-Bass, San Francisco, pp. 699-715.

Moses, R.P., and C.E. Cobb (2001), *Radical Equations: Math Literacy and Civil Rights,* Beacon Press, Boston.

Ochoa, G. L. (2007), *Learning from Latino Teachers,* Jossey-Bass, San Francisco.

Palk, S. J., and H. J. Walberg (eds.) (2007), *Narrowing the Achievement Gap: Strategies for Educating Latino, Black, and Asian Students,* Stringer Sciences + Business Media, New York.

Palmer, B. C., C.I. Chen, S. Chang and J.T. Leclere (2006), "The Impact of Biculturalism on Language and Literacy Development", *Reading Horizons,* Vol. 46, No. 4, pp. 239-265.

Pang, V. O. (2005), *Multicultural Education: A Caring-centered, Reflective Approach* (2nd edition), McGraw-Hill, Boston.

Pang, V.O., and L.R.L. Cheng (eds.) (1998), *Struggling to be Heard: The Unmet Needs of Asian Pacific American Children*, State University of New York Press, Albany.

Park, C.C. (2002), "Crosscultural Differences in Learning Styles of Secondary English Learners", *Bilingual Research Journal*, Vol. 26, No. 2, pp. 443-459.

Planty, M. *et al.* (2009), *The Condition of Education 2009* (NCES 2009-081), National Center for Education Statistics, Institute of Education Sciences, U.S. Department of Education, Washington, D.C.

Shade, B.J.R. (1997), *Culture, Style, and the Educative Process: Making Schools Work for Racially Diverse Students* (2nd edition), C.C. Thomas, Springfield, IL.

Shorr, P.W. (2006), "Teaching America's Immigrants", *Instructor*, Vol. 116, No. 1, pp. 46-48, 50-52.

Singleton, G.E. (2006), *Courageous Conversation about Race: A Field Guide for Achieving Equity in School*, Thousand Oakes, CA, Corwin.

Spindler, G.D. and L. Spindler (1994), *Pathways to Cultural Awareness: Cultural Therapy with Teachers and Students*, Corwin, Thousand Oaks, CA.

Steele, C.M. (1997), "A Threat in the Air: How Stereotypes Shape Intellectual Identity and Performance", *American Psychologist*, Vol. 52, No. 6, pp. 613-629.

Storti, C. (2001), *Old World New World: Bridging Cultural Differences, Britain, France, Germany and the US,* Intercultural Press, Yarmouth, ME.

Tharp, R.G. and R. Gallimore (1991), *Rousing Minds to Life: Teaching, Learning, and Schooling in Social Context* (2nd edition), Cambridge University Press, New York.

Tiedt, P.L., and I.M. Tiedt (2010), *Multicultural Teaching: Activities, Information, and Resources* (8th edition), Allyn and Bacon/Pearson Education, Boston.

Van Hook, C.W. (2004), *Preparing Teachers for the Diverse Classroom: A Developmental Model of Intercultural Sensitivity, http://ceep.crc.uiuc.edu/pubs/katzsym/vanhook.html*, accessed 13 August 2009.

Verma, G.K., C.R. Bagley and M.M. Jha (eds.) (2007), *International Perspectives on Educational Diversity and Inclusion: Studies from America, Europe, and India*, Routledge, London.

West, C.M. (1995), "Mammy, Sapphire, and Jezebel: Historical Image of Black women and their Implication for Psychotherapy", *Psychotherapy: Theory, Research, Practice, and Training*, Vol. 32, No. 3, pp. 458-466.

Woodard, J. B. and T. Mastin (2005), "Black Womanhood: 'Essence' and its Treatment of Stereotypical Image of Black Women", *Journal of Black Studies*, Vol. 36, No. 2, pp. 264-281.

Woodrow, D. (2007), "Impact of Culture in Creating Differential Learning Styles", in G.K. Verma, C.R. Bagley and M.M. Jha (eds.), *International Perspectives on Educational Diversity and Inclusion: Studies from America, Europe, and India,* Routledge, London, pp. 87-103.

Woodrow, D. and S. Sham (2001), "Chinese Pupils and their Learning Preferences", *Race, Ethnicity, and Education*, Vol. 14, pp. 377-394.

Part IV

The pending agenda

Chapter 13

Supporting effective practice: the pending agenda

Tracey Burns and Vanessa Shadoian-Gersing
Centre for Educational Research and Innovation, OECD
Paris, France

This chapter focuses on key issues in teacher education for diversity: the system and its governance, strengthening the research base, and improving teaching practice. Gaps in our knowledge and areas for improvement are identified and discussed for each of these areas. Orientations for addressing and improving the current state of affairs are also provided. These orientations are necessarily general as approaches to diversity in teacher education are context-dependent; therefore, it is argued that they should be used as a starting point for further thematic and contextual analysis. Policy makers, educators and research communities are encouraged to consolidate their efforts and resources to provide sound evidence for future decision-making on this important and sensitive topic.

From the OECD online consultation : evaluating what works

Most practitioners reported no formal evaluation of strategies used to address diverse student classrooms. Without evaluation, how can classrooms, schools and systems learn what works?

Introduction

This publication aims to shed light on teacher education for diverse student populations, with a particular focus on the changing role and expectations for teachers, the distinction between diversity and disparity, and the concept of multiple risks. Various options available in teacher education to address these themes have been discussed along with examples of particular country classroom practices.

One of the challenges in this field is that the available evidence base is not sufficiently robust, with an abundance of theoretical and descriptive research and a noticeable lack of empirical findings. In addition to calling for more empirical research on the general topic, this publication has identified areas in which more research is particularly needed.

The improvement of the evidence base is crucial and should in turn be used to connect research to practice and better inform policymaking. Although the need to better connect policy to research and research to practice is not unique to this topic, the sensitive – and often political – nature of diversity issues and debates makes doing so particularly complex. The difficulty in connecting research to practice and policy is also exacerbated by the complexity of the topic and a lack of connection among the various research disciplines doing work in this area, such as psycholinguistics, economics, sociology and the learning sciences, to name just a few.

This chapter focuses on areas that require further attention concerning the system and governance, the research base and teaching practice. It looks first at a number of transversal themes that have emerged across the chapters and discussions of this publication. Gaps in our knowledge and areas for improvement are then identified, followed by orientations for policy, research and practice on assessing and improving the *status quo*. These orientations are necessarily general in nature, as approaches to diversity in teacher education and the classroom are very much context-dependent. Devising a "one size fits all" response to an inherently multifaceted issue is thus neither possible nor desirable. The general orientations presented in this chapter will be complemented by further thematic and contextual analysis in the next stage of the Teacher Education for Diversity project.

Emerging transversal themes

Crafting an agenda (from a policy, school or research perspective) to best address the issues raised in teacher education for diversity is complex and encompasses a number of different disciplines. Throughout the chapters in this volume the following transversal themes have emerged:

- diversity is a broad term with multiple meanings. Charting courses of action for systems and classrooms can only be done with careful consideration of the particular context and tradition;

- when diversity is viewed as an asset rather than a liability, it becomes easier to consider and implement the advantages that it can bring to classrooms, schools and systems;

- changing attitudes and behaviours is neither simple nor rapid. Effective teacher education for diversity is thus an ongoing process in which diversity issues are embedded within training and development options rather than being presented as one-off optional modules;

- teacher education would benefit from systematic planning and structuring such that the links between initial and in-service teacher education are better articulated and offer a holistic approach to career development; and

- suggestions for reform (of curricula, programme design, teaching practice, etc.) must be considered also in light of the incentives available to support and encourage the change desired. One key element too often overlooked is the role of parents and communities in effecting lasting change.

Knowledge gaps and policy orientations

System-wide and governance issues

It is important to better understand characteristics of increasingly diverse populations so that they may be taken into account in education systems. Without clear indications of who is included in the diverse landscape, it is difficult to target efforts addressing disparities in educational performance to where they are most needed. To accomplish this, relevant data on diverse student populations must be collected and examined. However, overly broad data collection methods can distort the unique characteristics of diverse groups within the population as a whole. In addition, the analysis of the data may not be appropriately disaggregated, leading to inaccurate assumptions and conclusions of broad patterns that do not necessarily exist. Including and maintaining more detailed variables pertaining to diversity for all groups will benefit research, policies and practices pertaining to teacher education and student achievement.

> ➢ *Encourage timely, relevant and coherent data collection in order to provide clear indications of who is included in the diverse classroom landscape for more informed decision-making on how best to respond.*

As populations change across OECD countries, open and honest discussion about the nature and impact of these changes on society and classrooms can become embroiled in sensitive topics related to national identity and values. There is thus a tendency for these issues to become labelled as "difficult" and best avoided, particularly if political and ideological motivations become intertwined with suggested courses of action. Yet without open and active discussion, the impact of these demographic changes on schools and classrooms, and the pressure on teachers to address diversity issues, are unlikely to be adequately recognised. In order to design, develop and implement a cohesive, system-level approach to preparing teachers for diverse schools, open discussion among the relevant actors of changing realities and subsequent development needs is necessary.

> ➢ *Foster active dialogue in view of a shared vision, at different levels and with a variety of stakeholders, on the nature of increasingly diverse populations, how these are reflected in schools and classrooms, and how to accommodate the changing landscapes.*

Throughout OECD countries, demographic gaps between students and teachers are growing as student populations continue to diversify while teaching populations do not. A teaching force that more closely mirrors the student population can benefit both students and teachers. Diverse teachers can serve as powerful role models for diverse students, potentially motivating them to strive further in their achievements. Diverse teachers also bring to the classroom their unique experiences and perspectives, which can help them to better relate to their diverse students. Diverse teachers may also be more inclined to view student diversity in the classroom as a resource, and treat it as such.

> ➢ *Improve the diversity of student teachers and teachers. For this to be accomplished, there must be a holistic policy plan within countries*

and regions for attracting, retaining and inserting diverse student teachers into the teaching force.

Data on student achievement reveal that various characteristics of diverse populations, such as migration status, socio-economic status, parental levels of schooling, etc., can impact on student performance. While these data are of great importance, they must be augmented with other types of research evidence in order to provide teachers, schools and systems with timely and relevant information on what works for diverse student populations, and when. Within the classroom, the alignment of summative processes and formative assessment (or frequent interactive assessments of student progress and understanding) can assist teachers in helping their diverse students achieve their learning goals. They can also enable researchers and policy makers to better understand the links between teaching and learning, which can in turn inform and shape strategies for teaching diverse students at classroom, school and system levels.

➢ *Better link classroom, school and system assessment and evaluation to provide stakeholders with a more holistic view of how objectives are being achieved and to provide a more complete basis on which to make improvements.*

As is the case in other areas in education, research and evidence on teacher education for diversity are not very well linked to practice and policy. This missing element is crucial since a key benefit of research lies in its use and its implementation. Barriers to using research to inform practice can include resistance on the individual level, such as when teachers or policy makers do not believe that a suggested change is appropriate. Perhaps more importantly, it may not always be clear what research means and how it might be implemented. Even when stakeholders are clearly convinced of the utility of suggested changes, there may be practical barriers to implementation in terms of the time and resources required. On a system level, there may be resistance among policy makers on various levels, not because of mistrust of the research but due to reluctance to change existing teacher policy in an area that may not be viewed as under their own jurisdiction. As resistance to change on individual and system levels can be reduced with strategic interventions, efforts to encourage the use of research in policy and practice should be made accordingly, especially by local actors who can examine research results and determine the significance of these results within their specific context.

➢ *Encourage capacity-building throughout the system for using research to influence teacher education practice and policy, for example, through training for research literacy for practitioners, and/or helping to interpret and disseminate research results for a non-academic audience.*

Strengthening the knowledge base

Better teacher education for diverse student populations is a topic that requires learning from multidisciplinary evidence, but too often relevant research results are not disseminated widely enough. For example, teacher education institutions could greatly benefit from evidence from the linguistics field on how non-native speakers learn. However, research results too often remain in their original field without much further dissemination, making it difficult to create links between research findings. The dissemination of research results among relevant disciplines should be a planned and systematic process to allow for an interdisciplinary knowledge base that can better inform practice and policy. This could be fostered through the establishment of networks to stimulate dialogue and build communities among researchers themselves. This could also include creating or supporting brokerage agencies designed to provide the required links between research and practice as well as building relevant capacity both in the system and among stakeholders.

> ➤ *Create and support research networks and brokerage agencies to help foster dialogue and dissemination as well as improve the interdisciplinary nature of the knowledge base related to educating teachers for diversity.*

While the multidisciplinary domain of teacher education for diversity has inspired a great deal of research, it is predominately theoretical and descriptive in nature. Without rigorous empirical research on the key elements of teacher education for diversity, policy makers will not be able to answer crucial questions about what works and what does not. The importance of a strong evidence base on this topic is made more urgent given the political sensitivity and ideological motivations that often characterise these discussions.

> ➤ *Support relevant research, especially empirical research, on initial and ongoing teacher education as well as classroom practices for diversity in order to develop a richer knowledge base.*

In addition to calling for more empirical research overall, the analysis from the TED project reveals three major areas that require further investigation, as elaborated below.

1. Teacher educators are entrusted with the crucial task of preparing student teachers and teachers to face their classrooms. Yet there is a surprisingly sparse knowledge base on how teacher educators are themselves prepared. The limited evidence available suggests that in many countries there is minimal oversight on who can become teacher educators and that the required course of study is often ill-defined. Consequently, little is known about teacher educators and how they are prepared to teach in general, especially with respect to diversity.

> *Increase focus on the education of teacher educators, both broadly and for diversity in particular, in order to increase evidence of how they are prepared and how they in turn prepare student teachers and teachers.*

2. Diverse student teachers, who stay in the system and become diverse teachers, can bring numerous benefits to the classroom by serving as role models for diverse students, providing opportunities for all students to learn about diversity through their unique perspectives, enriching diverse students' learning through shared identities, and even serving as culture/diversity brokers in the school and broader community. Yet little is known about how best to attract diverse candidates to teaching careers, why many diverse student teachers do not continue on to become teachers, and the factors that could contribute to their retention. More targeted research would allow us to determine these factors and in turn develop strategies to address these issues.

> *Focus more on the factors involved in improving attraction and retention of diverse student teachers and teachers, who can serve as important role models and bring valuable perspectives into the classroom.*

3. In many OECD countries it is difficult to attract highly-qualified teachers to poorer performing schools. Even when the best teachers begin their careers at disadvantaged schools they often leave within a short period of time. Diverse student classrooms are in serious need of well-qualified teachers, but it is not always clear how to address this situation. For example, data on teacher retention both in general and in diverse schools is often lacking. So too is qualitative research that would meaningfully complement these quantitative data, such as research on contexts of hard-to-staff schools, incentives to keep the best teachers in the schools that need them most, and effective and targeted strategies for attraction and retention.

> *Further focus on the attraction and retention of highly qualified teachers in the schools that need them most, going beyond descriptive statistics to build explanatory evidence on key variables for attracting and retaining well-qualified teachers in diverse schools.*

Improving teacher practice

Initial teacher education, the induction period when teachers are first placed in the classroom, and continuing professional development are too often considered discrete stages in the professional life of a teacher. As such, they are developed and monitored by different bodies, often with minimal co-ordination among the various players. In order for teachers to reach their full potential and be best guided in their career progression, these "separate" stages must be linked in order to foster a more holistic process of career development and progression that more closely matches teachers' needs. A systematic approach to career progression and development also allows for an analysis of the best timing of development opportunities so that they can be offered when they would be most useful. For example, it may be premature to provide in-depth instruction on classroom management techniques if the student has not yet started practicing in classrooms. Waiting until a practicum begins and focusing on providing ongoing support during the induction phase (*i.e.* the first year of teaching) may be a far better use of student time (and programme budget) than separating the theory from its practical application.

> ➢ *Better connect the stages of teacher education to more thoroughly develop teachers' knowledge and skills, and plan the timing of interventions such that they are available when they are most needed.*

Improved teaching for diverse student populations is an increasingly important competency for current and future teachers. However, too often these topics are addressed through a sole course, often as an elective. As systems increasingly recognise the need to prepare teachers for a diversifying student population, there must be a systematic effort to integrate this topic and strategies into the curriculum. Moreover, a crucial component of teaching for diversity lies in examining one's own beliefs and how they influence behaviour. Much like any other teacher competency, the requisite skills for teaching and motivating diverse classrooms and attitudinal awareness cannot be simply absorbed through a one-off course during initial education or professional development. Instead, it is important to build on this training throughout teachers' careers, so that they gain transversal exposure to knowledge and perspectives that can have a meaningful impact on how they practice.

> ➢ *Ensure that teaching for diverse student populations is an integral component of both initial and in-service teacher education in order to foster and build on the ongoing behavioural changes necessary to respond to evolving classrooms.*

Firsthand experience in dealing with diversity issues can be a tremendous asset for teaching, curriculum design and class development. Student teachers would greatly benefit from participation in activities that expose them to practical situations of addressing diversity, especially classroom practice and placements in schools with highly diverse student populations as well as in schools that are already recognised for their use of good practices for addressing diversity. Another important way to better prepare student teachers to deal with diverse classrooms is by broadening their frame of reference with respect to diversity. Encouraging student teachers to experience another culture firsthand through foreign language study, sustained interaction with multicultural or indigenous communities, study abroad, etc. can help them better relate to diverse students. Another good approach would be to encourage understanding of diverse groups through the use of critical reflection in learning contexts and problem-solving simulations using student evidence. In turn, after the completion of such programmes or experiences, sharing such experiences within their own education programme through formal discussion with peers and instructors would help to disseminate lessons learned more broadly. It would also serve to encourage leadership within the population of student teachers on this issue.

> ➢ *Teacher education programmes should provide student teachers the opportunity to engage in activities that expose them to practical situations of classroom diversity and allow them to broaden their frames of reference. These experiences should be formally discussed and shared in order to maximise lessons learned.*

Mentoring schemes can be extremely helpful in supporting teacher candidates and new teachers by capitalising on guidance from veteran teachers, but this mechanism is not always properly implemented. Some mandatory mentoring programmes for new teachers function better on paper than in practice, while other voluntary mentoring schemes often have few incentives for teachers to volunteer, making it difficult to attract good mentors. However, when school leaders have the tools to design and implement them properly, mentoring programmes provide opportunities for new teachers and teacher candidates to work together and discuss new situations and difficulties encountered in the classroom. These measures have been shown to increase retention of new teachers, particularly in the induction phase, that is, the first year or two of schooling when attrition is most marked. It is important to fully develop mentoring schemes so that new teachers can learn constructively from experienced teachers in their field regarding the situations encountered in the classroom.

> ➢ *Develop new, or reinforce existing, mentoring programmes, so that new and veteran teachers, preferably at the same grade and subject level, can share experiences, with the aim of supporting new teachers and encouraging them to remain in the classroom.*

Teaching requires a tremendous amount of flexibility to respond to changing classroom needs, and teachers are constantly updating their practices to respond to their students. However, without proper evaluation, teachers and school leaders do not have feedback from which to learn and, thus, lack indications of what works well, what works less well, and why. While there may be very good practices being used by teachers in the field, the lack of formal record and evaluation means that potentially good practices are being lost. Proper evaluation helps us to learn from "what works" in practice and enables knowledge to be transferred back into schools and systems. Good evaluation practices can also serve to encourage critical self-assessment, which is an important element of improving teacher practice.

> *Better evaluate "what works" in the classroom by encouraging, and providing incentives for, the appraisal and feedback of teacher practices to feed knowledge back into classrooms, schools and systems.*

Teaching and learning take place in particular contexts. While general principles of teaching for diversity can transcend context, it is extremely important that particular classroom strategies be tailored to the learners in question. Determining universal best practices is thus neither possible nor desirable. Instead, it is important that pre-service and in-service teachers and teacher educators understand the importance of contextual specificity and be able to critically reflect on their own classroom contexts and practice. This will then allow them to apply general principles of teaching for diversity in ways that work for their classes and students. It should be noted that establishing this as a consistent practice takes time and repetition. Research has demonstrated that this process works best when it is supported in an ongoing manner throughout initial and in-service education. Furthermore, teachers report that they find this easiest to do when they have colleagues with whom they can collaborate and share experiences and reflections as well as leaders within the school body that support and champion these practices.

> *Promote awareness of contextual specificity when preparing pre-service and in-service teachers for diversity. Guide and encourage teachers and teacher candidates to adapt general principles of teaching for diversity to teaching their specific student populations.*

References

Ladson-Billings, G.J. (1999), "Preparing Teachers for Diverse Student Populations: A Critical Race Theory Perspective", *Review of Research in Education,* Vol. 24, pp. 211-247.

OECD (2005a), *Formative Assessment: Improving Learning in Secondary Classrooms,* OECD, Paris.

OECD (2005b), *Teachers Matter: Attracting, Developing and Retaining Effective Teachers*, OECD, Paris.

OECD (2007), *Evidence in Education: Linking Research and Policy*, OECD Publishing, Paris.

OECD (2008), *Improving School Leadership: Policy and Practice,* OECD Publishing, Paris.

OECD (2009a), *Creating Effective Teaching and Learning Environments: First Results from TALIS*, OECD Publishing, Paris.

OECD (2009b), *Working Out Change: Systemic Innovation in Vocational Education and Training*, OECD Publishing, Paris.

OECD (2010), *Innovative Learning Environments: The Reader on Learning* (provisional title), OECD Publishing, Paris.

Annex A

An international online consultation

From 17 November 2008 to 17 December 2008 the CERI Teacher Education for Diversity (TED) project ran an online consultation exercise with teachers, student teachers and teacher educators. The goal of this exercise was to hear the voices of practitioners about their day-to-day experience with diversity in the classrooms, the key challenges they face, as well as their best solutions and creative practices. It should be noted that this was not a representative survey with random sampling within and across countries as that was beyond the reach of both the budget and timeline of this project. The consultation was thus designed to use the voices of the responding practitioners to highlight keys areas for further research.

The questionnaire was composed of three separate branches, one each for student teachers, teachers, and teacher educators. All three groups were asked a series of multiple choice questions on:

- Demographic characteristics (gender, age, country of residence, name of region/institution, size of the town).

- Teacher education and experience (type of programme and length of time in studies (student teachers) or years of work experience (teachers and teacher educators), type of institution).

- Experience in and with diversity (diversity among their colleagues/ students, perceived importance of diversity issues, how well prepared they feel to address diversity in the classroom, and whether or not their training contained tools for working with parents and/or community members).

Teachers and teacher educators then went on to answer an additional series of questions on their current work and the relevance of any diversity training they may have received or provided as professional development or in-service education. They were also asked questions on the biggest challenges they experienced related to diversity in the classroom, the strategies that they used/devised to address these challenges, and the evaluation of such strategies.

In order to reach as many practitioners as possible, the consultation was hosted on the OECD website and available in English, French, Spanish and German. Social networking tools (*e.g.* Facebook and Linked In) were also used to contact practitioners and the call to participate was disseminated to other online discussion groups and fora, including Education Week's Teacher Magazine, Japan Society Education Programs; ELT Turkey; *Estudiantes, Graduados y Profesores de Ciencias de la Educación;* I am Teacher; *Tu Sais T'es Prof Quand*; Teacher2Teacher Network; and the Centre for Multicultural Education.

As already mentioned, the exercise was not designed nor intended to be a representative or random sample of the teacher, student-teacher, and teacher educator populations. In addition, as a web-based intervention there was concern that certain portions of the population (young, urban or at least those with access to broadband internet) might be more likely to respond than others.[1] The results should thus be interpreted with these limitations in mind.

Demographics

In just under a one-month period, 3 196 responses were received to the online consultation. Teachers comprised 53% of the respondents (N = 1750) while student teachers and teacher educators each comprised 23% (N = 723 for each group). Respondents identified themselves as living in over 40 countries, including 28 OECD countries. The breakdown of responses by country can be found in Figure A.1.

Overall, 73% of the respondents were female and 27% were male. The age distribution of respondents was quite broad, covering student teachers, teachers, and teacher educators. As might be expected, the age distribution is highly dependent on the category of respondent. The overall age breakdown for all three categories of respondents and from all countries can be found in Figure A.2.

Interestingly, the teacher respondents reported the same demographic profile as the teachers surveyed in TALIS in terms of gender composition, age range, the length of time employed as a teacher, and the percent working in public schools. However unlike TALIS, which targeted teachers in lower secondary schools (ISCED 2) the majority of the teachers that responded to this consultation reported teaching in primary and upper secondary schools (for more information see below).

Respondents were from a variety of communities, ranging from a village of less than 3 000 people (7%), a small town of 3 000 to 15 000 people (13%), towns of 15 000 to 100 000 inhabitants (24%), cities of 100 000 to 1 million (35%) and large cities (over 1 million) (21%).[2]

Figure A.1. **Respondents by country**

Absolute numbers

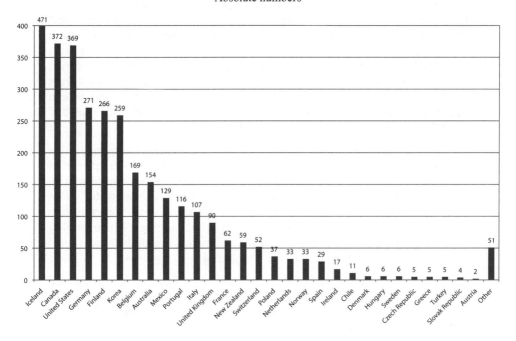

Figure A.2. **Breakdown of respondents by age and type**

Absolute numbers

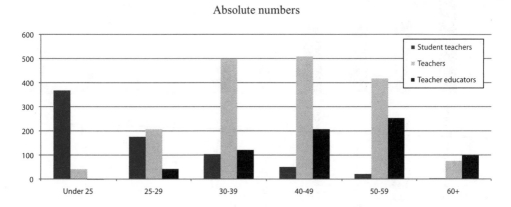

Work as a teacher and teacher educator

Most teacher respondents and teacher educator respondents reported teaching in primary and secondary education. 34% of teachers reported that they teach in "primary education", 27% in "lower secondary" and 34% in "upper secondary" education. Substantially smaller numbers of respondents were teaching in initial education and pre-school (7%) and tertiary education (8%).[3] Teacher educators show a similar profile: 55% reported that they train teachers to work in primary education, 42% in lower secondary and 38% in upper secondary education. 19 % reported preparing teachers for initial and pre-schooling and 17% for tertiary education.

In accordance with their reported age, 57% of teachers responded that they had more than 11 years working experience. Only 11% were in their first two years of teaching. This pattern was also true for teacher educators, with 22% reporting more than 20 years of experience as a teacher educator. More than eighty percent of the teachers (83%) and two-thirds of teacher educators work in full-time education programmes in school settings. Much smaller percentages report, for example, teaching online or through distance education (3% of the teacher educators that responded).

In terms of the content of their teaching, the teachers that responded to the consultation were spread across a wide variety of subject areas (see Figure A.3), with the heaviest concentrations in general subjects (primary school), mathematics or natural sciences, literature, history, and foreign

Figure A.3. **Subjects taught by teacher respondents**

Absolute numbers; N = 1 748; respondents free to choose more than one category

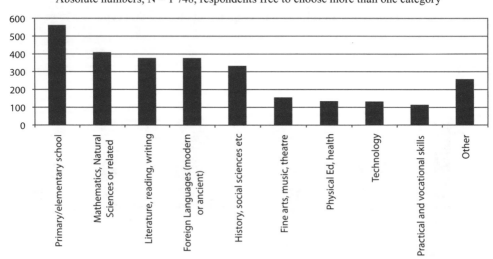

languages. For teacher educators, most of the respondents report that they focus on training teachers in pedagogical techniques (62%) and/ or on subject related knowledge (43%). Fewer respondents report that they focus on class-room management (30%) and interpersonal relations (27%).[4]

Preparation for diversity in the classroom

Perceived importance of diversity issues

All respondents were asked how important sensitivity to diversity issues (*e.g.* working with different languages, cultures, religions) was to effective teaching. The majority of the respondents across the three categories rated sensitivity to diversity issues to be of considerable importance for becoming an effective teacher. 96% of student teachers, 70% of teachers, and 96% of teacher educator respondents rated sensitivity to diversity issues as "extremely important" or "moderately important" for effective teaching. Female respond-ents across all categories were more convinced of the importance of sensitiv-ity to diversity across the three categories. Age did not change the pattern of responses for student teachers or teachers.

In the **teacher educator** category, there was some variation in impor-tance as a function of age, with a higher percentage of older respondents reporting that sensitivity to diversity was extremely important. Of the age group 30 to 39 years of age, 73% of the respondents stated that they find sensitivity for diversity extremely important, compared to 83% for the age group of 60 years and older. This also correlated with length of time teaching.

Perhaps not surprisingly, respondents across the categories from larger cities with a population of 100 000 to over one million generally reported sensitivity to diversity as more important than respondents from smaller cities and towns. As a general rule, the percentage of respondents from all three teacher categories (student teachers, teachers, teacher educators) rating sensitivity to diversity as extremely important became progressively lower for smaller cities and towns although as noted above the distribution of responses is not even across countries, and so this trend would need to be confirmed with a representative sample.

Diversity of student teachers

As classrooms become more diverse, questions have been raised regard-ing how best to diversify the teacher workforce to better reflect the compo-sition of the classrooms. In the online consultation, **student teachers** were asked to report on the diversity of the fellow participants in their teacher education programmes. The diversity of fellow student teachers was reported to be limited, with only 12% of student teachers reporting that those following their programme came from many different backgrounds. The majority of respondents were in programmes in which fellow student teachers were mostly (25%) or nearly fully (63%) from the same background.[5]

These responses were corroborated by the responses of the **teacher educators**, the great majority (83%) of whom teach classes where students are mostly (31%) or almost fully (52%) from the same background as themselves.[6] In addition, of the 89% of **student teacher** respondents who had already had practical experience in the classroom, greater diversity was reported among their students than among their fellow student teachers. Student teacher respondents were thus overall less representative of the populations that they teach – a result which raises the possibility of a continuing divergence in the composition of the teacher workforce and the students in the classrooms.

Coverage of diversity issues in education and training

Respondents were asked how diversity issues (*e.g.* working with different languages, cultures, and/or religions) were covered in their teacher education. Among **student teacher** respondents, only 7% stated that this was not covered at all in their teacher education programme. These responses coincide well with the responses of the **teacher educators,** of whom only 6% said their training did *not* address diversity issues. However the presence or absence of such training does not mean that this is systematically built into programmes. Of the student teachers, only 22% reported that this was *always* incorporated as part of the broader programme. Often the respondents reported that these issues were covered separately in courses or modules rather than integrated across the curriculum as a whole. While it is a positive sign that diversity is in fact addressed in teacher education programmes, the effectiveness of isolated courses or modules for creating or supporting lasting change in practice can be questioned.

When **teachers** were asked how diversity issues were covered in their initial teacher education, 45% of respondents said that they were *always* or *sometimes* incorporated as part of the broader programme. In addition 35% of teachers responded that these issues were *not covered* in their initial teacher education. One possible explanation for the difference in the responses of the teachers from the student teachers is that in many school systems training on diversity issues is relatively new, and so teachers who completed their initial training 20 or 30 years ago were reporting on systems that have since changed. However when examined more closely, there was a strong impact of country on the response. While some systems have been placing more emphasis on diversity issues more recently, others have very consistently offered such training and have been for quite some time, and still other systems do not currently emphasise this, at least not for the teachers that responded to this survey.

Assessing the effectiveness of preparation in initial teacher education

Respondents were asked how well prepared they felt by their teacher education to respond to diversity in the classroom. Although the vast majority of respondents reported that sensitivity to diversity was important to effective teaching, far fewer respondents reported feeling well-prepared to handle diversity issues in the classroom. This was particularly evident for the teachers who responded to the consultation.

As can be seen in Figure A.4, **student teachers** and **teacher educators** had similar patterns of responses, with around 50% of respondents from both groups reporting that they felt that student teachers were *moderately* to *extremely* well-prepared for diversity in the classroom. A small but nonetheless alarming proportion of student teacher and teacher educator respondents (13% and 10% respectively) reported that they felt that student teachers are *not at all* prepared by initial teacher education to deal with diversity issues in the classroom.

Teacher responses to the same question were far less positive: considerably less than half (34%) of the respondents reported feeling *extremely* or *moderately* well-prepared by their initial teacher education. Of the 66% that reported feeling only *somewhat well* or *not at all* prepared, a full 30% reported that they felt *not at all* prepared by their initial teacher education to handle diversity in the classroom. Given how highly the importance of this subject was rated by all groups of respondents, these responses suggest that more could be done to help student teachers feel better prepared during and after their initial teacher education. They also suggest that for teachers currently in the workforce, there might be unmet need for ongoing guidance and support on these issues.

Figure A.4. **"How well do you feel your [initial] teacher education is preparing/ prepared you to effectively handle diversity issues?"**

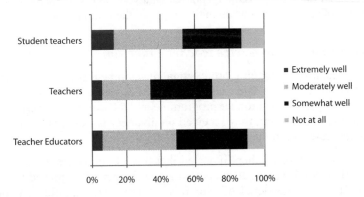

Note: For teacher educators, the question was "How well do you think student teachers are prepared to effectively handle diversity issues?"

When probed about how they felt they were best prepared, **teachers** and **teacher educators** (reporting on student teachers) gave similar patterns of responses, although as with the previous question, teachers were overall less positive than teacher educators. This may indicate that the teachers themselves, experiencing classroom life day-in and day-out as they do, are slightly more realistic about how well elements in their initial teacher education prepared them for diversity in the classroom. Not surprisingly, both groups reported that real world experience in schools was the number one reason for feeling prepared, followed by good theoretical courses, practice in teacher training courses, and diversity of students and teachers in the study programme.

Student teachers had a slightly different assessment, attributing the most importance to good theoretical courses, followed by real world experience in schools. A much lower ranking was given to both practice in teacher education (*e.g.* role playing with other student teachers) and diversity of students and teachers in their study programme. Unlike the other two groups, student teachers more often chose having good theoretical coursework than having real world experience, which may be indicative of what they spend the most time on during their studies. This raises an important question on finding the right balance of theory and practice in the education and preparation of teachers.

Figure A.6 presents the responses given by those respondents who did not feel well prepared by their initial teacher education when asked *how* they did not feel well prepared. All three groups chose a "lack of practice in teacher training (*e.g.* role playing with other student teachers)" most often to account for feeling unprepared for diversity issues. Overall, **student teachers** and **teacher educators** (reporting on the preparation of student teachers) gave very similar patterns of responses, with "lack of diversity of students and teachers in study programme" as the second most frequent response. Teachers who did not feel well prepared rated all possible responses relatively highly, perhaps reflecting on the lack of such training when they completed their initial teacher education.

Diversity issues in in-service teacher education

When looking at ongoing professional development for in-service teachers, 50% of respondents said that diversity issues were *always* or *sometimes* addressed as part of the broader programme and 64% of teacher respondents reported that the training they received on diversity issues was *extremely* or *moderately* relevant to their needs.

However 18% of teachers reported that these issues were not addressed at all in their professional development and a further 8% reported that they did not receive professional development of any kind. Additionally, of the 1 100 respondents who did receive diversity training during their professional development, 8% reported that it was *irrelevant* or only *somewhat relevant* to

Figure A.5. **"If extremely or moderately well prepared, how?"**

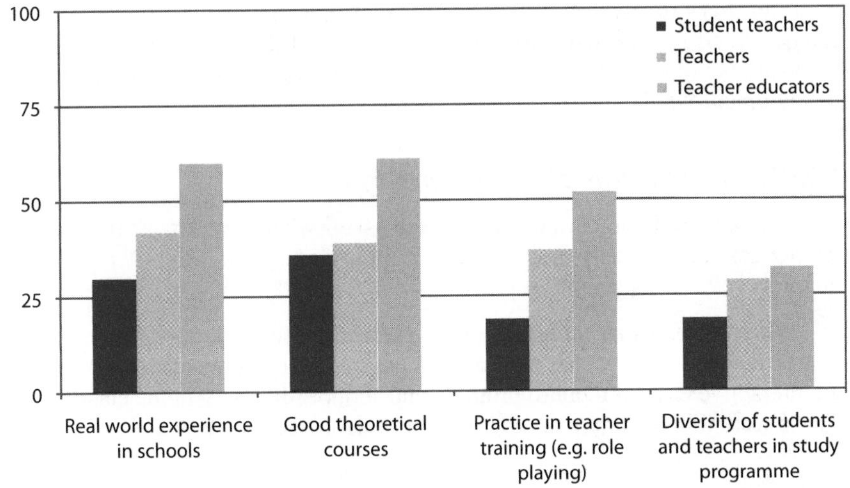

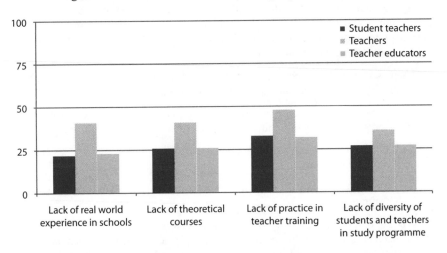

Note: Respondents were free to choose as many options as applied; thus, the sum of category percentages is greater than 100%.

Figure A.6. **"If somewhat or not at all prepared, why not?"**

Note: Respondents were free to choose as many options as applied; thus, the sum of category percentages is greater than 100%.

their needs. These figures are similar to those coming from the large representative sample of TALIS, which probed the kinds of professional development teachers received and how well it met their needs. There is thus very likely a need to look carefully at the professional development options that are available to teachers and to develop a systematic approach to indentifying development needs and training provision.

Challenges and strategies developed by teachers

Teachers and teacher educators were asked what they saw as the biggest challenges related to diversity issues in their classroom. Table A.1 provides an overview of their responses.[7]

When asked what strategies were currently used to address these challenges, teachers and teacher educators' most frequent responses were: "creating an interactive environment to promote and support diversity in the classroom". These were followed by a number of other factors (see Table A.2).[8]

Box A.1. **Working with parents and communities**

Teachers (and student teachers once they enter the classroom) interact with not only their students but also parents and community members, and there is growing evidence that involving parents and community can be an effective strategy for addressing diversity in the classroom and helping with the integration of new arrivals to the school system.

When asked whether or not they were given tools or strategies for working with parents or community members in their initial teacher education:

- 53% of student teacher respondents reported that they received training for working with these important constituents in their programme;

- 60% of teacher educators stated that their teacher training includes such strategies and/or tools;

- HOWEVER, only 31% of teachers reported that they had received such training.

As classrooms open up and involve more outside actors, working with communities and parents is becoming more important for teachers, and the education that student teacher respondents are receiving seems to be beginning to reflect this. For many, however, and especially for teachers who have not received such guidance, working with parents and communities may be a next but unfamiliar step.

One-tenth of the respondents also chose to add a preferred strategy of their own. Strategies frequently mentioned included:

- increasing the interaction between students (games, role play and group work);

- diversifying pedagogical techniques so that children with different backgrounds and abilities will all be able to understand teaching content better; and

- recognising, valuing and addressing diversity in the classroom.

A final important topic highlighted by this consultation is the lack of systematic formal evaluations of strategies to address challenges related to diversity. Over three-quarters of teachers responding to the consultation reported no formal evaluation of the strategies they used to address diversity in the classroom. Of the 22% that did report a formal evaluation, 9% reported receiving formal institutional evaluations and 13% conducted formal evaluations themselves (*e.g.* through an evaluation tool). The situation was similar for teacher educators (see Figure A.7).

Table A.1. **Diversity challenges rated by teachers and teacher educators**

Teachers	Teacher Educators
Lack of fluency in the classroom language (49%)	Cultural differences (62%)
Cultural differences (42%)	Socio-economic differences (50%)
Physical or behavioural differences (42%)	Lack of fluency of the language of instruction (49%)
Socio-economic differences (41%).	Physical or behavioural differences (30%)
Gender (16%)	Religious differences (22%)
Religious differences (15%)	Gender (16%)

Table A.2. **Diversity strategies identified by teachers and teacher educators**

Teachers	Teacher Educators
Creating an interactive environment to promote and support diversity in the classroom (48%)	Creating an interactive environment to promote and support diversity in the classroom (58%)
Flexibility for students whose first language is not the majority language (47%)	Using an inclusive curriculum (56%)
Using an inclusive curriculum (45%).	Flexibility for students whose first language is not the majority language (37%)
Participation in community events or contests aimed at promoting diversity (26%).	Participation in community events or contests aimed at promoting diversity (26%).

Figure A.7. **Type of evaluation reported**

Percentage of respondents

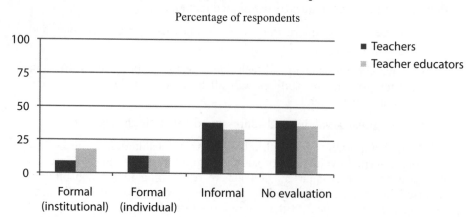

These responses imply that the teachers and teacher educators who responded to this consultation were often choosing their preferred strategies without formal feedback on how well they work. Although teachers can know what works and what doesn't without requiring a formal evaluation, the lack of evaluation is troubling in that evaluation procedures also offer opportunities for learning and clear feedback. In relying on informal evaluation, there is very little institutional structure to aid teachers in their assessments, and the link between skill needs and options for professional development is weakened. It is also a missed opportunity in the form of knowledge transfer, as without formal or at least explicit appraisal mechanisms, it is not possible to systematically distribute the informal knowledge that individual teachers gain from such assessments to other teachers who could benefit from that knowledge.

Conclusion

The results of the online consultation are meant to shed light on the experiences and challenges faced by practitioners in their day to day work which can then be interpreted in light of available research. The student teachers, teachers, and teacher educators that generously gave their time to compete the survey have underlined the importance of diversity issues in effective teaching, and expressed their concerns about their level of preparation before entering the classroom. They have also suggested that moving from theory to practice (*i.e.* from student teacher courses to real world teaching) is not always easy, and ongoing support throughout this period (by fellow teachers, school leaders, and professional development) is important. The key messages from this exercise are used to highlight or counterpoint the research contributions of experts in this volume, and thus appear at the start of each chapter.

The short discussion in this Annex presents aggregate responses from all countries due to the nature of the sample. Given the different contexts and approaches to diversity among the systems, one would expect to see rather different profiles from particular countries or regions. It would thus be very interesting to examine these kinds of questions with a large-scale representative sample. Indeed, TALIS can be examined more closely for questions related to professional development and appraisal and feedback, and Ben Jensen does this is Chapter 3 of this volume. On many other questions, such as the link between initial teacher education and in-service teacher training and the effectiveness of teaching strategies for diverse classrooms, much work remains to be done.

Box A.2. **Support by school administration**

Teacher respondents were asked how well supported they felt by school administration in their attempts to address diversity issues in the classroom. 41% of teachers that responded to the consultation reported that they felt *extremely* or *moderately* supported, while an almost equal proportion (42%) reported feeling only *somewhat* or *not* supported by school administration.

Clearly there is room to improve the support and guidance that these teachers receive, and if this pattern of responses were to be found in a representative sample, this would suggest that there is a need for school administration to provide more leadership in this area. Of course, it should be noted that the strategies mentioned by these respondents were focussed on the learning process directly and thus take place within the confines of the classroom. Teachers thus often have both the capacity and the autonomy to pursue these strategies.

Notes

1. Interestingly, a number of studies, including the 2009 Teaching and Learning International Survey (TALIS), have showed no difference in the profiles or types of responses obtained from either online or pen and paper survey instruments.

2. The relatively high number of respondents located in a village or rural area of less than 3 000 people is not evenly distributed across countries (e.g. 39% of teachers from such small villages come from Iceland).

3. Note that respondents can report that they teach in more than one category.

4. Respondents were free to choose as many options as applied; thus, the sum of category percentages is greater than 100%.

5. Here students were defined to come from the same background if 90% or more are from the majority background, mostly from the same background if 65% or more were from the majority background, or from many different backgrounds if less than 50% were from the majority background.

6. *Ibid.*

7. Respondents were free to choose as many options as applied thus the sum of category percentages is greater than 100%.

8. *Ibid.*

Biographies of contributing authors

Russell Bishop is Professor for Maori Education in the School of Education at the University of Waikato, Hamilton, New Zealand. He is also a qualified and experienced secondary school teacher. Prior to his present appointment he was a senior lecturer in Maori Education in the Education Department at the University of Otago and Interim Director for Otago University's Teacher Education programme. His most recent book, with Mere Berryman, *Culture Speaks*, examines the experiences of Maori students, their families, their principals and their teachers with the schooling of Maori students. He is currently the project director for Te Kotahitanga, a large New Zealand Ministry of Education funded research/professional development project that seeks to improve the educational achievement of Maori students in mainstream classrooms through the implementation of a culturally responsive pedagogy of relations.

Tracey Burns is a research and policy analyst in the OECD's Centre for Educational Research and Innovation in Paris, France. She is responsible for the CERI work on evidence-based research in education, teacher education for diversity, and also works on systemic innovation in vocational education and training systems. Previous to this she worked on social determinants of health and on education and social inclusion issues at both the OECD and in Vancouver, Canada. As a Post-Doctoral Fellow at The University of British Columbia, Dr. Burns led a hospital-based research team investigating newborn infants' responses to language, and was an award-winning lecturer on infant and child development. Tracey holds a BA from McGill University, Canada and a PhD from Northeastern University, USA. Her most recent OECD publications are *Evidence in Education: Linking Research and Policy* (2007) and *Working out Change: Systemic Innovation in Vocational Education and Training* (2009).

Bruce Garnett has been an ESL teacher of both adult and teen-age immigrant students since 1990, and has taught pre-service teachers at the University of British Columbia. Currently he is employed in the Surrey School District in British Columbia, Canada. He holds a doctorate in Educational Studies from the University of British Columbia; his research examines the social and academic integration of ESL students, and their academic trajectories through high school. He frequently speaks to decision-makers in Canada's educational communities where his empirical work has been generating growing interest.

Miquel Angel Essomba has a PhD in Education regarding diversity issues. He is currently professor of Pedagogy at the Autonomous University of Barcelona, director of ERIC (a research team on diversity and education) and director of the Master in Intercultural Education at the same university. He has extensive experience in giving postgraduate and doctoral courses on diversity and education in Spain as well as in countries in the Americas (Chile, Mexico and Argentina). From an international perspective, he is currently the team leader for the training of trainers on Intercultural Education at the Council of Europe, where he is also an expert in research teams on teacher training and diversity. He also has experience in non formal education, community development and co-operation programmes, especially between Spain and African countries. He is a consultant for several local and regional authorities in Spain on education, teacher training and diversity.

Geneva Gay is Professor of Education at the University of Washington-Seattle, USA, where she teaches multicultural education and general curriculum theory. Dr. Gay is known for her scholarship in multicultural education, particularly as it relates to curriculum design, staff development, classroom instruction, and intersections of culture, race, ethnicity, teaching, and learning. Her writings include numerous articles and book chapters; editor of *Becoming Multicultural Educators: Personal Journey Toward Professional Agency* (Jossey-Bass, 2003); author of *Culturally Responsive Teaching: Theory, Practice, & Research* (Teachers College Press, 2000) which received the 2001 Outstanding Writing Award from the American Association of Colleges for Teacher Education (AACTE).); author of *At the Essence of Learning:Multicultural Education* (Kappa Delta Pi, 1994); and the co-editorship of *Expressively Black: The Cultural Basis of Ethnic Identity* (Praeger, 1987).

Ben Jensen is the Director of the School Education Program of the Grattan Institute, a newly-established independent Australian think tank. Grattan aspires to contribute significantly to Australian public policy through objective, evidence-driven analysis. Before joining Grattan, Ben worked at the OECD on a number of projects, producing *Creating Effective Teaching and Learning Environments: First Results from TALIS* and *Measuring Improvements in Learning Outcomes – Best Practices to Assess the Value-added of Schools* among others. Prior to joining the OECD, Ben was a Senior Analyst at the Department of Premier and Cabinet at the Victorian Government, Australia and a Research Fellow at the Melbourne Institute of Applied Economic and Social Research where he led the education research programme. Ben has a PhD in Economics from the University of Melbourne.

Mikael Luciak is assistant professor in the Department of Education at the University of Vienna, Austria. His research and teaching have an emphasis on intercultural education, the schooling of ethnic minorities in comparative perspective as well as special needs and inclusive education. Aside from the University of Vienna, Dr. Luciak received his education from the University of California at Berkeley and San Francisco State University. He previously worked at the University of Economics in Vienna, and served as educational expert for the European Monitoring Centre on Racism and Xenophobia, as A World of Difference trainer for the Anti-Defamation League and as psychotherapist in independent practice. He is Board Member of the International Association for Intercultural Education and Editorial Advisory Board Member of the journal Intercultural Education. He has written for different journals and books on diversity, inequality, school achievement, and integration related to minority schooling. His current research concentrates on the educational situation of the Roma.

Claire McGlynn lectures at the School of Education, Queen's University, Belfast, Northern Ireland. She gained a BSc (Hons) in Biochemistry from the University of Newcastle-upon-Tyne, a PGCE from the Institute of Education, University of London and a PGDip, MEd and EdD from the University of Ulster. She has taught in a variety of educational settings in England and Northern Ireland for twenty years and was a founder teacher of New-Bridge Integrated College in 1995. Her research interests include integrated education in Northern Ireland, multicultural and intercultural education, education for social cohesion in conflict and post-conflict societies and teacher education for diversity. She is the co-editor of *Peace education in conflict and post-conflict societies: comparative perspectives* (Palgrave Macmillan USA 2009) and *Addressing ethnic conflict through peace education: international perspectives* (Palgrave Macmillan USA, 2007). She is currently the Chair of the Peace Education special interest group of the American Educational Research Association and a member of the editorial board of the Journal of Peace Education.

Marieke Meeuwisse has worked as a researcher at RISBO, a research institute of the Erasmus University in The Netherlands, since February 2007. Marieke is working on her PhD project on diversity in higher education. This project contains four empirical studies that attempt to explain in detail why students from ethnic minority background on average are less successful academically compared to ethnic majority students in terms of progress, grade point average and dropout rates. Marieke graduated in September 2001 from the Psychology Department at the University of Utrecht and from the Erasmus University Rotterdam in Sociology in June 2006.

H. Richard Milner IV is Associate Professor of Education in the Department of Teaching and Learning at Vanderbilt University, United States of America. Dr. Milner's research, policy, and teaching interests are urban education, race and equity in society and education, and teacher education. In 2006, he was awarded the Scholars of Colour in Education Early Career Contribution Award of the American Educational Research Association. He is the editor of three books: *Culture, Curriculum, and Identity in Education* (in press, Palgrave Macmillan), *Diversity and Education: Teachers, Teaching, and Teacher Education* (2009, Charles C. Thomas Publisher), and *Race, Ethnicity, and Education: The Influences of Racial and Ethnic Identity in Education* with E.W. Ross (2006, Greenwood/Praeger).

Milena Santerini is full Professor of Education, Ph.D, Faculty of Education Sciences in the Catholic University of the Sacred Heart of Milan, Italy. She is Director of the Master for "Intercultural Training" in the same University. She is member of the Italian Scientific Committee for Intercultural education (Ministero della Pubblica Istruzione), member of the Council of ARIC (Association pour la Recherche Interculturelle), CDEC (Centro di Documentazione Ebraica Contemporanea) and other international bodies. Her recent publications on intercultural issues include: P.Branca, M.Santerini (2008), *Alunni arabofoni a scuola*, Carocci, Roma; M.Santerini, P.Reggio (editors) (2007), *Formazione interculturale: teoria e pratica*, Unicopli, Milano; M.Santerini (2003), *Intercultura, La Scuola*, Brescia.

Sabine Severiens has devoted most of her research life to diversity and inequality in education. Her main studies were a four-year longitudinal study on women in engineering education, and a three year study on ethnic minority students in higher education. Most recently, together with a team of five researchers in Rotterdam, The Netherlands, she conducted a large scale research project on drop out of ethnic minority students in teacher education. Before she started working for RISBO (Rotterdam Institute for Social science Policy Research, Erasmus University Rotterdam) in 2001, she worked for 10 years at a teacher training institute (University of Amsterdam). This is where she conducted her PhD research on a study on inequality in secondary education. Since 2005, Sabine Severiens has been general director of RISBO. In this job she combines her research activities with managerial tasks.

Vanessa Shadoian-Gersing is an analyst in the OECD's Centre for Educational Research and Innovation, where she focuses on Teacher Education for Diversity and systemic innovation in education systems. Prior to this, she was a researcher on CERI's external evaluation of the Youth Empowerment Partnership Programme. At the OECD, she previously worked on social innovation in the Local Economic and Employment Development programme. She has researched public-private partnerships in youth employment in West Africa at the UN sub-regional office in Dakar, and has worked on access to education at UNESCO headquarters. Vanessa studied political economy and economic development at the State University of New York and Université de Paris IX-Dauphine. She completed her graduate studies at the University of North

Carolina-Chapel Hill and Institut d'Etudes Politiques (Sciences Po) de Paris, focusing on social policy and sociology of education.

Anne Sliwka is a professor of Education in Heidelberg, Germany. She trained and worked as a secondary school teacher of history and social studies. After her Ph.D. at Oxford University, Anne worked for the Bertelsmann Foundation's International Network of Innovative School Systems (INIS). Anne's research in recent years has been focussing on education for democracy. Her 2008 book *Bürgerbildung: Demokratie beginnt in der Schule* [Citizenship education: democracy begins at school] advocates citizenship education as a means of turning a fragmented society into one that perceives diversity as an asset.

F. Blake Tenore is a doctoral candidate in Language, Literacy, and Culture at Vanderbilt University. His research and teaching interests are equity in education, teacher education, and English education.

Rick Wolff is a senior researcher at the research institute RISBO (Rotterdam Institute for Social science Policy Research), Erasmus University Rotterdam. His work focuses on study success of students from ethnic minority background in Dutch higher education, compared to that of White Dutch students. He is writing his PhD thesis on the subject, based on findings of several research projects in which he participated. At present he is also involved in setting up the Dutch Consortium of Research on Urban Talent, together with three partner institutes.